IMAGES
of America

LEWISVILLE

I0792666

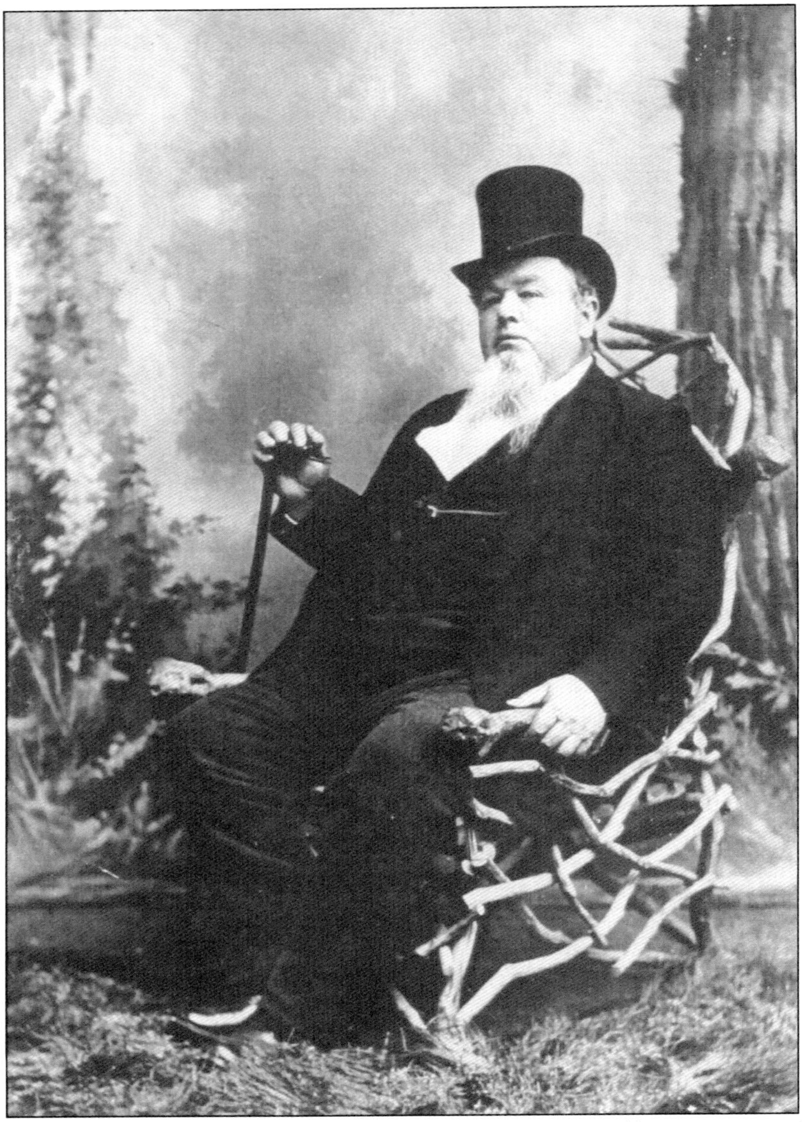

Lewis Case Laugenour (1826–1893), founder and namesake of Lewisville, grew up in a family that had settled in the Moravian community of Friedland, located in the Wachovia Tract. He and three of his brothers left home to travel to the California Gold Rush in 1849. In 1857, with a fortune of $10,000, Lewis returned to North Carolina. He settled in the southwestern area of Forsyth County, about 5 miles from the Yadkin River, and started a town there. According to Laugenour's nephew, Dr. Philip Fletcher Laugenour of Statesville, North Carolina, Lewis weighed 300 pounds and stood at a height of 5 feet and 6 inches. Dr. Laugenour describes his uncle as "distinguished for his large heart and kindness to the poor for whom he did many kind acts." Lewis Laugenour was known for his hospitality and never tired of entertaining guests at his spacious home. (PB.)

On the Cover: A Prohibition rally was held at Eugene Harley "E. H." Wright's General Store around 1908. Adults, teens, and children gathered together with signs proclaiming "The Saloon or the Boys and Girls—The Real Issue." (LHS.)

IMAGES
of America

LEWISVILLE

Merrikay Everett Brown and
Darla Morgan Johnson in association
with the Lewisville Historical Society

ARCADIA
PUBLISHING

ISBN 978-0-7385-6629-0

Published by Arcadia Publishing
Charleston, South Carolina

Printed in the United States of America

Library of Congress Control Number: 2009927056

For all general information contact Arcadia Publishing at:
Telephone 843-853-2070
Fax 843-853-0044
E-mail sales@arcadiapublishing.com
For customer service and orders:
Toll-Free 1-888-313-2665

Visit us on the Internet at www.arcadiapublishing.com

To the members of the Lewisville Historical Society, in honor of all the fun we have had over the years, learning about and sharing the rich history of Lewisville

—Merrikay Everett Brown

To Kathryn Burke Morgan and Lela Fulk Burke, who first told me stories about Lewisville

—Darla Morgan Johnson

Contents

ACKNOWLEDGMENTS

Since the Lewisville Historical Society was founded in 1991, an Archives Committee has been working steadily to collect, organize, preserve, and label documents, photographs, and audiovisual materials that comprise the Lewisville Historical Society Archives Collection. It is impossible to thank all the volunteers who have helped over the 18 years of the society's history, but we would like to thank the Historic Archives Committee members: Frank Bailey Jr., Margaret Boggs, Reba Dull, Mary Gaines, Mabel and Maurice Hall, Ruth Hartle, Linda King, Margaret Lee, Nancy Lloyd, the late Nell Trivette, and Mary Alice Warren. Without the consistent efforts of these dedicated people, the preservation of the history of Lewisville and this book would not have been possible.

The authors would also like to thank members of the society who have loaned, donated, and helped to research photographs for this book: Frank Bailey Jr., Margaret Boggs, Nick and Grace Conrad, Floyd and Polly Craft, John and Ruth Craft, Mary Haynes Dalton, Ruth Hartle, Darriell Hauser, Jarvis and Johnnie Hauser, Herbert and Judy Hudson, Laura Huffman, Dan Jennings, Mike Jones, Sally Jones, Susan Linker, Deb Phillips, Dub and Dare Reich, the late Stella Reich, Duran Stimson, Mary Alice Warren, and Lanier Williams.

The authors would like to thank the following citizens who have contributed photographs and information for this book: Tom Albert and the Union United Methodist Church, Kathleen Barr, Nancy Jones Beauchamp, Margaret Petree Boggs, Wake Burke, Ed and Levita Craft, Reid Craft, Gladys Conrad Doub, Shantina Shore Hairston, Lynn Hall, Leo Harrell, Eugene Holder, Rex Jennings, Monroe Jones, Henry Land, Jerry Loafman, Chris Mackie, Susan Mathis, Zeke Mock, Fred Moser, Clendon Newsome, Pearl Whitman Norman, Molly Rawls and Forsyth County Public Library, Patty Bailey Sheets, Gwynne Stephens Taylor, Shirleen Transou, and Mozell Voss. And special thanks to the many citizens who provided valuable information that filled in pieces of the puzzle.

The late Philip Brown and his family—wife Jewel and daughter Libby—of Troutman, North Carolina, must also be thanked for generously providing the Lewisville Historical Society with the Laugenour genealogy, family documents, and photographs.

Special thanks to Molly Grogan Rawls for sharing her knowledge and experience of publishing and access to the Forsyth County Public Library Photograph Collection.

John Reynolds and Jeffrey Rawls have provided valuable technical assistance to this project, which is greatly appreciated.

Sincere thanks go to Arcadia Publishing and the editors who have worked diligently with us: Maggie Tiller Bullwinkel and Lindsay Harris.

And very special thanks go to Tom Brown and Brent Johnson for their vision, support, and patience throughout this photographic history journey.

INTRODUCTION

The area that became Lewisville, North Carolina, was a popular venue for the life of many Native American tribes, including the Saponi Indians, who researchers believe flourished near the Yadkin River. According to Frank Tursi in his book, *Winston-Salem: A History*, the tribe's name meant "flowing" or "gentle." Around 1 CE, or the time of the birth of Christ, these Native Americans began settling in the area that would become Lewisville, nestled in the bounty of the Yadkin River Valley. They thrived on the plentiful game animals, such as buffalo, deer, and elk. They named the river "Atkin," meaning "where the many cottonwoods grow." They earned their livelihood partly from rock fish traps built in the river, remnants of which exist today. Life in the fertile bottom lands near the river was good. The Native Americans not only feasted on a plentiful supply of fish and mussels, but began farming, raising beans, squash, and corn. By the early 1700s, these gentle people were gone from the riverbanks.

In the mid-1700s, settlers from the north began arriving as they traveled south on the Great Philadelphia Wagon Road, which was routed through the Wachovia Tract of the Moravians. Daniel Boone, who lived with his family on the other side of the Yadkin River in the Bryan Settlement, blazed the Daniel Boone Trail in 1769 across the Shallow Ford, a link in the Great Wagon Road. The Shallow Ford, a wide shallow place in the Yadkin River, was vital to settlement patterns in the area. As frontiersmen camped alongside the river waiting for the water level to lower so they could cross with their wagons, equipment, and families, many people stayed to settle this area with its abundant wildlife and natural springs. When the old Ford Rock was visible above the water, the campers knew that the river was safe to cross.

In the mid 1750s, Col. Joseph Williams, an Indian fighter and Revolutionary War hero from Hanover County, Virginia, acquired 8,000 acres of land and built a sprawling plantation house called Panther Creek. He raised eight sons, many of whom served in local, state, and federal government: Robert as adjutant general of North Carolina; Joseph Jr. as clerk of court for Surry County, North Carolina; Colonel John as U.S. senator from Tennessee and later appointed minister to Central America; Lewis, who was elected to Congress 14 times, serving 28 years without defeat. Many prominent people of the time dropped in for visits at Panther Creek, including Henry Clay, John Caldwell Calhoun, and Daniel Boone.

Around 1777, German settlers established a new church that was known locally as the Old Dutch Meeting House. At that time, the area that would later become Lewisville was called "The German Settlement on the Yadkin." Many German family names, such as Dull, Hauser, Conrad, Leinbach, Ketner, and Pfaff, still exist in the area. The church became Shiloh Lutheran Church, the oldest Lutheran church in Forsyth County.

At the Battle of the Shallow Ford on October 14, 1780, Tories were defeated by Whigs. In 1781, Gen. George Cornwallis was slowed down by having to wait to cross the Shallow Ford. These events contributed to his eventual defeat and the victory of the new United States of America.

In the late 18th and early 19th centuries, frontier settlement continued. Waggoner's Chapel was established in the 1780s and became Concord United Methodist Church, the oldest Methodist church in Forsyth County.

The story of the founding of Lewisville can be said to have started in Friedland, a Moravian settlement on the eastern edge of the Wachovia Tract. The Laugenour family had settled there, and Tycho Nissen and his wife, Maria Salome, moved from Salem to minister to the community for five years. Tycho's grandson, John Philip Nissen, would found the Nissen Wagon Works in 1834 on a hill in Waughtown outside of Salem. Lewis Case Laugenour went to work as a young man for Nissen in the wagon factory. In 1849, he and three of his brothers left for the Gold Rush in California. By 1857, Lewis returned to North Carolina a rich man. He joined Nissen family members living to the west of the Wachovia Tract near the Yadkin River. With his money, he bought 750 acres from the Conrads and built a large brick house by 1860. He offered land cheaply to any farmer who would grow corn and tobacco, and so a town was born. The area became known as Lewisville in honor of the big man with the big heart. The year 1859 is the earliest date that can be established as the first use of "Lewisville" for this area. Laugenour and his wife, Mary Elizabeth "Betty" Nissen Laugenour, fostered the establishment of many historic churches, including the Lewisville Baptist Church, the Lewisville United Methodist Church, and the New Hope AME Zion Church. They helped establish the Lewisville School, the oldest high school in Forsyth County.

With his brother-in-law George Elias Nissen, Lewis Laugenour operated the Laugenour and Nissen Sawmill, one of the largest business enterprises in the area during the 1800s. George Nissen also ran a gristmill in the Lewisville area, which in 1870 was the fourth largest industry in Forsyth County. George Nissen, who built a large house in Lewisville around 1876, was a well-known industrial pioneer in North Carolina. He inherited his father's business, and it operated as George E. Nissen's Wagon Works for 36 years, until it passed on to his younger brother William Nissen.

As time passed, many businesses were established in the area, including a trading post, a blacksmith shop, and a tavern. There were two early mills: Edward Hughes's (1760) and Frederick Miller's (1798). Lewisville was a popular stopover for early farmers who were carrying goods to sell in Winston and Salem, having just crossed the Shallow Ford. Campgrounds were established near the Shallow Ford and in the middle of Lewisville to accommodate the travelers. Many commented that "All roads lead to Lewisville." Crossing the river was treacherous by ford, so in time, many ferries were established in the mid- to late 1800s. Three notable ones were in the Lewisville area: Nading's, Conrad's, and Styers'. Many individuals who operated ferry service also operated a mill near the river. Some mills operating in the area in the late 1800s were Eugene Conrad's, Richard Craft's, and Abe Styers's.

In the late 1700s, Col. Joseph Williams began distilling whiskey on his plantation. His youngest son, Nicholas Lanier Williams, established Williams Distillery in the 1800s and began producing Old Nick Whiskey. This industry led to the establishment of the town of Williams in 1903 when the North Carolina General Assembly passed a law stating that a brewery or distillery could only operate in an incorporated town. Other early businesses in the area included brick companies, lumber companies, sawmills, a tobacco company, a furniture company, and several grocery and general stores.

The post office in Lewisville was established on January 2, 1861. John H. Stoltz was the first postmaster. Philip Laugenour, the father of Lewis, served as the third postmaster from 1867 until his death in 1869. The post office was located in several different venues through the years, depending on which political party was in power in Washington, D.C. Notably, the post office was located in Eugene Harley "E. H." Wright's store and trading post in the 1880s and 1890s.

In the Lewisville community, there were five early schoolhouses in the late 1800s with one or two rooms: Lewisville, Blackburn's, Grapevine, Black's, and Warner's. The Lewisville Academy was established by the Methodist Conference of the Lewisville Circuit in 1901. Students came from many of these one- and two-room schoolhouses in the area to attend the academy, which provided elementary through high school classes. The academy became the Lewisville School in 1907, which included the oldest high school in Forsyth County. In the West Bend community, named after the west bend of the Yadkin River, there were the West Bend, Slater's, and the Howard-Brann Schools. In 1890, the Masons in West Bend Lodge No. 434 established the West Bend Lodge and Academy. Students from the local one- and two-room schoolhouses began attending classes at the academy in the downstairs of the large two-story building.

In the mid-1930s, Anna Ogburn built a large home in Lewisville, calling it Sunny Acres. This stately home included several acres of land. Ogburn, a philanthropist from a wealthy tobacco family, brought underprivileged children to Sunny Acres on weekends and during the summers to enjoy outdoor recreation in the country. They helped care for her gardens, and she made sure they attended Sunday school and church. Later the home was used as a Methodist church retreat and eventually as a community center for the growing town.

The Holder Furniture Company began operation in the mid-1930s on Lewisville-Clemmons Road across from today's Jack Warren Park. Matthew and Ervin Holder left the family farm and invested in equipment to manufacture kitchen and dinette sets. The manufacturing business prospered, selling their products throughout the Southeast. During World War II, they manufactured tables and chairs for the military. The Holders built a retail furniture store on Shallowford Road in the 1940s where the Fulk blacksmith shop once stood. The Holder brothers eventually moved the manufacturing business to Kernersville.

Established by the Sprinkle family in 1910 as Fairview Roller Mill, the mill was acquired in 1925 by the Jennings family and was a major employer in the town for almost 60 years as Lewisville Roller Mills. The L. A. Reynolds family business enterprises established in Lewisville in the early decades of the 1900s have prospered into the 21st century.

In 1945, as the veterans came home from World War II, the spirit of community began to grow even more. In July of that year, the Lewisville Civic Club was established and in 1948, began publishing a newspaper, the *Lewisville Citizen*. This newspaper symbolized the new community spirit and continued publication until 1961. On December 2, 1945, the Lewisville School tragically burned. It was a watershed event for the community to lose their school. Many citizens in the community realized there was a critical need for a fire department. Led by the Civic Club, the community raised money, the Lewisville Volunteer Fire Department was established in 1951, and a station was built. Later a rescue squad was established, housed in the volunteer fire department building. The Civic Club made its mark early as a community leader. Included among its many projects that improved the community were the establishment of a Boy Scout Troop, the building of a Scout Hut, school improvements, fund-raising for the fire department, petitioning for the paving of many roads in and around Lewisville, establishing a local baseball league, and partnering with other community groups to raise funds for improvements in the community. The Civic Club held events such as an annual Fall Festival and parade with the Parent Teachers Association, horse shows, and country fairs. The Lewisville Home Extension Club had established a volunteer library in a small house near the Sunny Acres home in October 1945. They doubled their efforts after the Lewisville School burned to provide the children of the town access to library books and resources. As the population grew over the years, more faith communities emerged in the Lewisville community, including Presbyterian, Moravian, Quaker, Pentecostal Holiness, and other denominations.

In 1970, after a grassroots campaign by community leaders, a county public library branch was established. Westbend Vineyards was established in 1972, setting a business precedent for the emerging Yadkin Valley wine industry today. The Civic Club raised money and in 1978 built a community center for Lewisville. Then in 1991, in order to preserve the small town and inviting atmosphere, the citizens of Lewisville led by the Civic Club incorporated the town. This led to the establishment of sidewalks, a Town Square, several parks, a new town hall, a new public library building, and a regular schedule of recreational activities. Lewisville today is a quiet village with a good quality of life in which families thrive, and citizens of all ages enjoy their lives. The community meets for many events at the Town Square, including family picnics, outdoor theater productions, movies, music programs, an annual tree lighting and Christmas parade, and a Fourth of July fireworks event. The town has many challenges ahead as it grows, but it stands out as a true gem in the crown of Forsyth County. Lewisville's proud heritage is a fitting base upon which to face a future filled with promise beyond 250 years of heritage.

LEGEND TO PHOTOGRAPH CREDITS

CM—Chris Mackie and the Clemmons Courier
DCH—Darriell Cornelius Hauser
DMJ—Darla Morgan Johnson
DP—Deb Phillips
DS—Duran Stimson
EH—Eugene Holder
ELC—Ed and Levita Craft
FB—Frank Bailey Jr.
FCPL—Forsyth County Public Library Photograph Collection
FM—Fred Moser
FPC—Floyd and Polly Craft
GCD—Gladys Conrad Doub
GGR—Glen Galloway Reynolds
GST—Gwynne Stephens Taylor
HJH—Herbert and Judy Hudson
HL—Henry Land
JRC—John and Ruth Craft
JL—Jerry Loafman
JLW—Joseph Lanier Williams
KDB—Kathleen Dull Barr
LCC—Lewisville Civic Club
LCH—Laura Conrad Huffman
LH—Leo Harrell
LHL—Lynn Hall and the Lewisville Town Hall
LHS—Lewisville Historical Society
MAFW—Mary Alice Fulk Warren
MIJ—Michael Jones
MOJ—Monroe Jones
MPB—Margaret Petree Boggs
MRB—Margaret Reich Boggs
MV—Mozell Voss
NGC—Nick and Grace Conrad
NJB—Nancy Jones Beachamp
PB—Philip Brown
PBS—Patty Bailey Sheets
PWN—Pearl Whitman Norman
RC—Reid Craft
RJ—Rex Jennings
RRH—Ruth Reynolds Hartle
SJ—Sally Jones
SL—Susan Linker
SMC—Susan Mathis and the Clemmons Courier
SSH—Shantina Shore Hairston
ST—Shirlene Transou
TAU—Tom Albert and Union United Methodist Church
WBL—West Bend Lodge No. 434

One

The Journey Begins

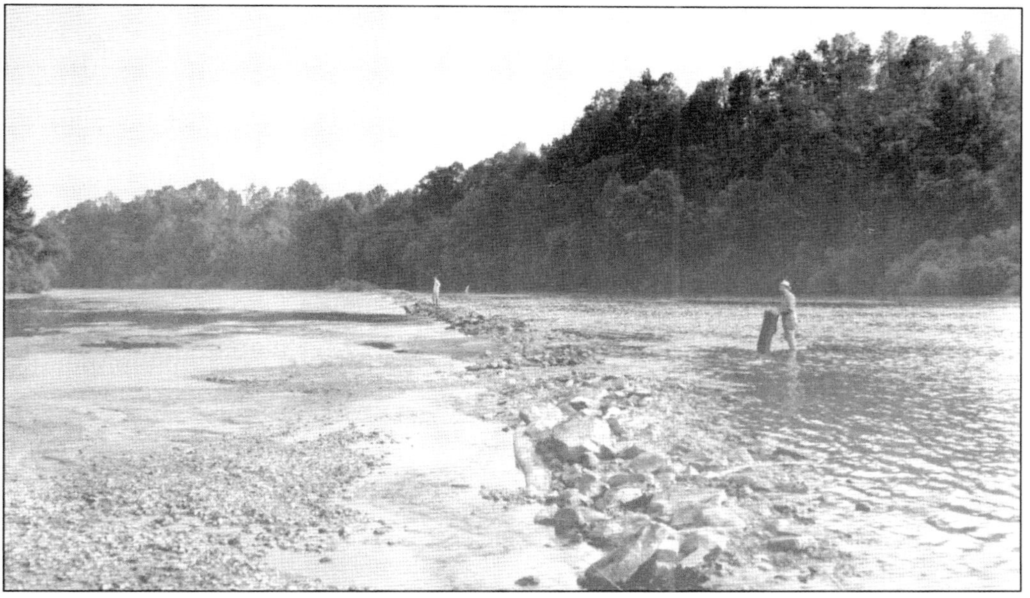

The Shallow Ford is a natural rock formation in the Yadkin River that allowed travelers to cross the waters safely when water levels were low, revealing the Ford Rock. The Shallow Ford, a link in the Great Philadelphia Wagon Road frontier migration route, was an important factor for the location of Lewisville and Winston-Salem. Lewisville residents wading across this passage in 1953 are, from left to right, Shermer Martin, Robert Martin, and Gwyn Jennings. (GGF.)

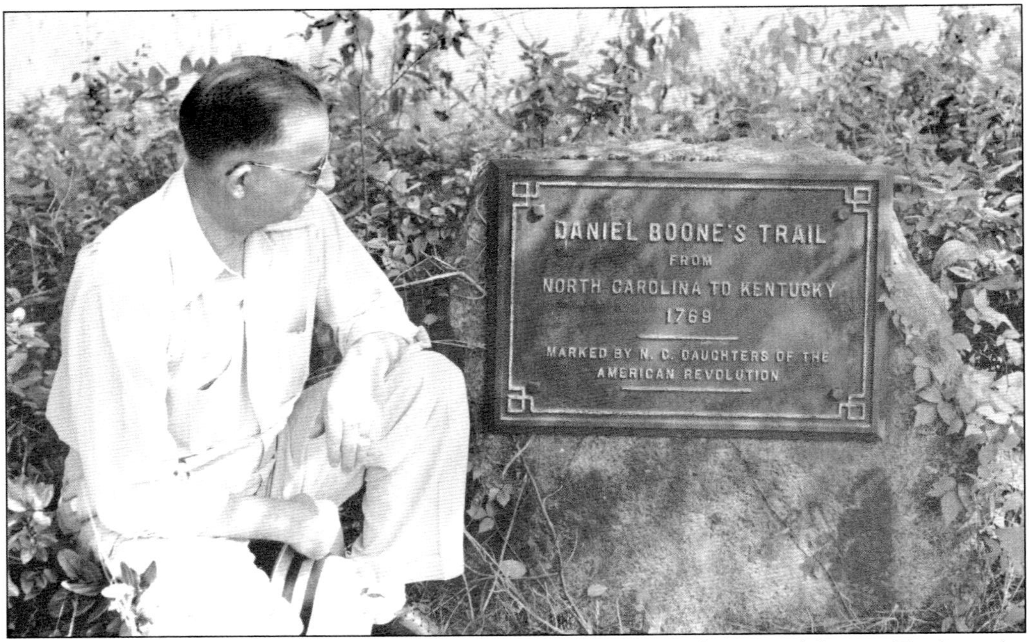

In 1953, Floyd Hauser examines the DAR marker designating the Daniel Boone Trail on the western bank of the Yadkin River. At the time of its installation in 1913, the members of the organization did not foresee this vital roadway would one day be bypassed by modern roads and highways. (GGR.)

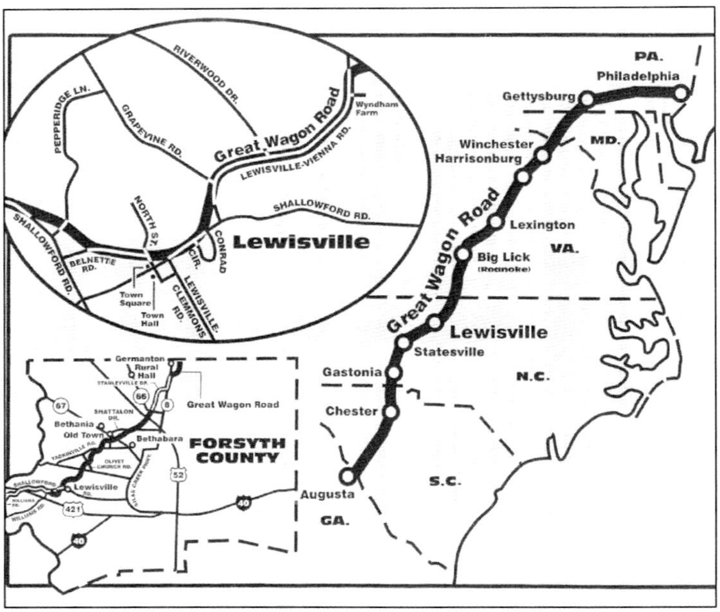

The map of the Great Wagon Road illustrates the major frontier highway by which thousands of American settlers traveled from Pennsylvania to Georgia, establishing new homes in the open territories of the United States. The Moravians cut the Forsyth segment of the road in 1754. The road entered the Lewisville community north of Shiloh Lutheran Church, passing through the Shallowford Square area and on through the countryside to the Shallow Ford crossing of the Yadkin River. (LHS.)

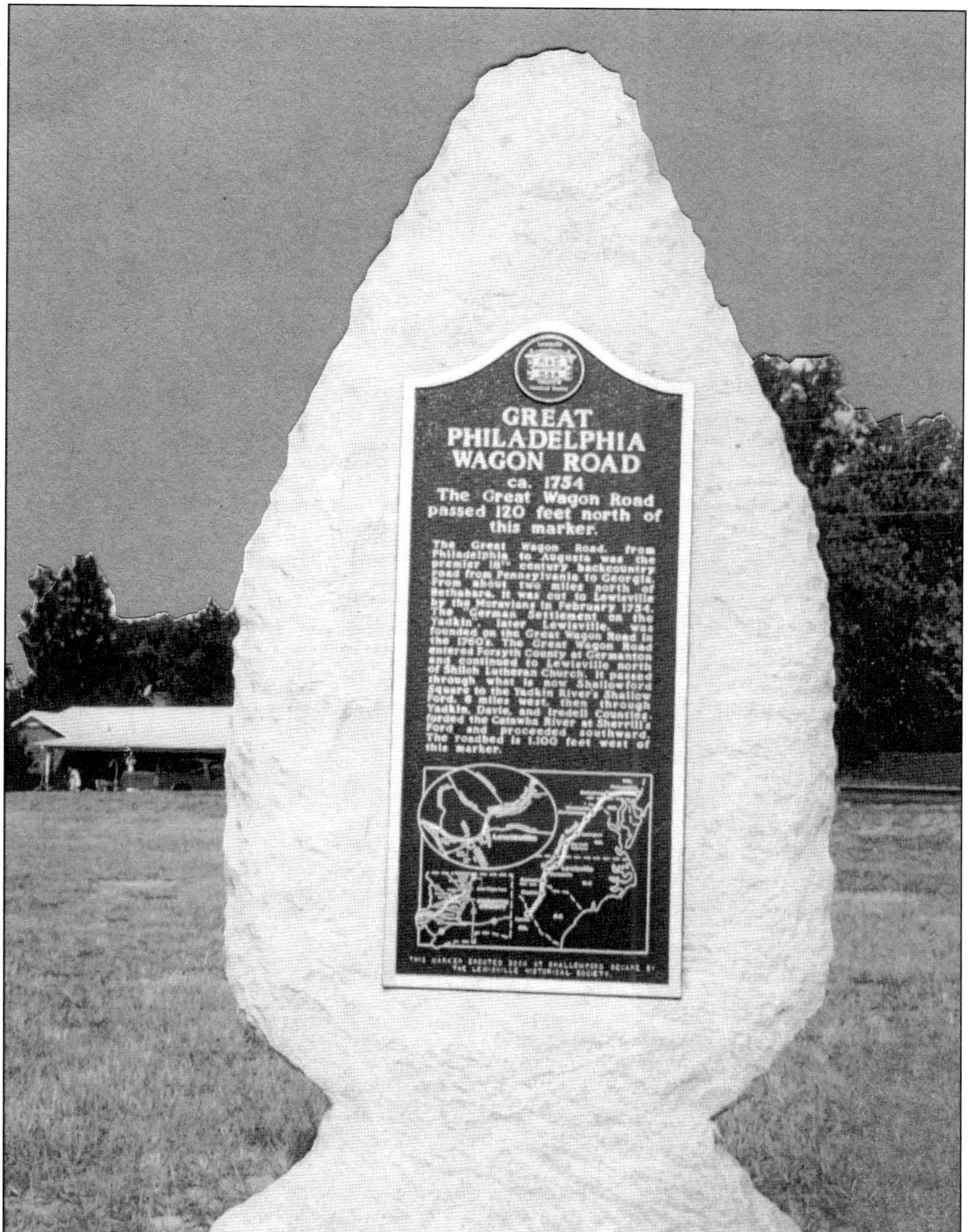

An arrowhead monument designating the passage of the Great Wagon Road through the eastern states, Forsyth County, and Lewisville, North Carolina, was erected at the Lewisville Town Square in 2000. Its dedication along with a Nissen Wagon Museum, featuring an authentic Nissen wagon, symbolized the importance of wagons and roads in the development of Lewisville. Lewisville is the only location in Forsyth County where the path of the Great Wagon Road follows current existing roads. (LHS.)

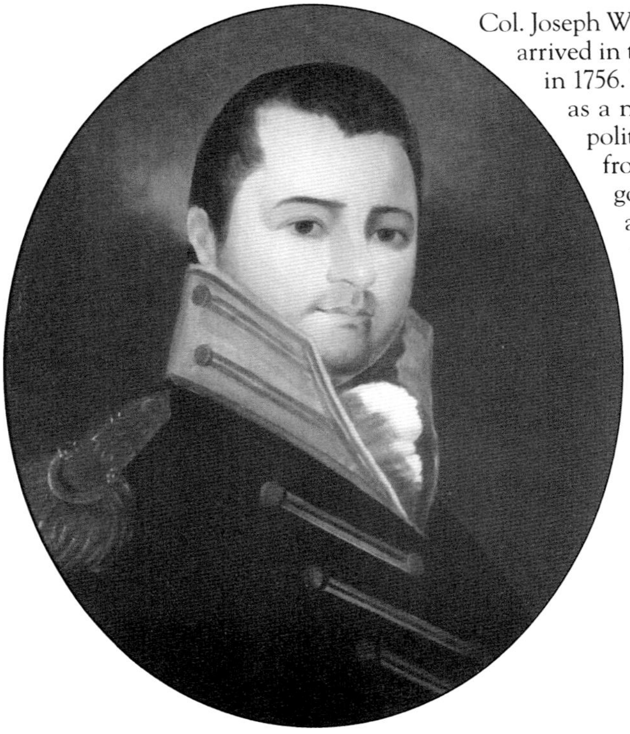

Col. Joseph Williams of Hanover County, Virginia, arrived in the piedmont area of North Carolina in 1756. He served in the Revolutionary War, as a noted Indian fighter, and in several political positions, including as a delegate from his county to set up a provisional government for North Carolina. He and his bride, Rebekah Lanier, raised a family of 13. They are buried together in the family cemetery at Panther Creek. (JLW.)

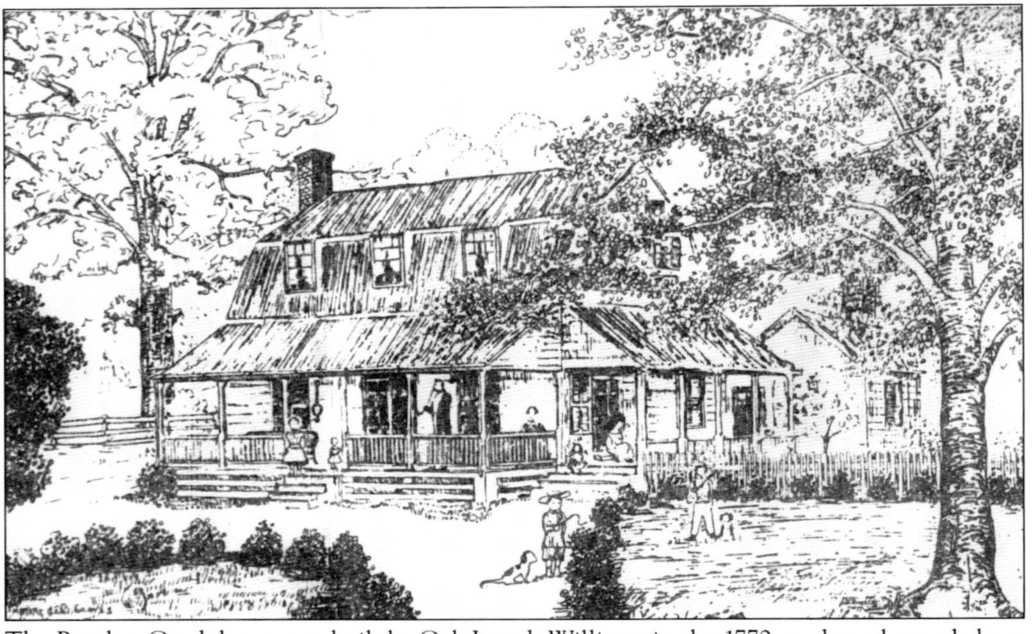

The Panther Creek home was built by Col. Joseph Williams in the 1770s and was located about a mile from the Yadkin River on his estate of several thousand acres on the east side of the river. Williams named his plantation after a panther he killed near a stream. The Williamses were famous for their hospitality and welcomed many prominent visitors to "The House Beside the Road." The stately home burned in 1885. (JLW.)

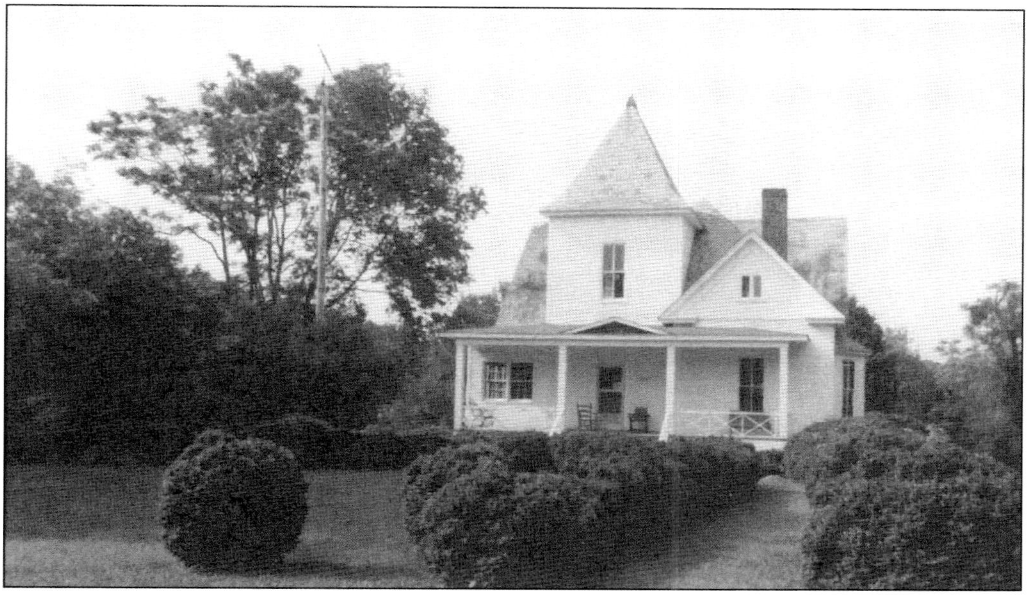

The second Panther Creek home was built in 1906, using the Queen Anne style of architecture. It was built by Sarah Alef "Sallie" Smith Williams Lillington and Nicholas Williams Lillington. Sallie married Nicholas, the nephew of her first husband and her first beau. Nicholas had been born at Panther Creek, in the old home in 1842. After their marriage, they retired to the old home place and enjoyed farming the rest of their lives. (GGR.)

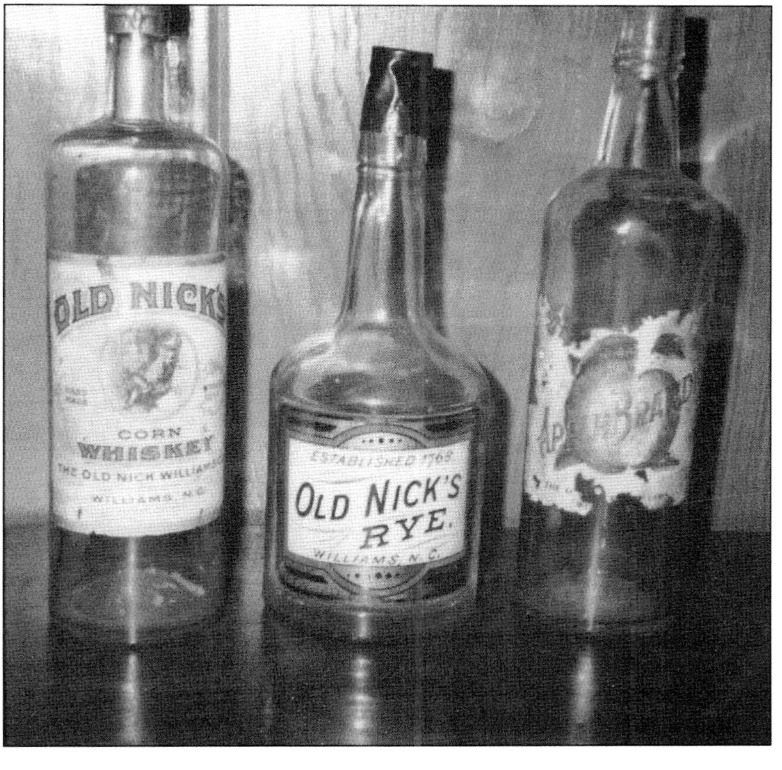

The Old Nick Whiskey Company produced a variety of whiskeys. The area where these spirits were manufactured became known as Williams, North Carolina, from 1903 to 1908, as the laws at that time required distilleries to operate in incorporated towns. Nicholas Lanier Williams, the youngest son of Col. Joseph Williams, established the company in the 1800s. In 1903, Nicholas Glen Williams organized the town of Williams and was the first mayor. (JLW.)

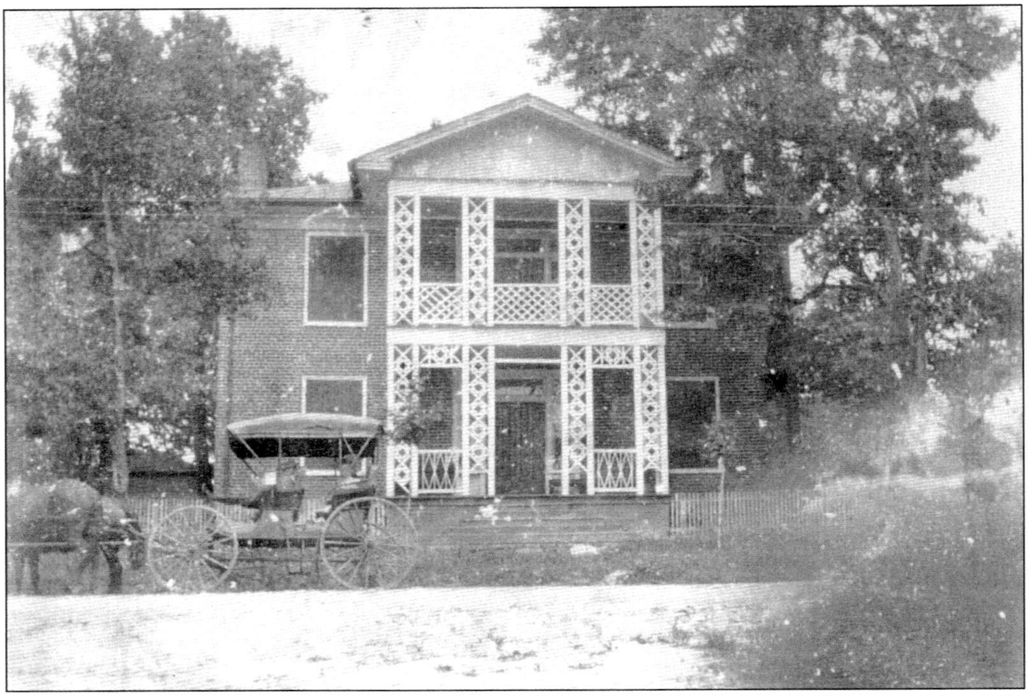

The Lewis Case Laugenour House was built around 1860, and the double porches were originally trimmed with white lattice work. Horse-drawn buggies were the transportation mode of the day when this photograph was taken, probably in the late 1800s or early 1900s. The house is one of the best examples of Greek Revival architecture in the county. The walls are 26 inches thick of locally made brick. (PB.)

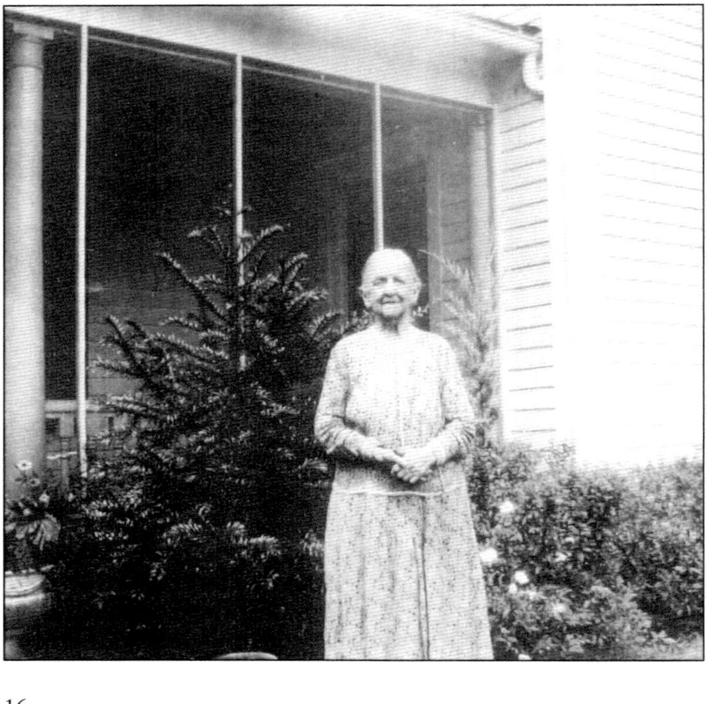

Mary Elizabeth "Betty" Nissen Laugenour (1843–1933) moved to Lewisville as a young bride in 1860. She was the daughter of Nissen Wagon Works founder John Phillip Nissen. Betty Laugenour worked with her husband in establishing churches in the community to encourage families to live and worship in the growing town. Betty was a charter member of the Lewisville Baptist Church. She loved needlework, entertaining friends, and playing cards. This photograph was taken at her home in the Waughtown area of Forsyth County on her 90th birthday. (PB.)

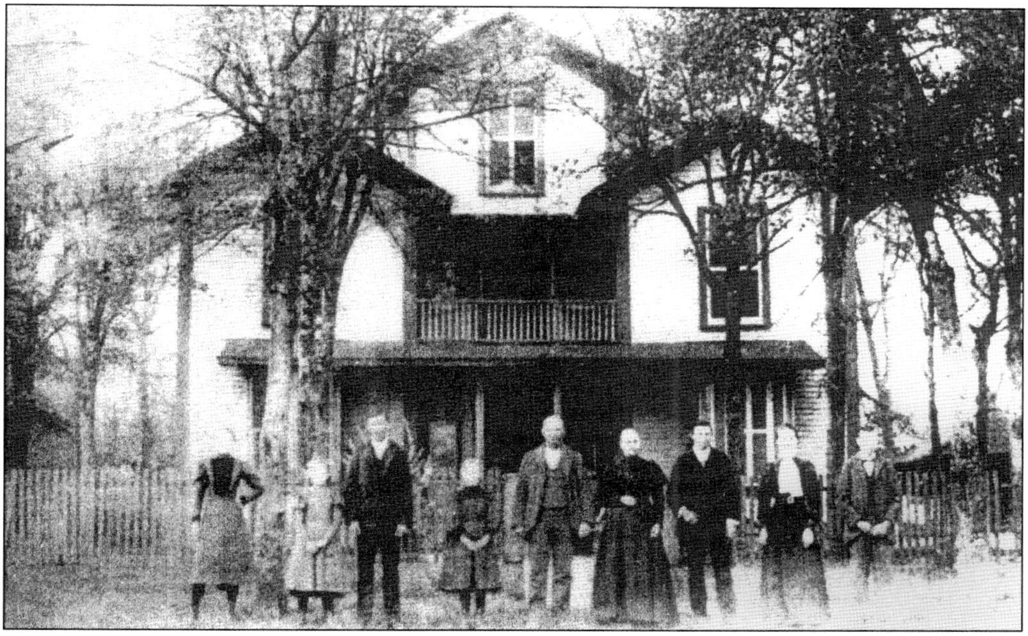

The George Elias Nissen House was built around 1876 by industrial pioneer George Nissen of the Nissen Wagon Works family. The house has been home to many families and individuals including a minister, doctor, and businessmen. The John Joe Jackson "Jack" Kiger family is posing around 1900 in front of their home. Family members, standing from left to right, are Carrie Alice, Laura Catherine, Jasper Lee, Della Sue, Jack, Elmira Styers, William Stedman, Eliza Jane, and Jackson Eugene. (LHS.)

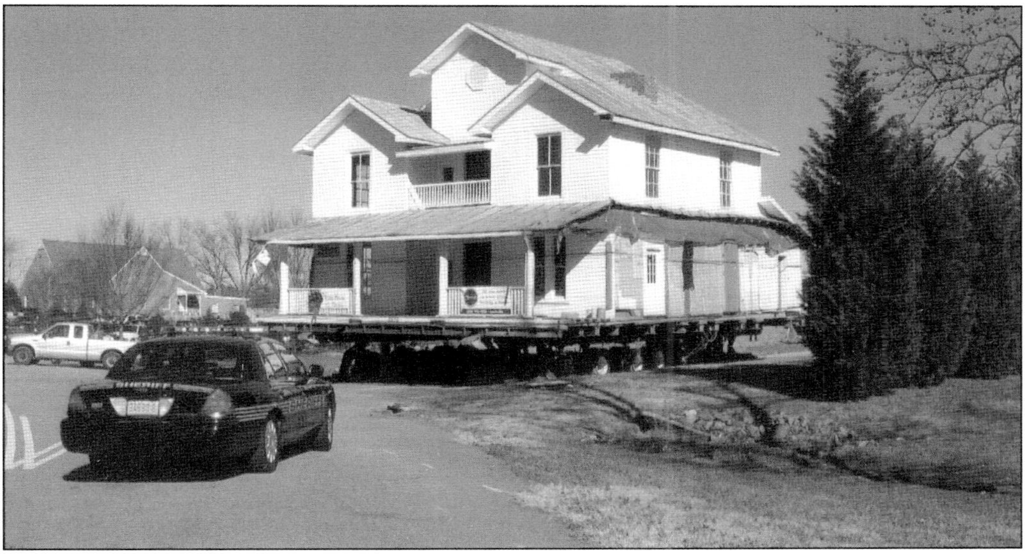

The Nissen House was relocated on January 1, 2009, to prevent demolition of the structure. Moved several hundred feet from its original location at 6570 Shallowford Road to 213 Arrowleaf Drive, the Nissen House is being restored into a cultural and educational center, which will also house the Lewisville Historical Society Archives. The unique Italianate and Greek Revival architectural style is one of few remaining houses in North Carolina from this time period. (DMJ.)

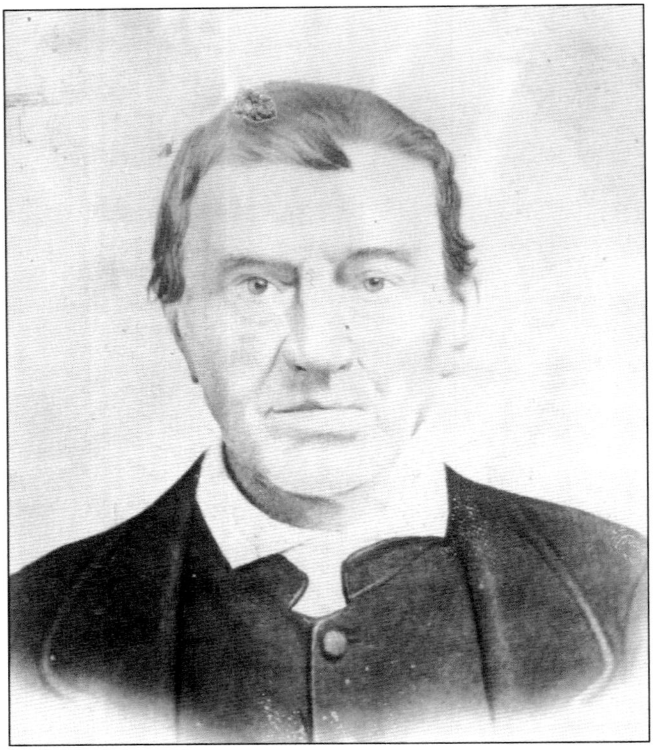

Philip Laugenour (1796–1869) was the father of Lewis Case Laugenour, the founder of Lewisville. He was a well-to-do farmer who ran a large plantation in Friedland, a Moravian community in the Wachovia Tract. He married Phebe Davis in 1823, and they raised seven children to adulthood. In 1857, he moved to his son George's land on the Yadkin River, near the Shallow Ford. He served as Lewisville postmaster from 1867 to 1869. (PB.)

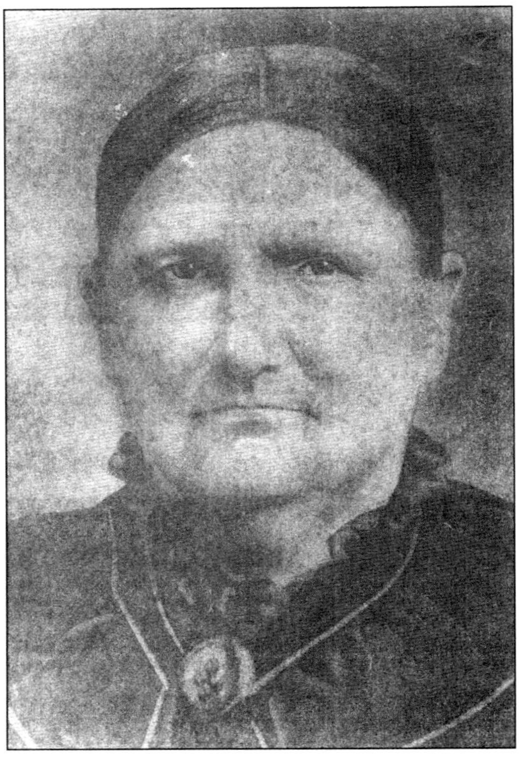

Phebe Davis Laugenour (1801–1865) was the mother of Lewis Case Laugenour. Her mother died in childbirth, so she was adopted by Samuel and Nancy Davis, who brought her up as their own. Phebe's physical build was short, plump, and fleshy. She passed her physical traits on to most of her seven children. She and her husband, Philip Laugenour, were buried in the New Friendship Baptist Church cemetery. (PB.)

Two

Come and Worship

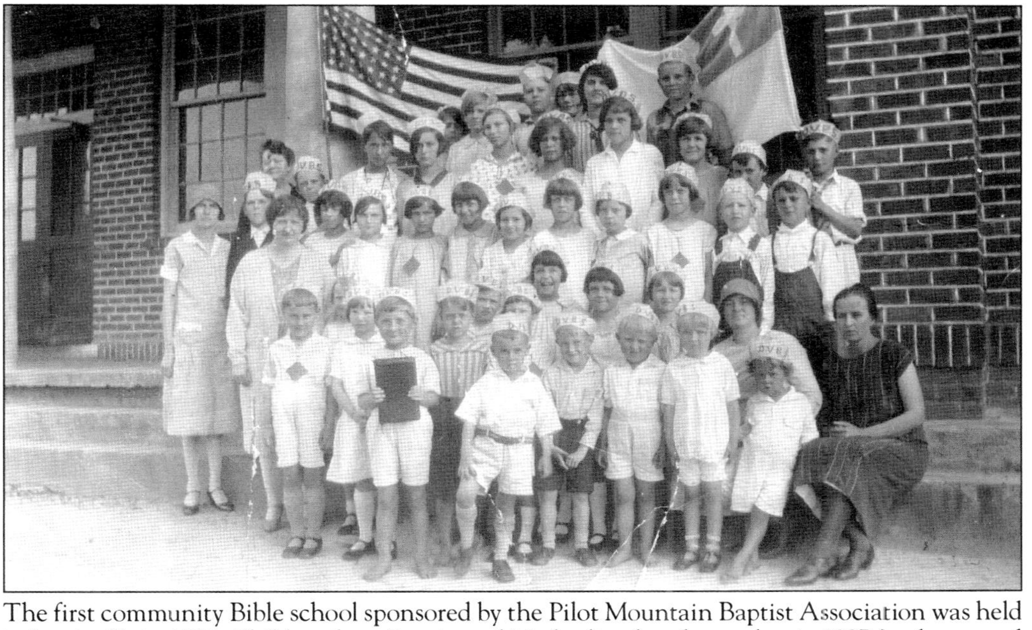

The first community Bible school sponsored by the Pilot Mountain Baptist Association was held in Lewisville in 1926. Children from Baptist and Methodist churches gather in 1927 for the second year of Bible School, standing in front of Lewisville School with their teachers. (DS, LHS.)

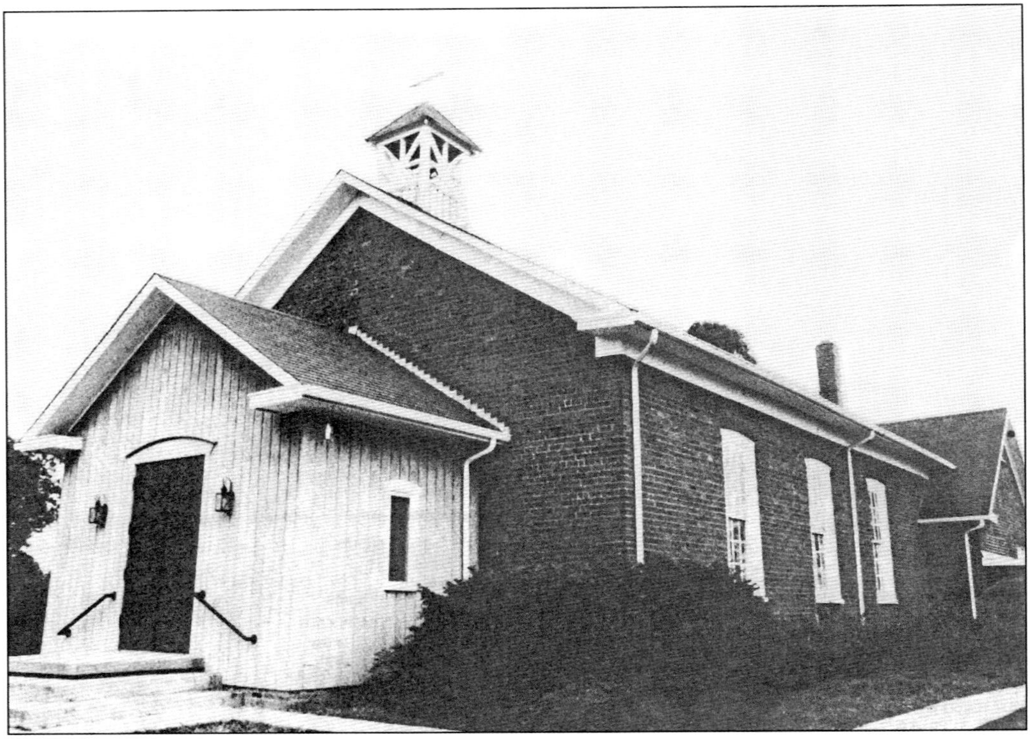

Shiloh Lutheran Church is the oldest church in Lewisville and the first Lutheran church built in Forsyth County. It was organized around 1777 by Rev. Adolph Nussman with the help of Reverend Arends. The first church was located a quarter-mile south of the present structure and built of logs, just across from the old cemetery. Shiloh was also called "the German Church beyond Muddy Creek" in the Moravian diaries and later known as Gerber's Church in 1813 for George Gerber, who gave 2 acres of land to the congregation. (SMC.)

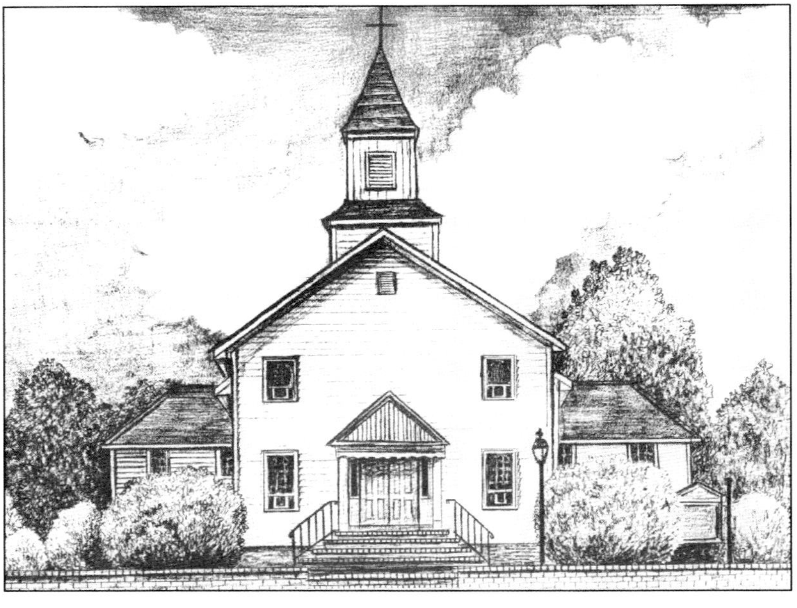

Concord United Methodist Church is the oldest Methodist congregation in Forsyth County, North Carolina, founded in about 1782. It was originally called Waggoner's Chapel by Bishop Asbury. The present church sanctuary was built in 1908. Unique hand-carved gravestones can be found in the church cemetery. (PBS.)

Sharon United Methodist Church was organized in 1813, although religious services were held in the area prior to 1800. Charles Vest provided land for the church and cemetery. The church was rebuilt about 1849. In 1897, the log church building was removed and a brick church was built. (SJ.)

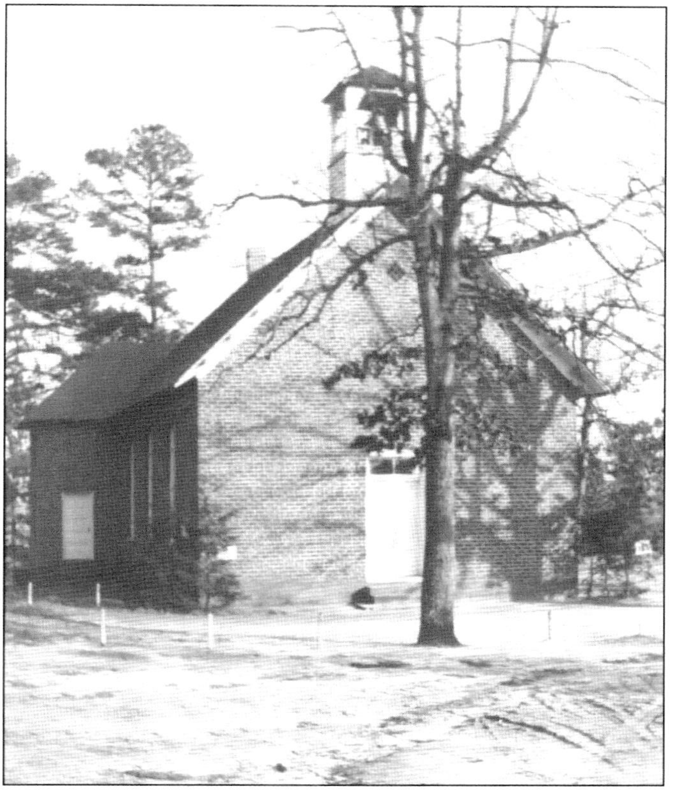

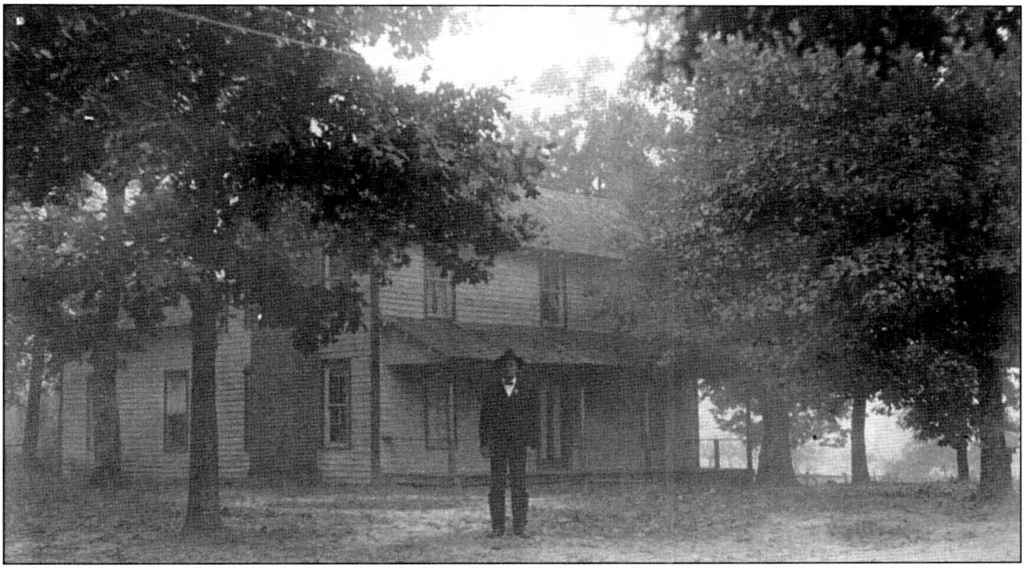

In 1884, the Forsyth Circuit of the Methodist Church bought the former Wesley Vogler house on Shallowford Road to use as a parsonage for their traveling minister. From 1901 to 1935, the building served as a parsonage for the Lewisville Circuit (later Charge), until a new brick parsonage was built next to the Lewisville United Methodist Church. This building then became a private residence. (LHS.)

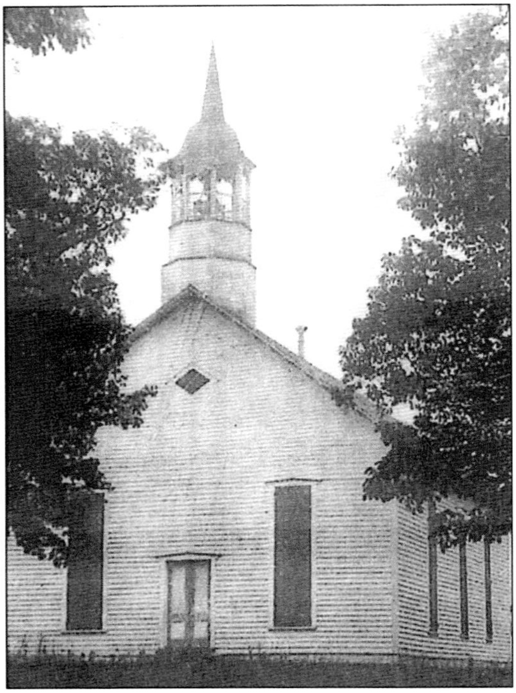

Organized in 1878 under the leadership of Augustine Eugene Conrad and Rev. Moses J. Hunt, Lewisville United Methodist Church constructed its first building in 1881 on land acquired from the Laugenours. This structure served the congregation until 1930. (RRH.)

Lewisville United Methodist Church's second building served the congregation from 1931 to 1983. Early in the morning of September 7, 1954, a fire broke out and nearly destroyed this church. It took months to repair the building. A third brick structure built in 1984 stands on the site today, providing worship services and a weekday preschool. (RRH.)

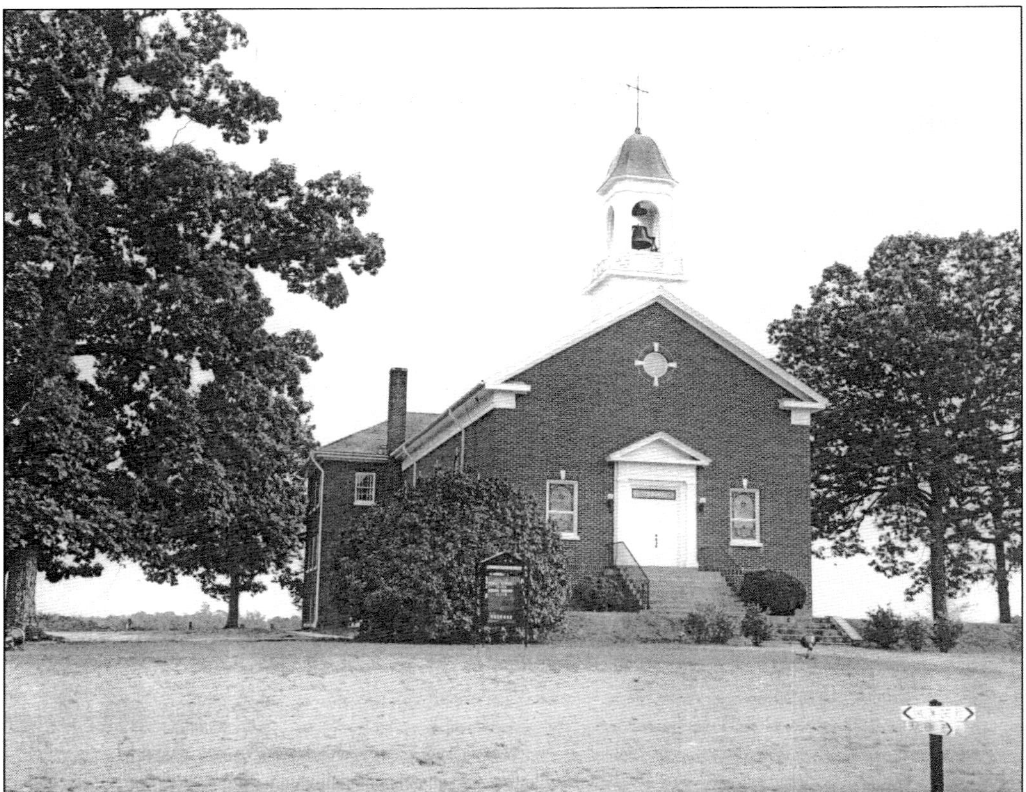

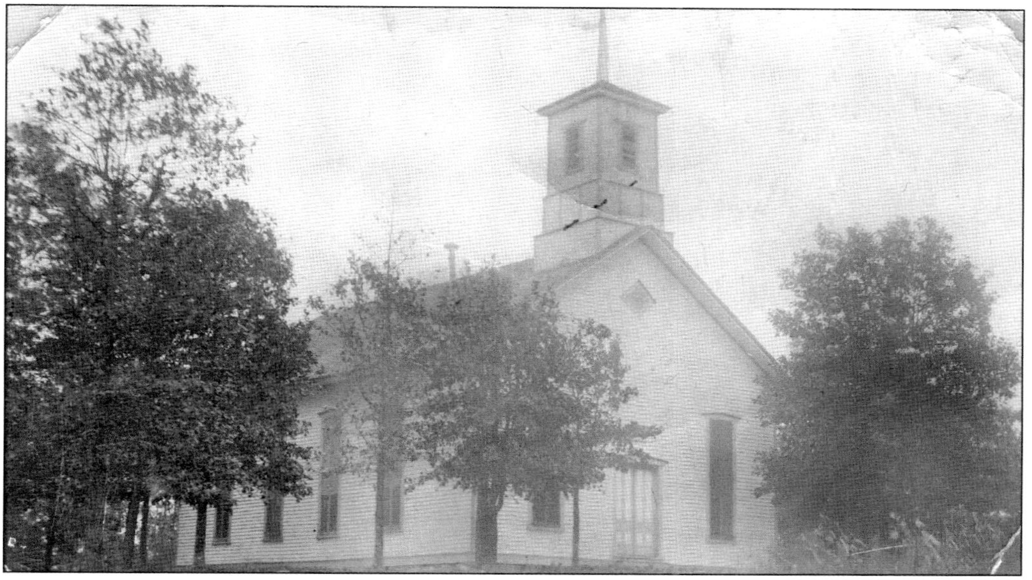

Lewisville Baptist Church was organized in 1881, acquiring land from the Laugenours to build atop the highest point in the village. In 1936, lightning struck the bell tower and the church burned to the ground. All was lost, except the collection plate and the original minutes book, not in the church at the time. By 1937, a second brick church was built. A third church structure stands today, where multicultural services are attended. Lewis and Betty Laugenour were charter members of the church and are buried in the cemetery. (LHS.)

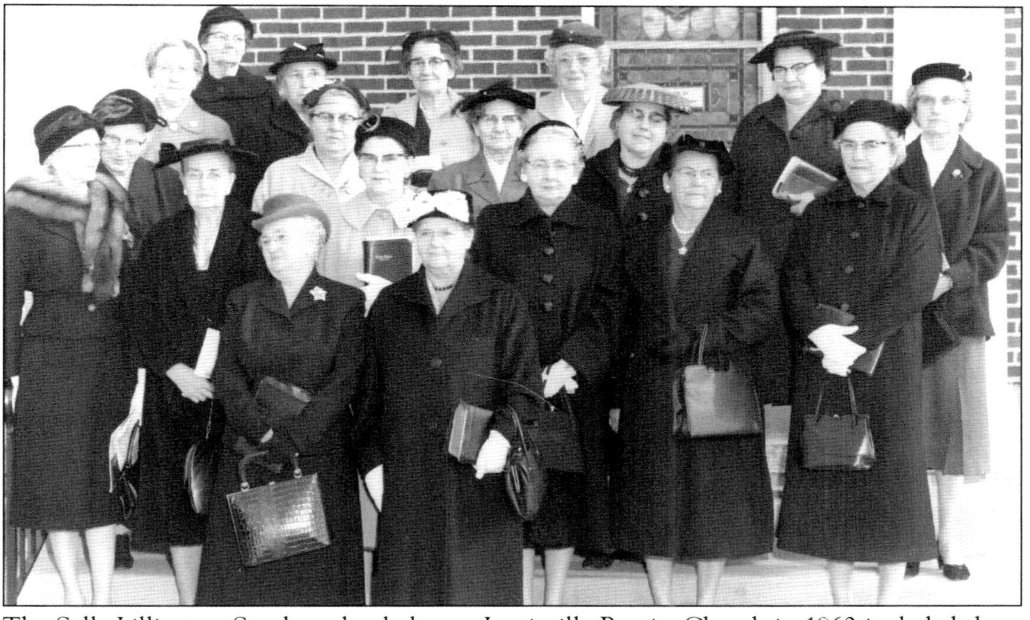

The Sally Lillington Sunday school class at Lewisville Baptist Church in 1960 included these members, from left to right, (first row) Myrtle Stimson and Sadie French; (second row) Maude Fulk, Fannie Conrad, Metta Redding, Lela Burke, Nela Harbin, and Anna Mock; (third row) Nell Sprinkle, Flora Dull, Flora Whitman, Millie Thrush, and Mary Lawrence; (fourth row) Nora Hailey, Jennie Clayton, Della Kiger, Esther Hunter, Bertha Martin, and Edna Craft. (MAFW.)

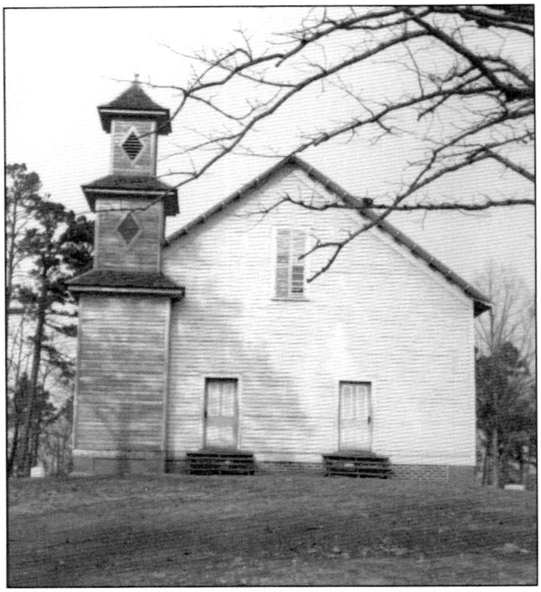

Organized gatherings at Union Meeting House in the West Bend community are recorded in the 1830s, in which Baptists and Methodists worshipped together, hence the "Union" of two denominations. In 1876, Union United Methodist Church in West Bend and West Bend Baptist Church organized two separate congregations. From 1921 to 1950, this church structure served the Union United Methodist Church congregation. (TAU.)

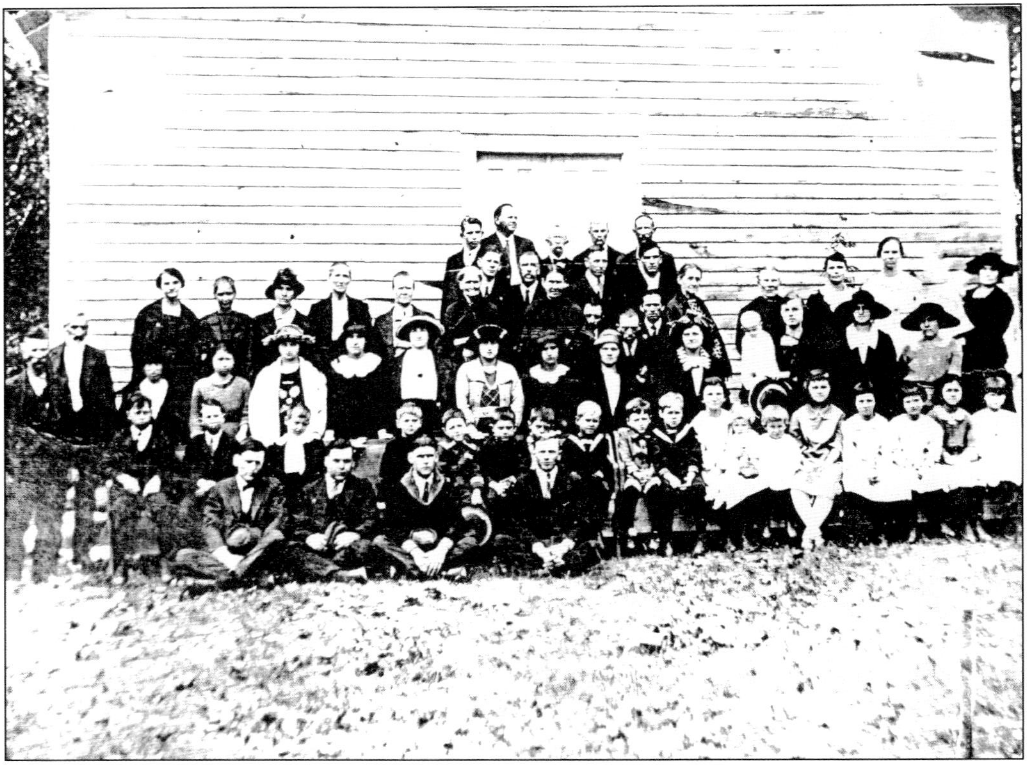

Harmony Grove United Methodist Church was built in 1887 on Styers Ferry Road near the intersection at Lewisville-Clemmons Road. The congregation gathers in the 1920s for a portrait at the first church building, with members of the Craft, Jarvis, Ketner, Ridings, Sheets, and other families. The church was rebuilt in 1936. A brick structure has replaced the original buildings. (ELC.)

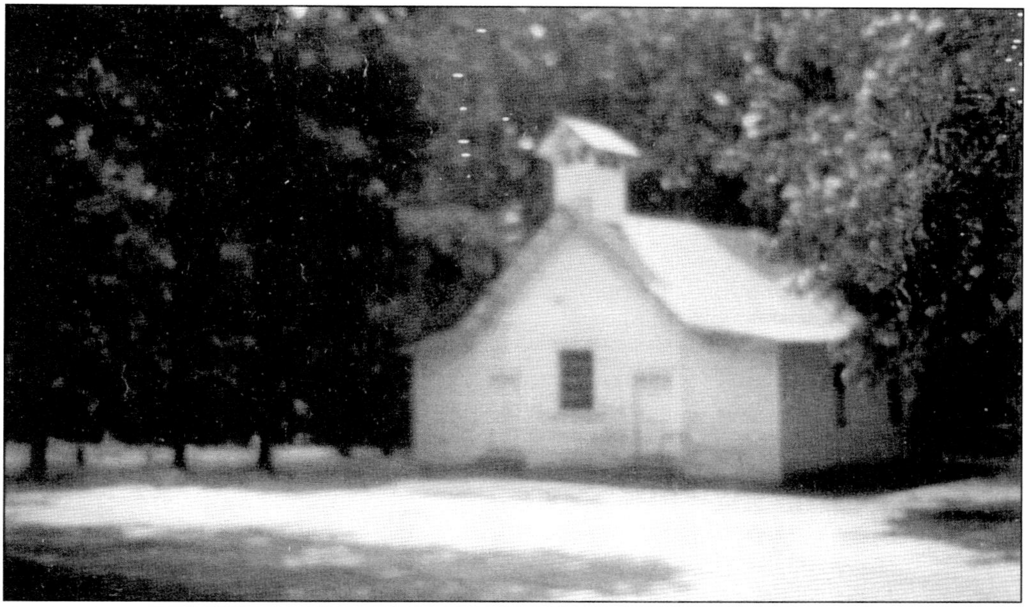

Double Springs AME Zion Church was founded by former slaves living on the neighboring Williams plantation. The church fell into disrepair in the 20th century with vandalism in both the church and historic cemetery. Many members joined the New Hope AME Zion Church in time. The church was eventually burned and buried by the former members and the cemetery restored with permanent fencing around the grave sites on Double Springs Road. (SSH.)

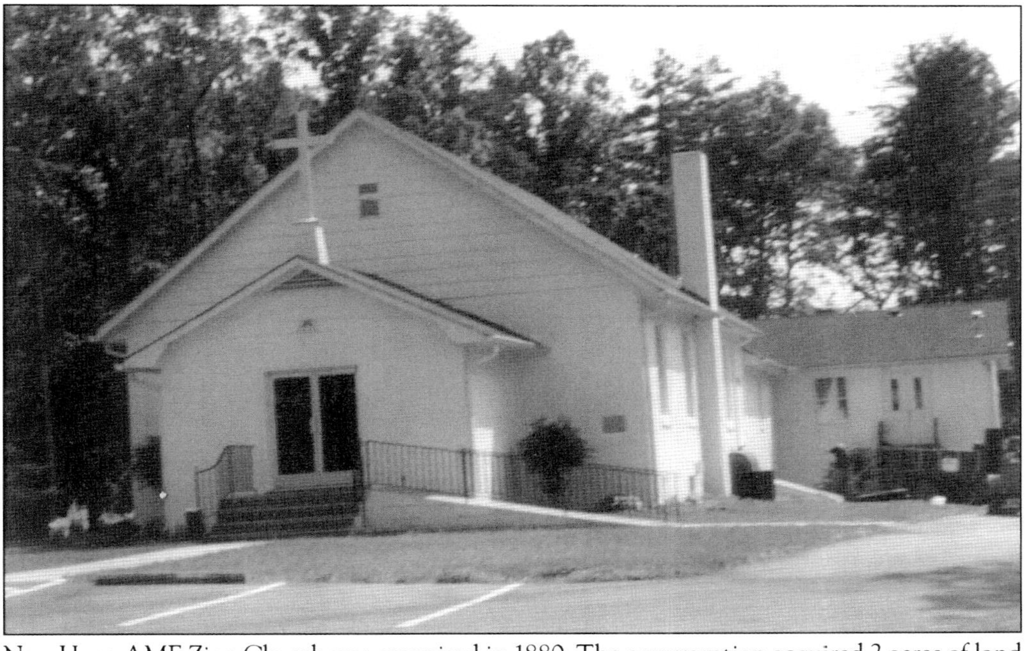

New Hope AME Zion Church was organized in 1880. The congregation acquired 2 acres of land from Lewis Laugenour to build the church on Shallowford Road. Additional land was acquired later for use as a cemetery. It is one of the oldest AME Zion churches in Forsyth County. The current sanctuary was built in 1953 under the leadership of Rev. Howard Mayberry. (LHS.)

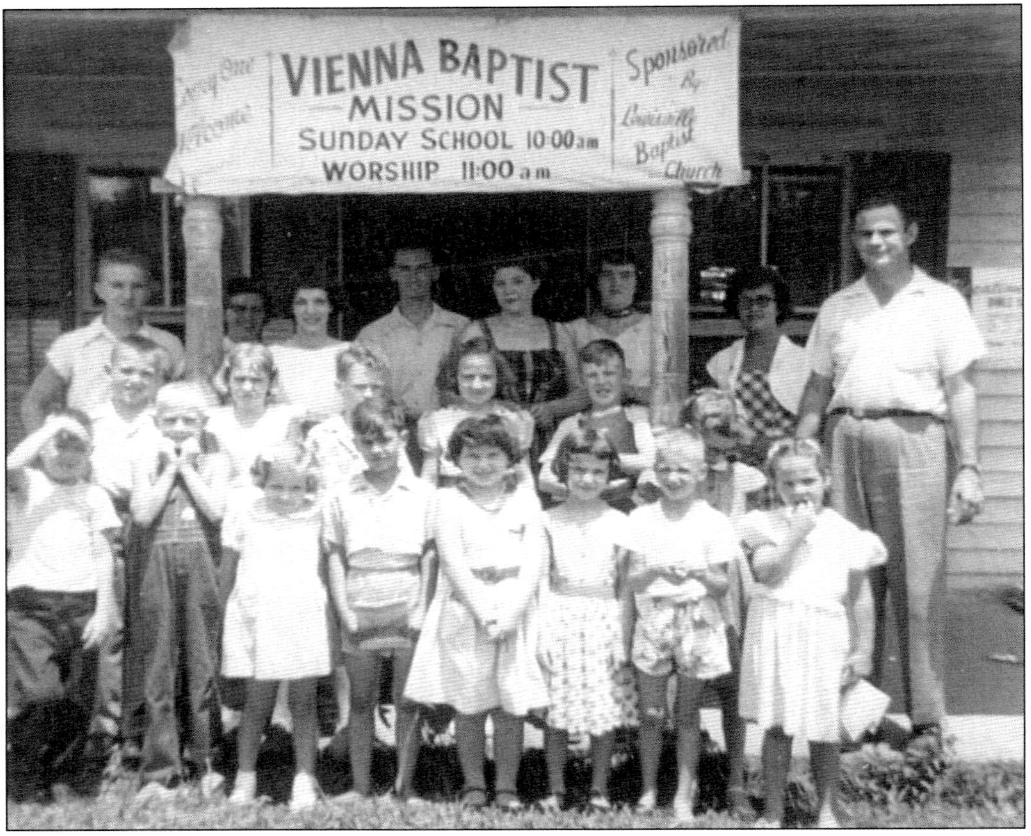

Vienna Baptist Mission, sponsored by Lewisville Baptist Church, first met in a store building. The growing congregation later became Vienna Baptist Church. Today this building serves as a Boy Scout hut. (JL.)

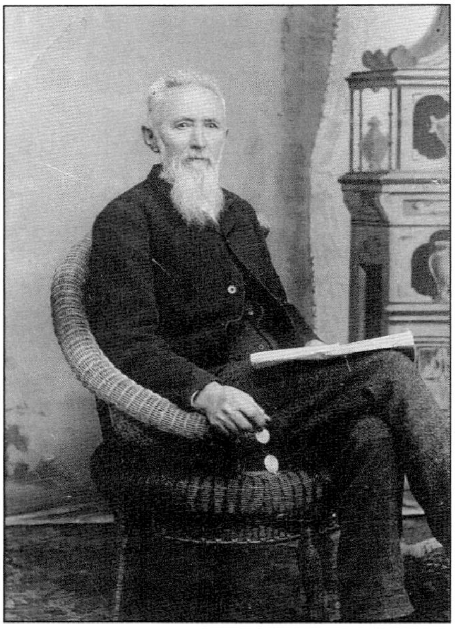

Brookstown United Methodist Church was built on 1 acre of land given by Philip Mock near his home in the 1850s and became part of the Lewisville charge of Methodist congregations. The first church was a one-room building with backless benches for pews, with a second church constructed in 1914. One of the early ministers at Brookstown poses for a portrait. (JL.)

Three

School Days

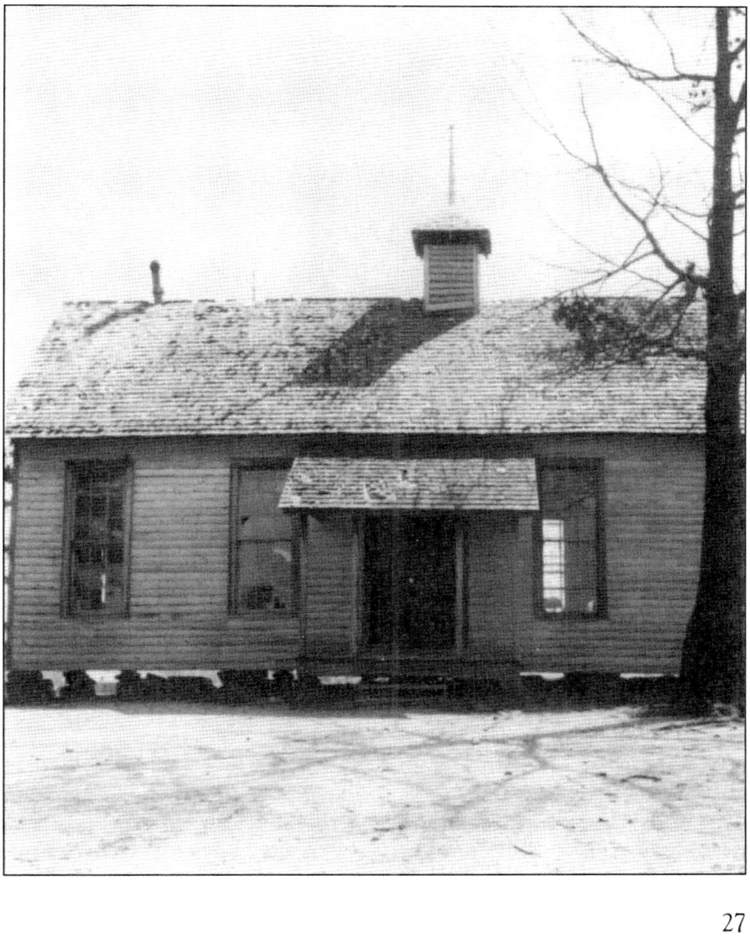

West Bend School was located on Panther Creek Road, now West Bend School Road. It opened in 1902 and was used until 1927, when West Bend (or Little Yadkin Township) was taken into Forsyth County from Yadkin County. (LHS.)

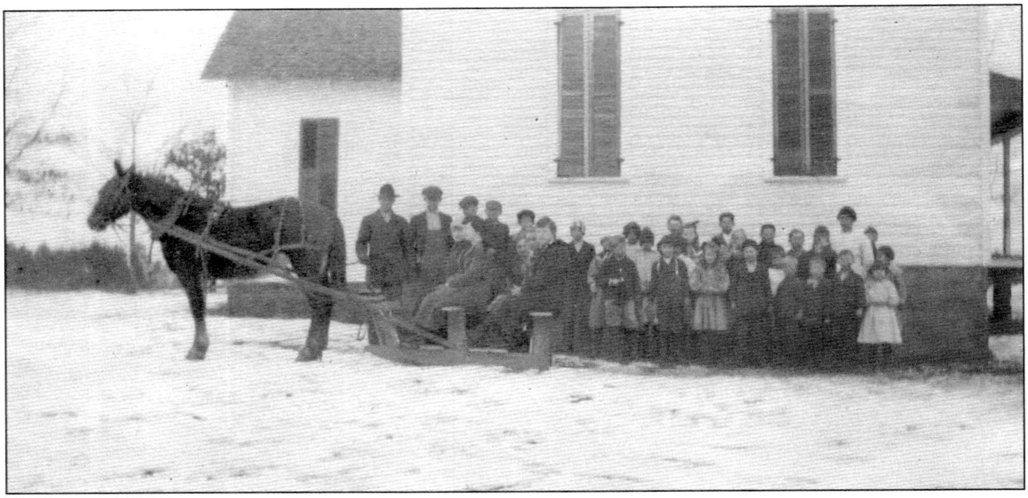

Black's School was located in the Concord United Methodist Church community. Students and teachers gather in the winter season for rides in the snow with a horse-drawn sled. (MRB.)

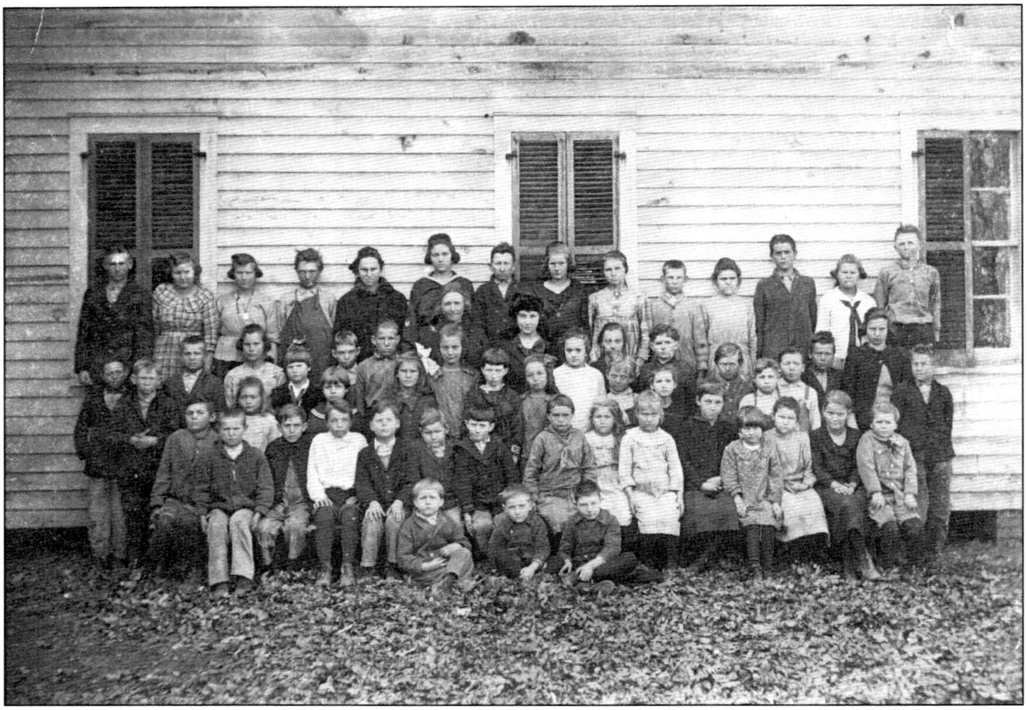

Students assembled for a portrait at Brookstown School as it appeared in 1919. The school closed in 1921 when Vienna School opened in the community. (JL.)

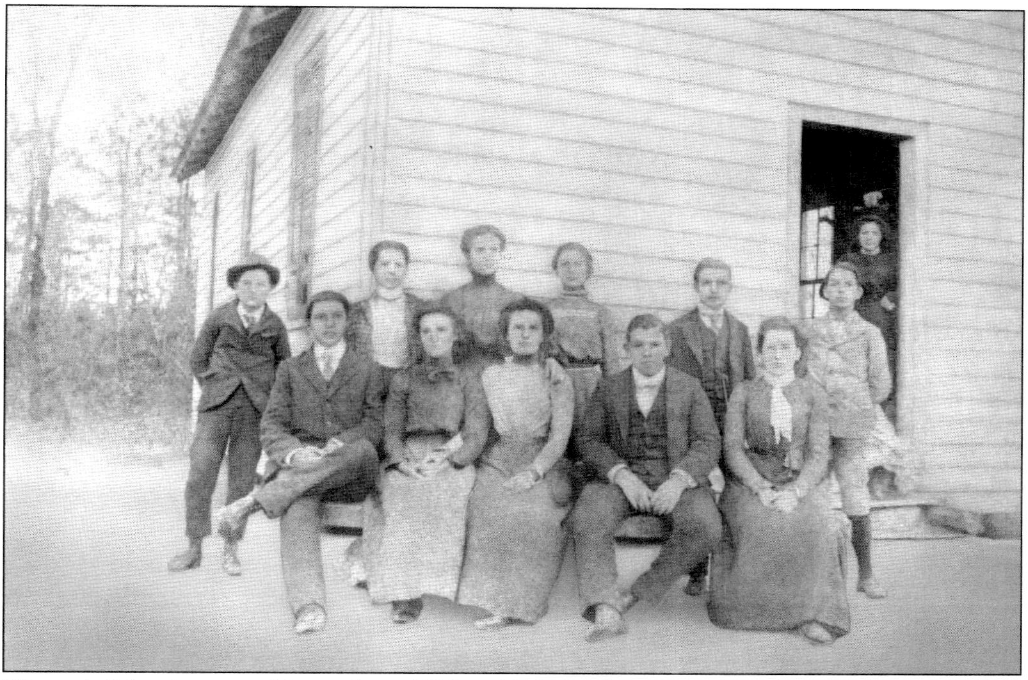

Warner's School operated from about 1890 to 1908. Students posing at the school are, from left to right, (first row) Herman Warner, Lula Tesh, Bessie Binkley, Carl Warner, and Lily Binkley; (second row) Mangrum Brown, Bessie Phillips, Bessie Tesh, Stella Harper, Syd Holder, and J. Marvin Binkley Sr. An unidentified teacher stands in doorway. (RRH.)

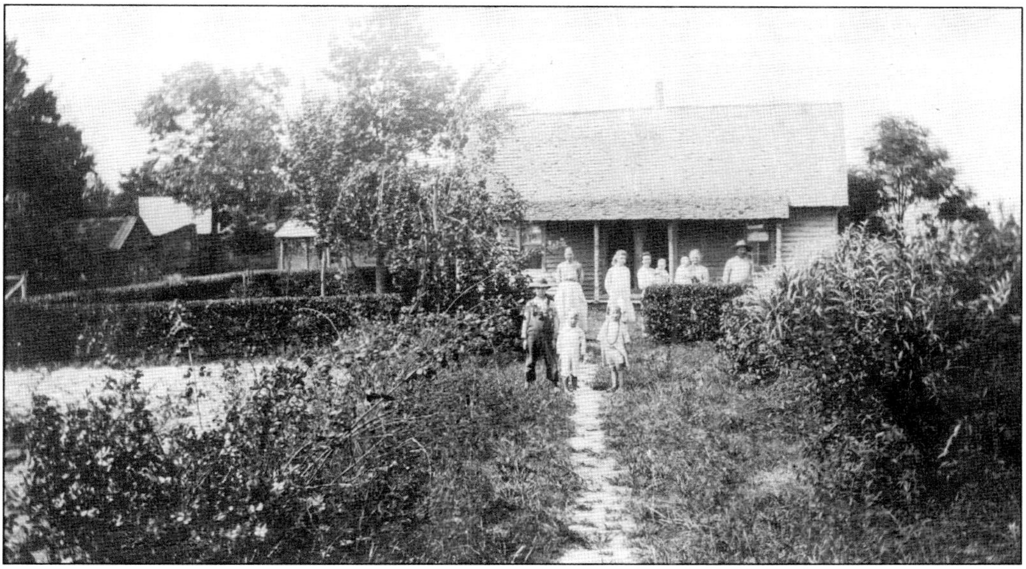

In 1902, Leon Reid Jones purchased 44 acres of land from Mary S. Harper. The family moved the old Blackburn's School House, which sat near Harmony Grove United Methodist Church, to their property on Styers Ferry Road. They moved into their new home in 1903. The house was moved again in 1931 about 150 feet north for construction of a new family home. The structure is still standing today on the Jones property. (SJ.)

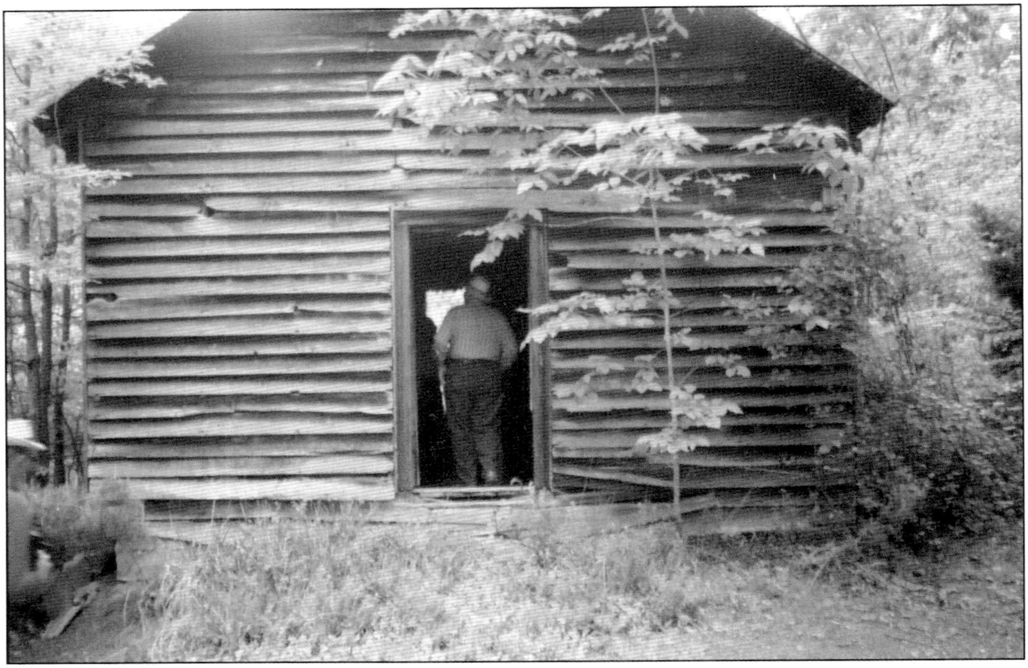

Students who attended the Howard-Brann School in West Bend later transferred to the West Bend Academy. Members of the Lewisville Historical Society visited the schoolhouse in the 1990s. (LHS.)

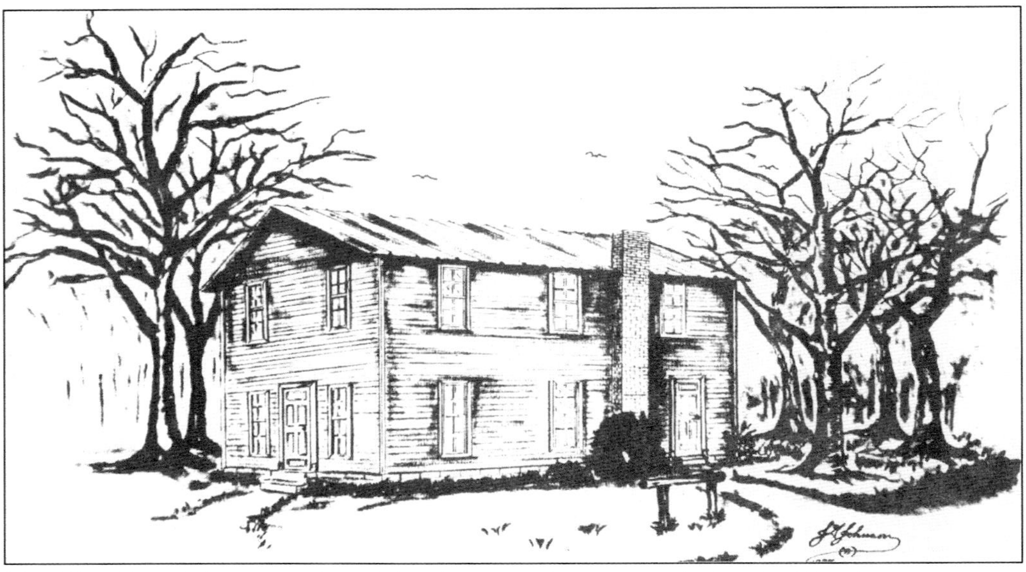

The West Bend Masonic Hall and Academy was located on Shallowford Road in a two-story structure. The school with elementary and high school classes operated from 1892 to 1900 on the downstairs floor. The upstairs floor was used by the Masons from 1890 to 1931. Today the structure is a private residence. (WBL.)

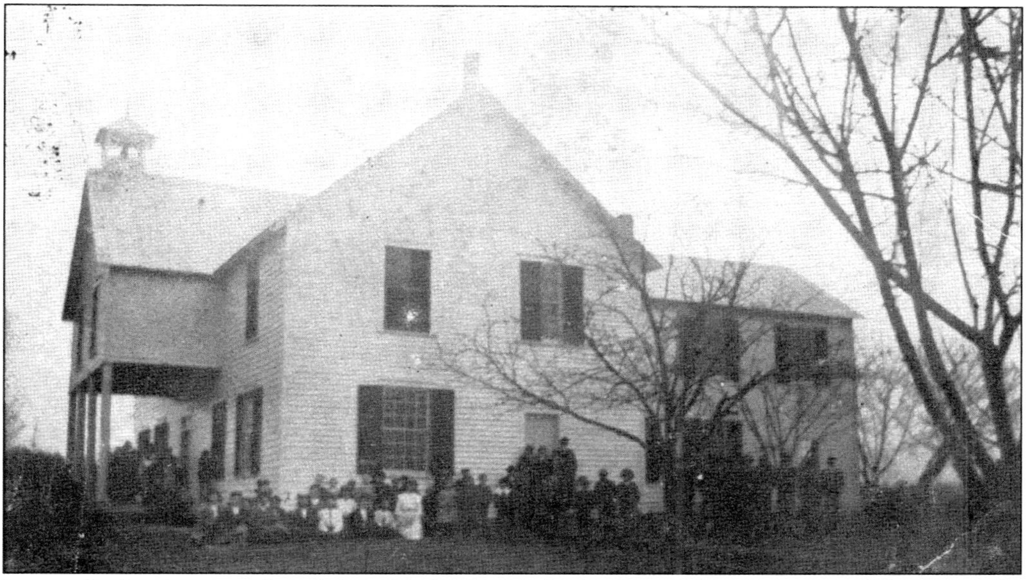

Lewisville Academy was founded in 1901 by the Methodist Quarterly Conference of the Lewisville Circuit. The Caleb Thomas home place was purchased for $350, consisting of a two-story house and 6 acres of land. J. Wilson Carroll was the first principal. Lewisville Academy was the first high school in Forsyth County, North Carolina, depicted on this early-1900s postcard. Additional rooms were added to accommodate elementary through high school classes and assemblies. A bell in the roof tower rang to summon students to class. (LHS.)

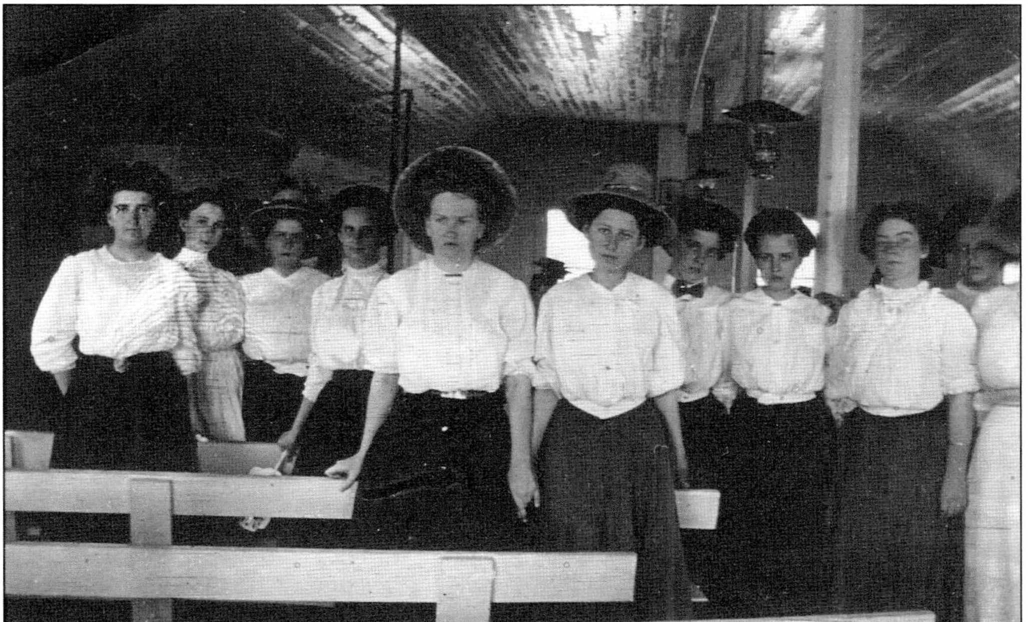

High school students gather inside the Lewisville Academy building in the early 1900s. Possibly assembled in an auditorium, the girls stand among benches, with wooden ceilings and supports visible. (LCH.)

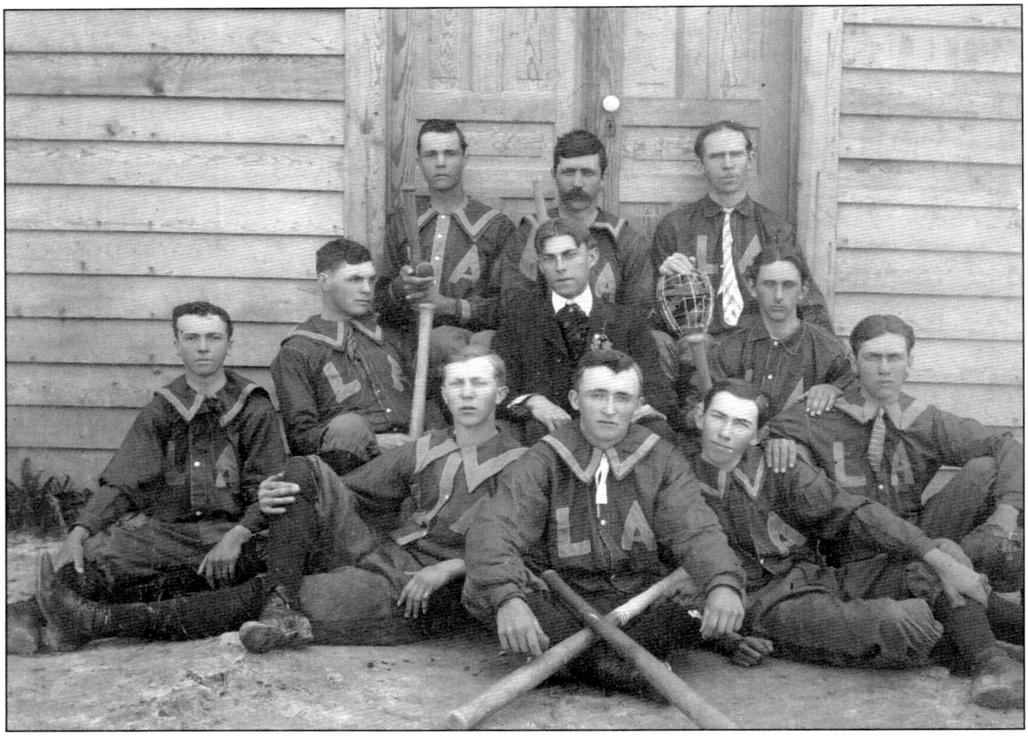

The LA baseball team in the early 1900s may have been the Lewisville Academy team of high school boys or a community team of young men. The players in the center of each row are Ernest Peacock (first row), Robah Stimson (second row), and Howard Moser (third row). Coy Dull is at left on the second row. (DS.)

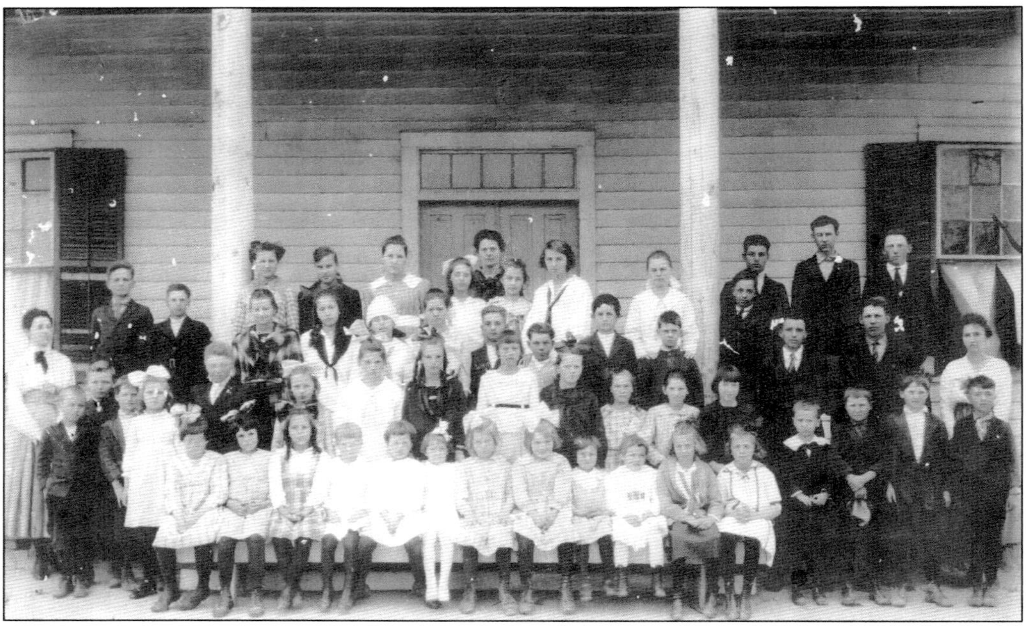

Students gather in front of Lewisville Academy in the early 1920s. (LHS.)

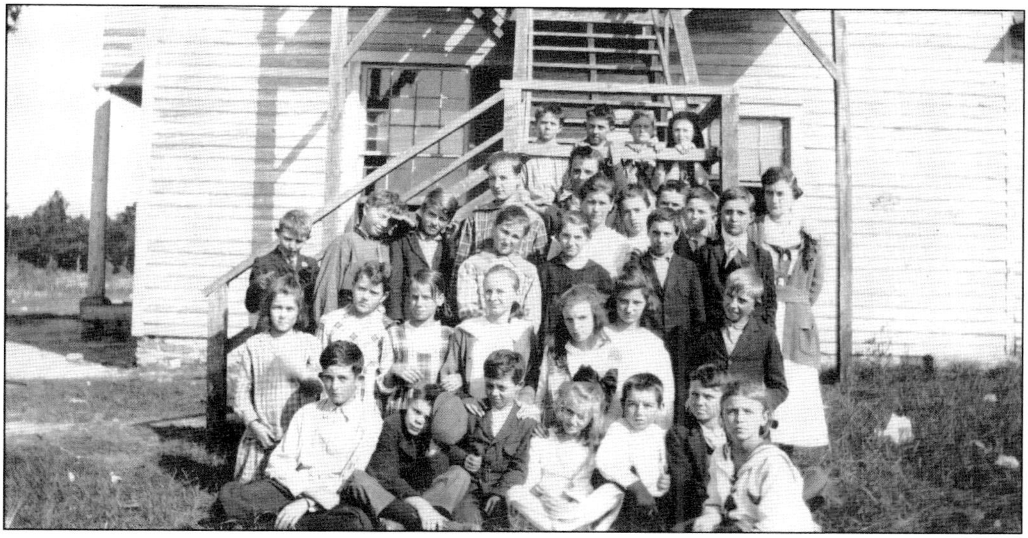

At the side stairwell entrance at Lewisville Academy, students assemble about 1921 for a class portrait. (LHS.)

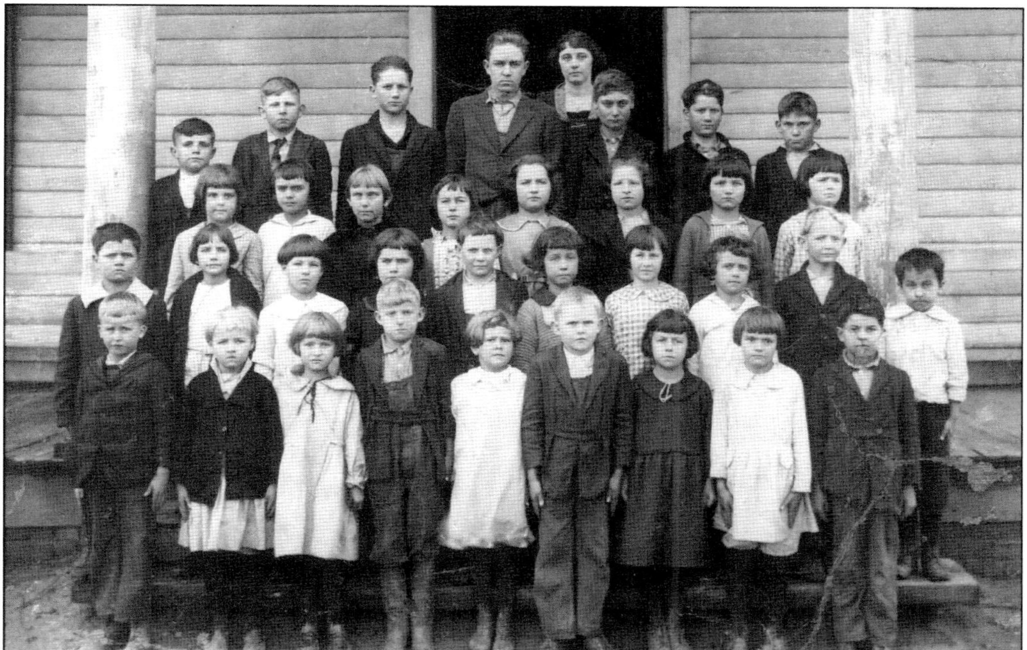

In 1922, the last year Lewisville Academy conducted classes in this building, elementary students posing together include, from left to right, (first row) Herbert Moser, Laura Conrad, Mary Carter, Robah Carter, Sarah Martin, Claude Moser, Alma Wilson, Ruth Whitman, and Jack Tuttle; (second row) James Hicks, Macy Boles, unidentified, Albert Craft, Carson Boles, Lillian Mock, Clara Kiger, Myra Dull, Osborne Boles, and Philip Mock; (third row) Dorothy Moser, Annie Ruth Dull, Nellie Clayton, Blanche Craft, Annie Gertrude Moser, Kate Warner, Lettie Hicks, and Mildred Warner; (fourth row) Howard Moser, Lemuel Carter, Andrew Holder, Jack Freeman, teacher Alverta Hunt, ? Hicks, Ervin Holder, and Lester Clayton. (LCH.)

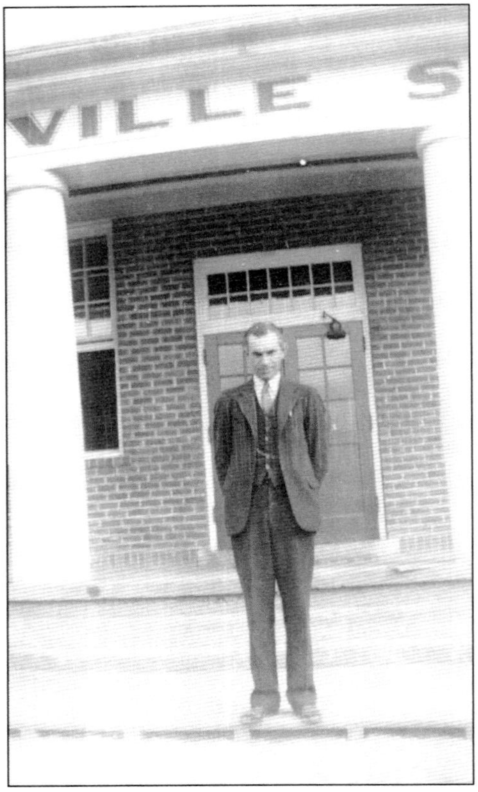

Principal Sidney A. "S. A." Winslow served for many years as principal of the second Lewisville School, built in 1923. Along with his duties as principal, he taught classes and coached sport teams, the standard work ethic for educators of his day. (LHS.)

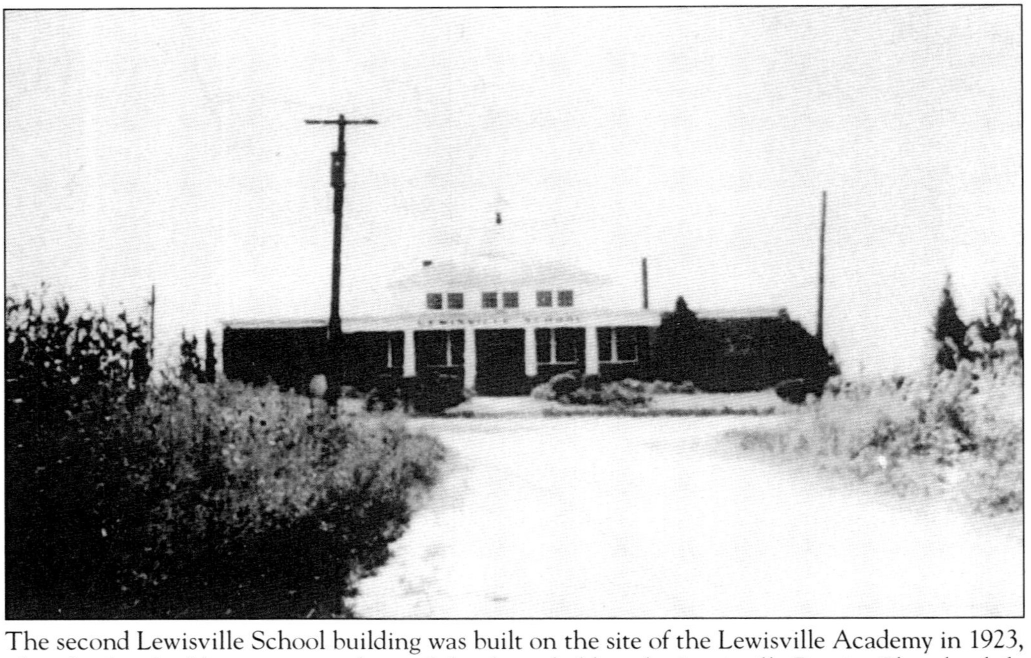

The second Lewisville School building was built on the site of the Lewisville Academy in 1923, after the first building was torn down. School was held in the Lewisville Baptist Church while the new brick structure was built. This building burned on December 2, 1945. (LHS.)

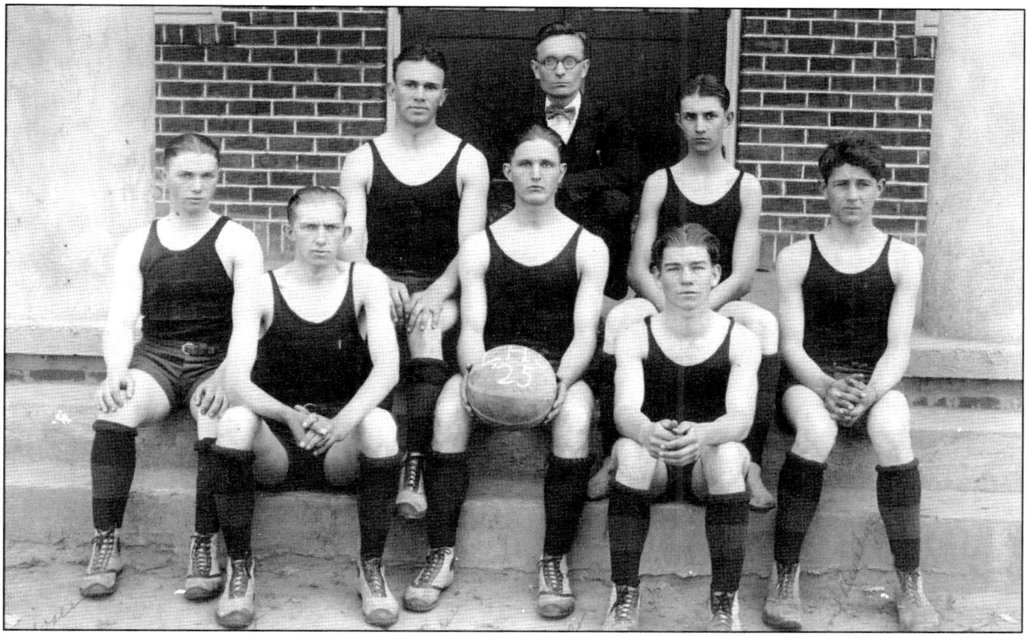

The winning Lewisville High School basketball team in 1925 included, from left to right, (first row) Clarence Moser, Fletcher Craft, Clarence ?, Tom Craft, Sherrill Beauchamp; (second row) Frank Reynolds, unidentified coach, and Allen Moser. (RRH.)

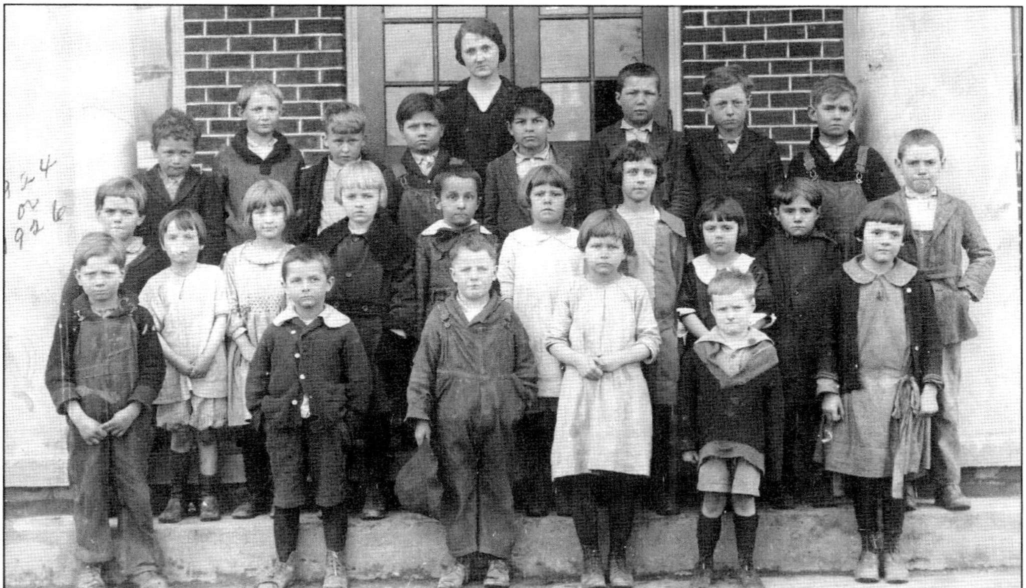

Students in four grades at Lewisville School in 1924 or 1926 included, from left to right, (first row) Charlie Hicks, Allen Mock, ? Stewart, Hattie Black, Smith Williams, and Ruth Whitman; (second row) Joseph Craft, Frances Williams, Mary Carter, Laura Conrad, Philip Mock, Sarah Martin, Myra Dull, Annie Ruth Dull, Horace Moser, and Terry Kimel; (third row) Henry Petree, Osborne Boles, Herbert Moser, James Hicks, Jack Tuttle, James Black, Charlie Hicks, Fred Craft; and teacher Carrie Sprinkle. (LCH.)

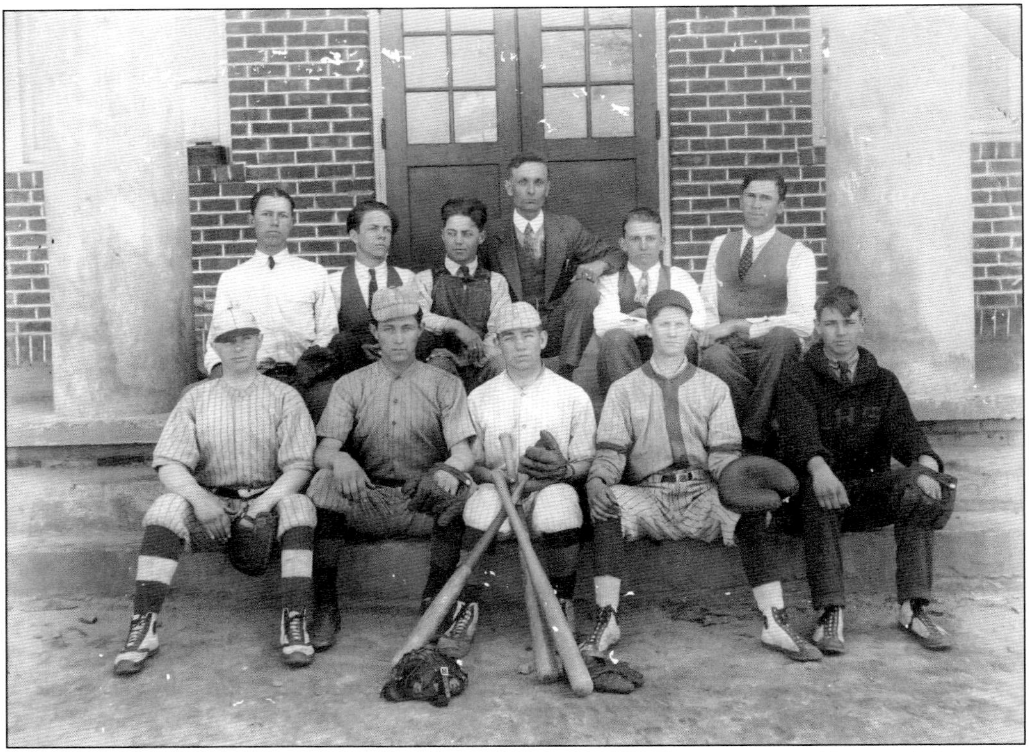

The 1927 Lewisville School baseball team seated at the school entrance are (first row) Clarence Moser, Sherrill Beauchamp, Tom Craft, Ervin Holder, and Talmadge Kimel; (second row) Delbert Craft, Allen Lasley, Bill Wagoner, Principal J. Hugh White, Aubrey Kinney, and Dan Reynolds. (RRH.)

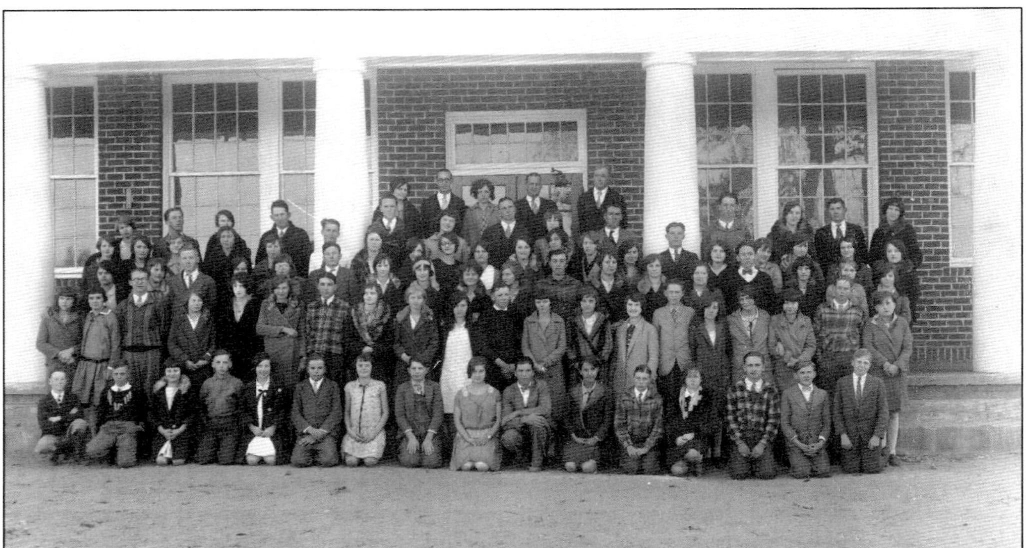

The high school students in 1927 pose together on the steps of the Lewisville School. (RRH.)

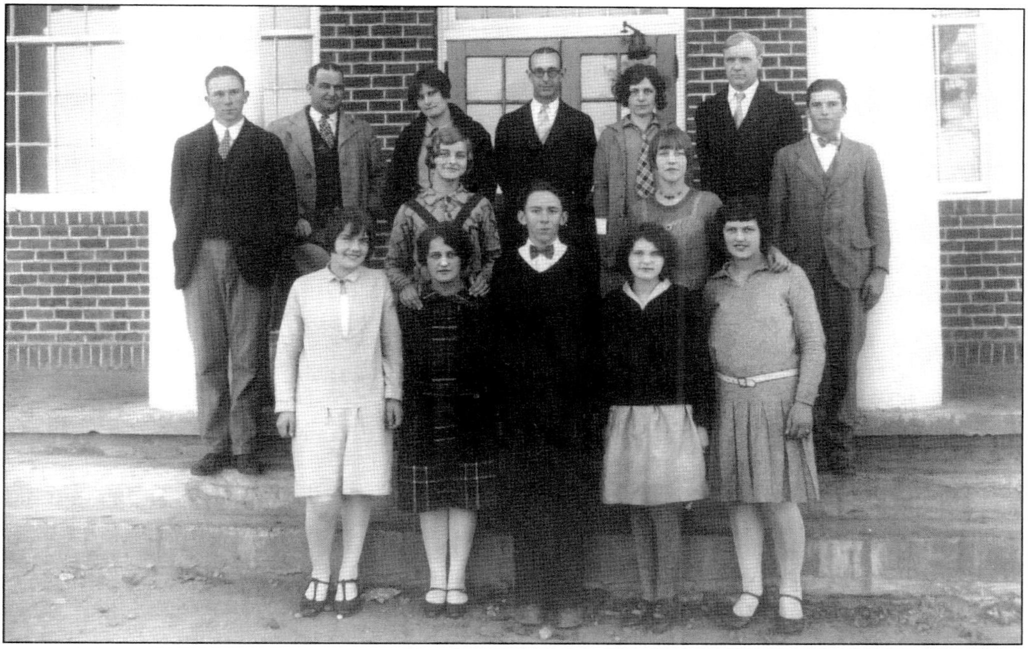

A Lewisville School class of students standing with their teachers in 1929 include, from left to right, (first row) Lucy Craft (Sheets), Johnsie Martin (Kinnamon), Fred D. Hauser, Elizabeth Jones (Saunders), and Annie Laurie Conrad (Holcomb); (second row) Tom Reynolds, Pauline Moser (Longest), Stella Reich (Casey), and Clifton Warner; (third row) Principal George Dewey Shore, Vivian Wheless, Lonnie Clifton Elmore, Elizabeth Hahn (Smith), and Wesley Speas. (MHD.)

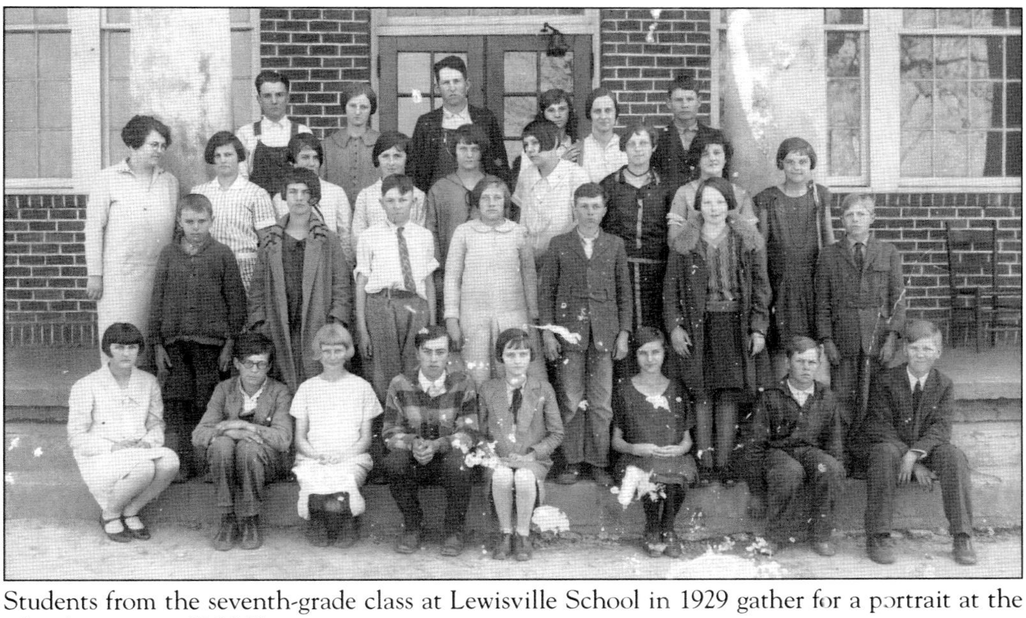

Students from the seventh-grade class at Lewisville School in 1929 gather for a portrait at the school entrance. (RRH.)

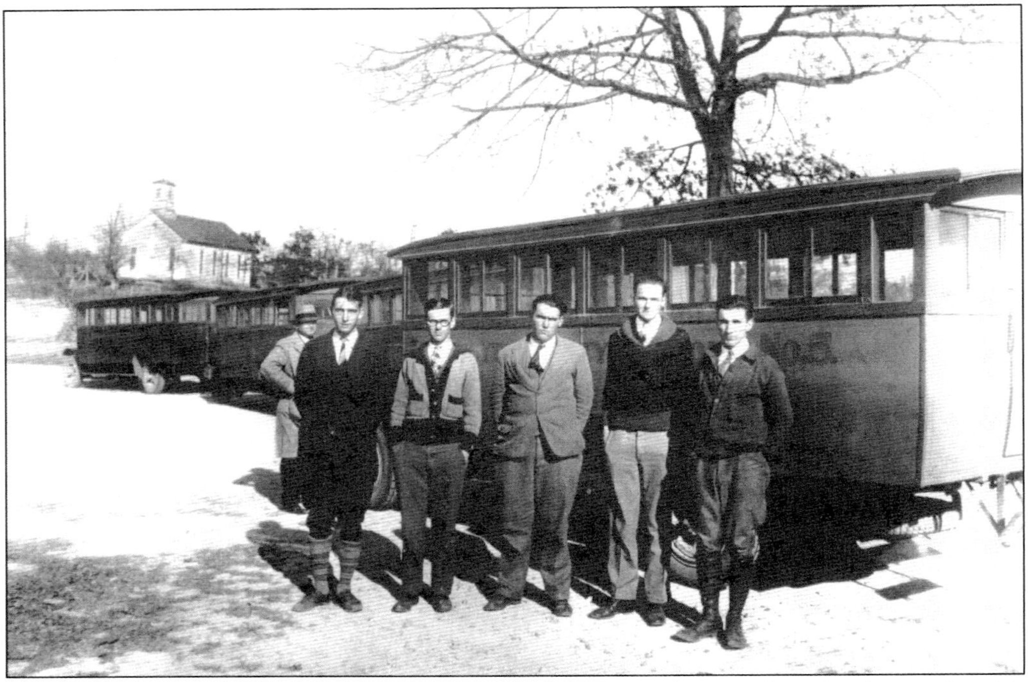

The 1927–1928 Lewisville School student bus drivers are standing on the school grounds, with Lewisville Baptist Church in view upon the hill. Principal George Dewey Shore is standing in back with a hat and overcoat, with student drivers, posing from left to right, A. C. Mock, Herman Landreth, Bruce Harbin, Porter Reynolds, and Andrew Harper. (RRH.)

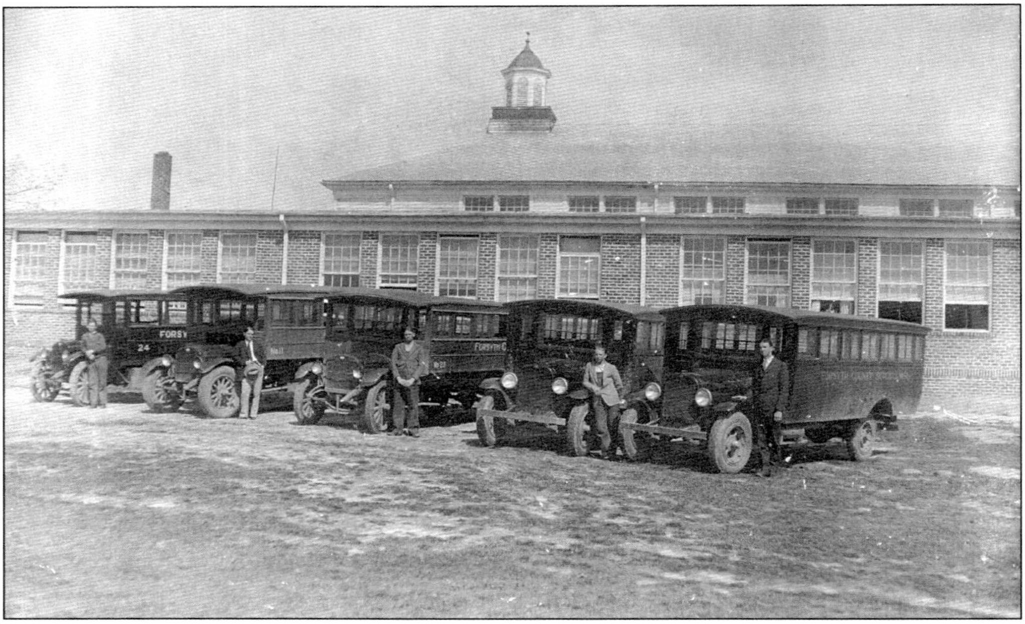

High school student bus drivers standing near the second Lewisville School building are, from left to right, Jimmie Butler, Talmadge Kimel, unidentified, Aubrey Kinney, and Dan Reynolds. (RRH.)

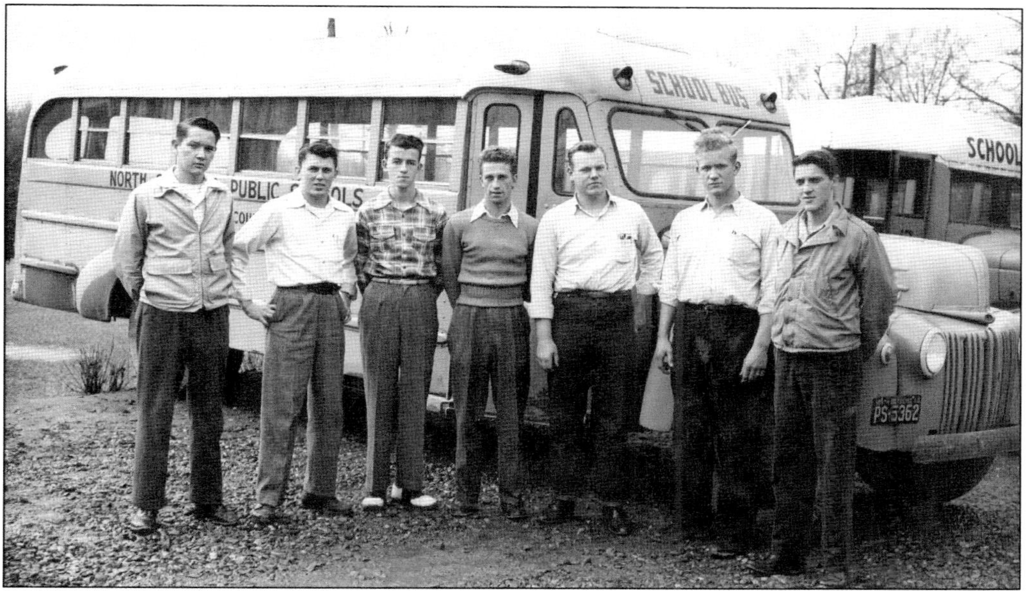

Lewisville School student bus drivers in 1947–1948 transported high school students to South Fork School and elementary students to Vienna School while Lewisville School was being rebuilt after fire destroyed the facility in 1945. Some elementary students also attended classes in the agricultural building on the Lewisville School campus. Seniors officially graduated from Lewisville School during the years at South Fork. Standing from left to right are Leo Pegram, Charlie Hauser, Wake Burke, Phillip Jones, Lee Bailey, Arvil Hensley, and Bruce Flynt. (DCH.)

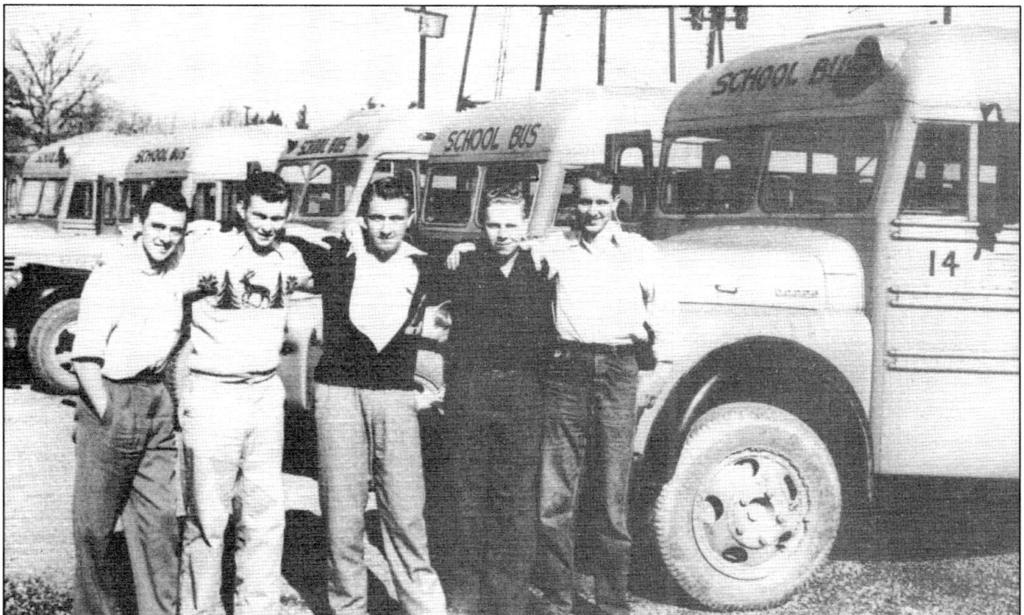

Lewisville School student bus drivers standing arm in arm together with their buses in 1950 include, from left to right, Bobby Jordan, Billy Reid, Bruce Harper, Frank Holder, and Bobby Harper. (LHS.)

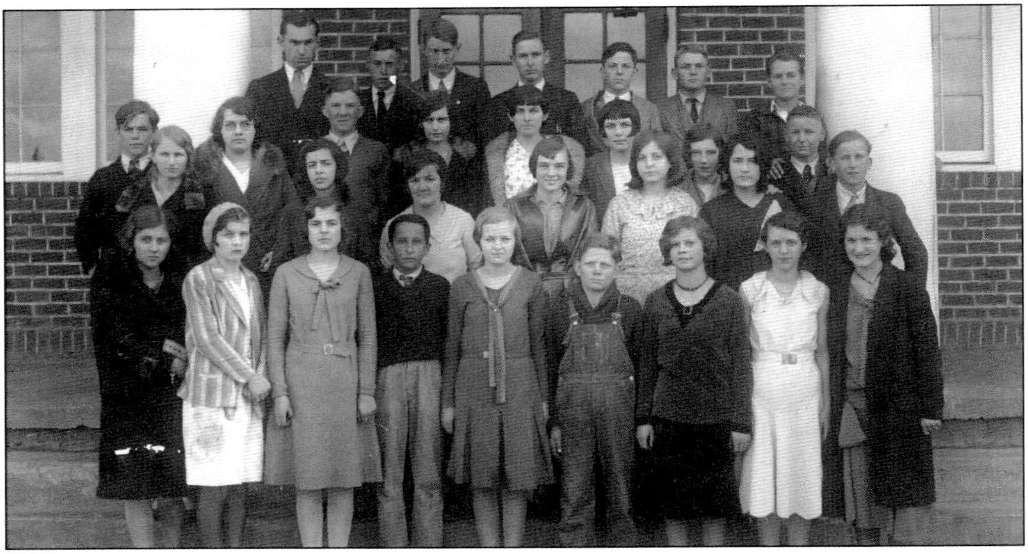

Ninth-grade students at Lewisville School in 1930–1931 included, from left to right, (first row) Virginia Fink, Gladys Binkley, Adeline Hauser, Philip Mock, Laura Conrad, Charlie Hicks, Sarah Martin, Myra Dull, and Nell Robertson; (second row) Elizabeth McBride, Annie Gertrude Moser, Robah Stimson, Marie Landreth, Pauline Mullican, Viola Rothrock, Lola Warner, and Herbert Moser; (third row) Odell Robertson, Louise Bryant, Evola Cumby, Adeline Seats, Blanche Harper, and William Rock; (fourth row) Principal S. A. Winslow, Robert Oakley, Harold Conrad, Roy Hutchins, William Jones, and Elmo Reich. (LCH.)

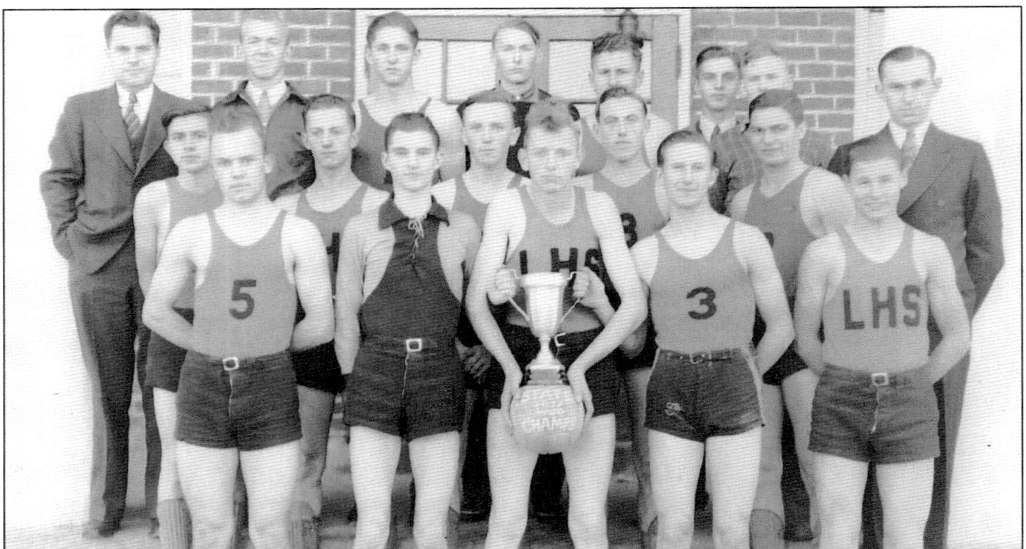

The Lewisville School soccer team won the North Carolina High School Soccer Championship in 1936–1937. Displaying their trophy are team members, from left to right, (first row) James Transou, Pete Slater, Tom Jones, Hubert Crater, and Jim Binkley; (second row) Raeford Groce, Virgil Jones, Tom Foster, Herb Speas, and Walt Harbin; (third row) coach C. W. Dinkins, Carl Robertson, Rob Beauchamp, Don Dalton, Dave Rock, William Henry Moser, Memory Redding, and Principal S. A. Winslow. (MOJ.)

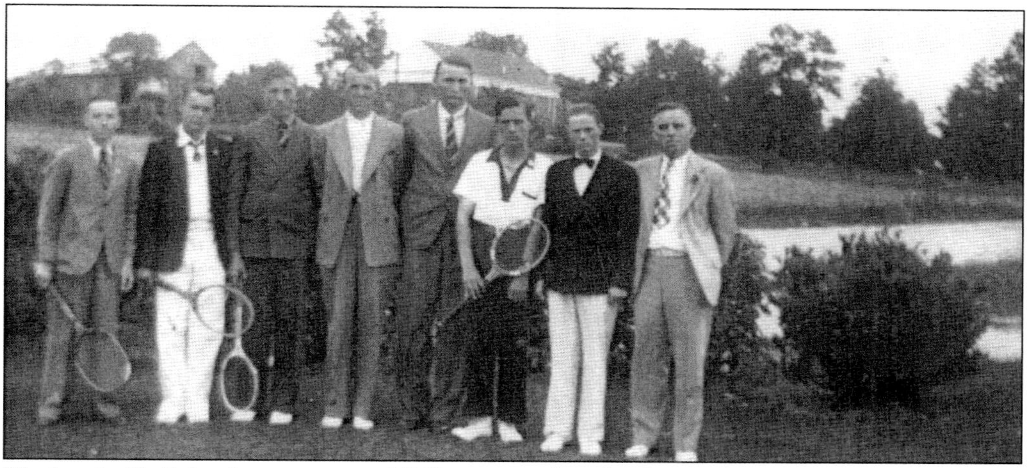

The Lewisville School tennis team of 1937 poses on the school grounds with the second Lewisville Baptist Church building in the background. Students are, from left to right, Lanier Williams, Edward Fulk, Herbert Speas, Carl Robertson, Donald Dalton, Transou Conrad, Smith Williams, and coach Hokey Hunter. (NGC.)

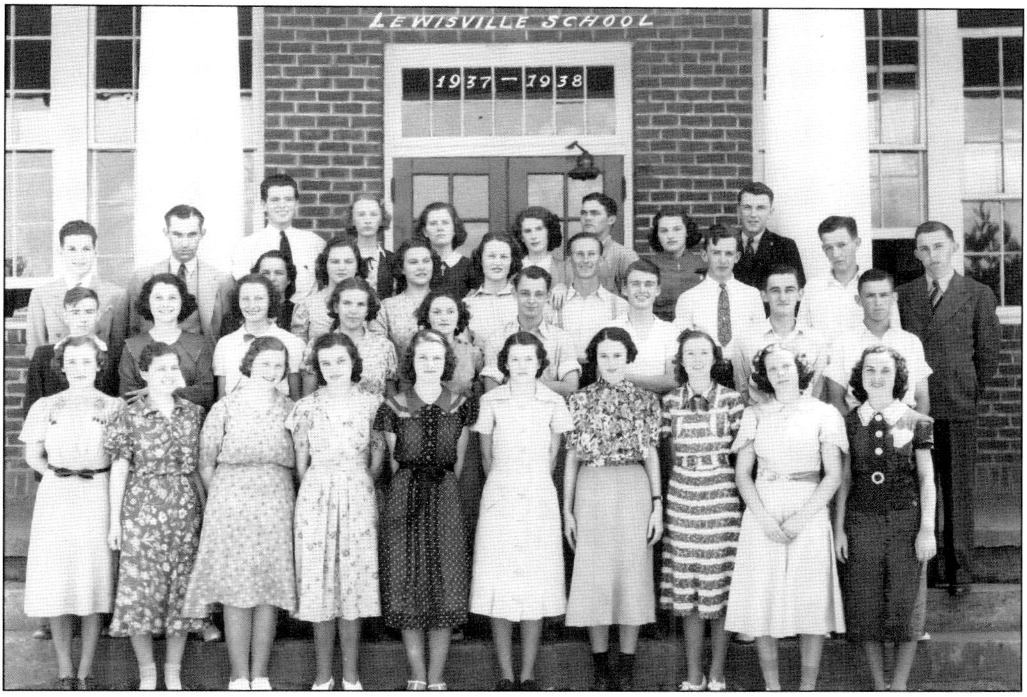

Lewisville School class of 1938 graduates included, from left to right, (first row) Carrie Scott, Eunice Reeves, Virginia Dalton, Edith Allgood, Dorothy Vogler, Miss Singletary, Nell Tuttle, Mary Alice Fulk, Pansy Steelman, and Mabel Smith; (second row) Lanier Williams, Katie Lee Mock, Dovie Dull, Eunice Doub, Dora Fulton, Edward Fulk, Grady McBride, J. Henry Craft, and W. D. McBride; (third row) Odell Conrad, S.A. Winslow-principal, Annie Mary Harbin, Margaret Petree, Anna Foster, Cleo Ziglar, Hubert Crater, Frank Conrad, Luther Hege, Jesse Flynt; (fourth row) Oneal Reich, Kathryn Burke, Virginia Orrell, Kathleen Grubbs, Walter Harbin, Lucille Transou, and Gray Conrad. (MAFW, MPB.)

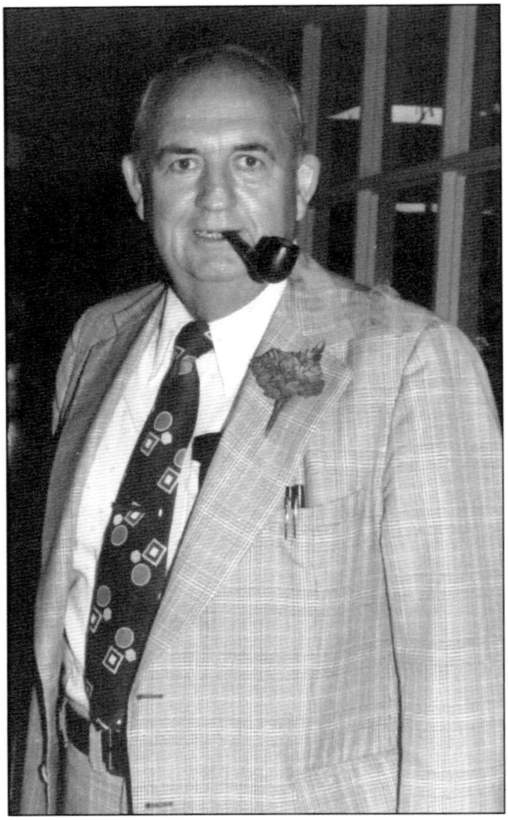

Harold Simpson was a well-known citizen in Lewisville, having served as principal at Lewisville School, Southwest High School, and West Forsyth High School during his career. A native of Hyde County in North Carolina, he taught and coached in Hamlet, North Carolina, served in the U.S. Navy, then earned a masters degree at UNC Chapel Hill. He was principal at Cherry Point, near the North Carolina coast, before taking the post as principal of the new Lewisville School building in mid August of 1949. This photograph shows him near the end of his career. (LHS.)

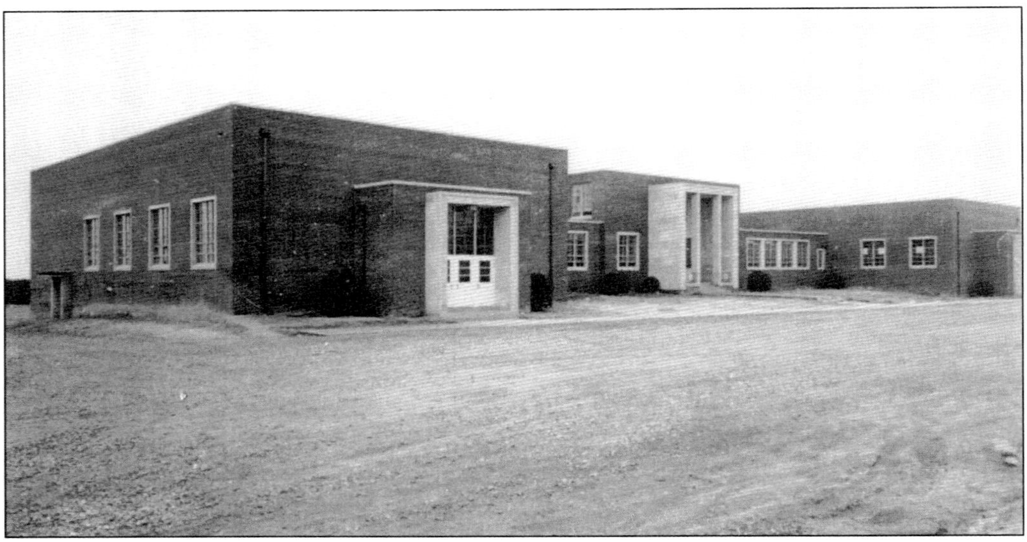

After a fire on December 2, 1945, burned the school to the ground, a third Lewisville School building was constructed on the same site. It opened for the 1948–1949 school year, and the graduating class became known as the "forty-niners." Harold Simpson served as the first principal in this building and elementary through high school students attended classes together. Today this school serves elementary grades. (LHS.)

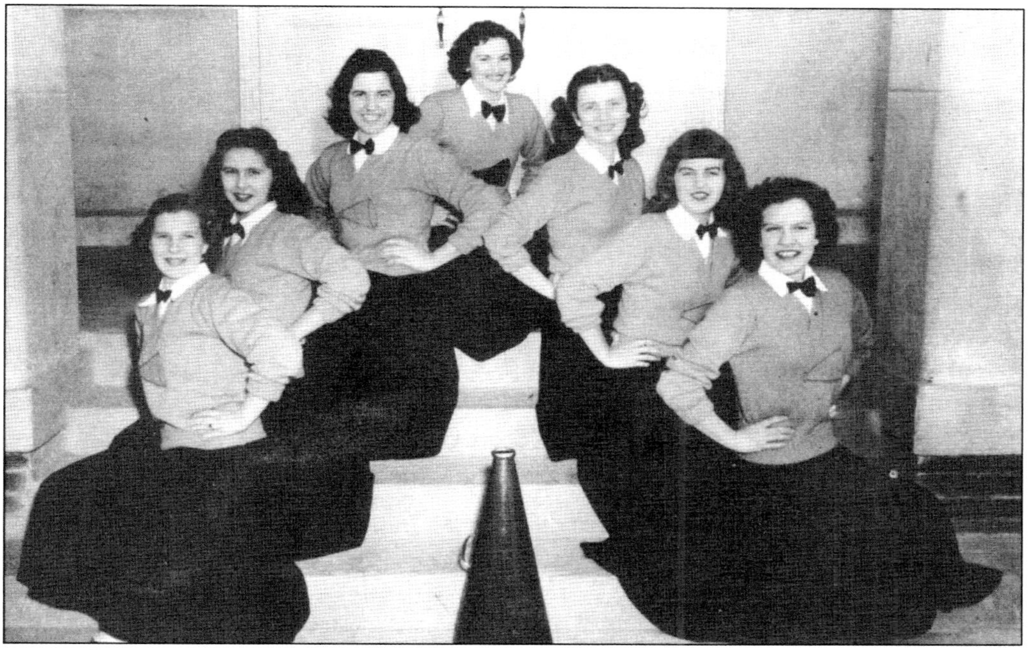

Lewisville School cheerleaders led energetic students to cheer on their teams in 1948–1949. Gathered around a megaphone are, from left to right, Nancy Hauser, Dora Harper, Polly Brewer, chief Anna Jones, Julia Ann Mock, Norma Jean Bowen, and Catherine Prince. (LHS.)

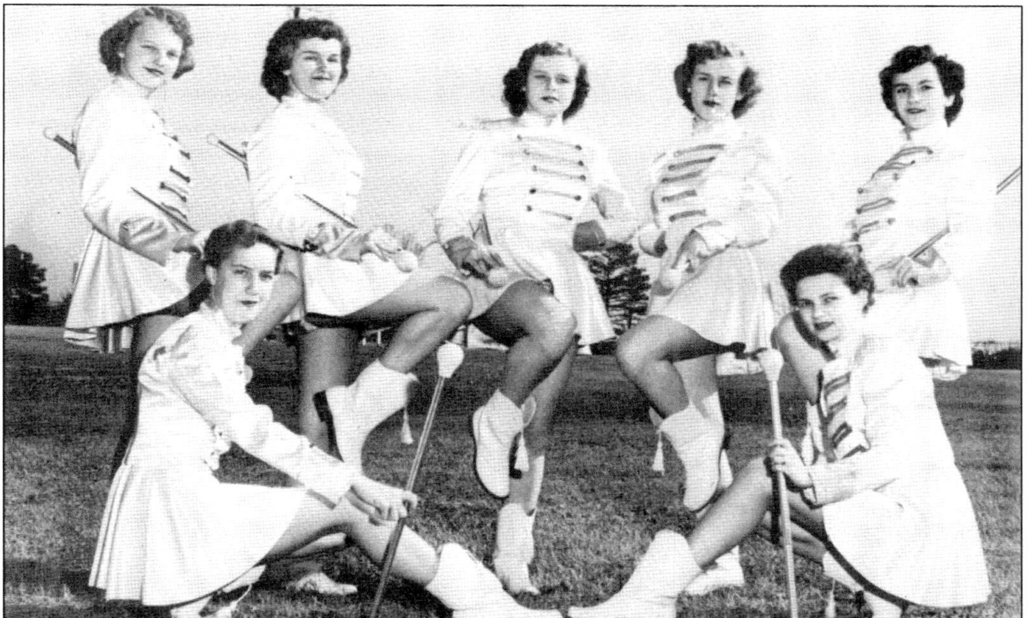

Majorettes led the Lewisville School band in parades and performed at sporting events. Posing on the school grounds in 1952 are, from left to right, (first row) chief Joanne Casey and Rachel Snow; (second row) Audrey Kinney, Catherine Williams, Paige Jones, Joyce Binkley, and Patsy Roberson. (LHS.)

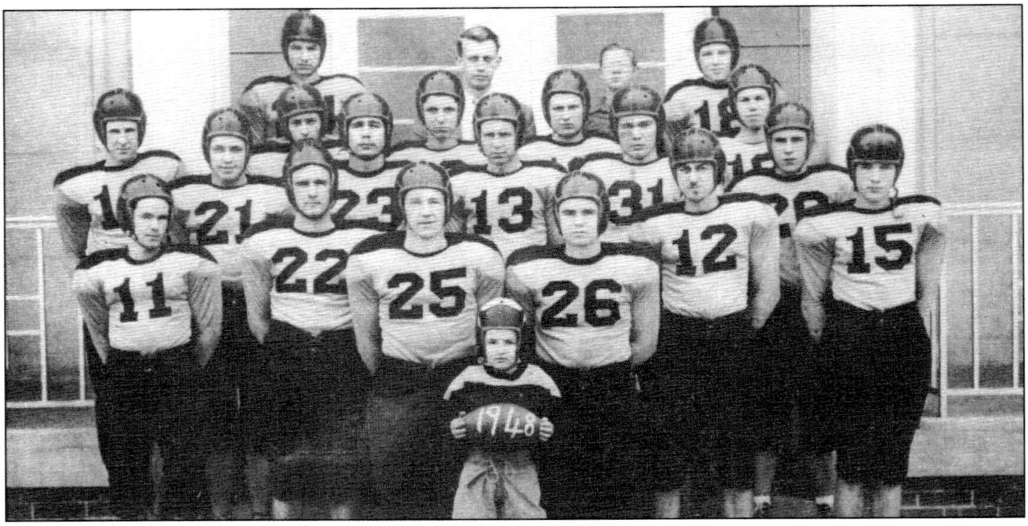

The 1948 Lewisville football team competed with other Forsyth County schools. Mascot Danny Jennings holds a football with cocaptains Lloyd Caudle (left) and Ray Plunkett (right) standing behind him. Team members included, from left to right, (first row) Foy Jennings, William Southern, Floyd Craft, and Glenn Lasley; (second row) Jack Dull, Bob Fox, Edwin Craft, Bobby Harper, Billy Lasley, and Franklin Mathis; (third row) Bob Huffman, Jake Nifong, Billy Fred Harper, and James Mullican; (fourth row) Roy Jennings, coach Gale Lemly, manager Ted Fulp, and Don McMordie. (LHS.)

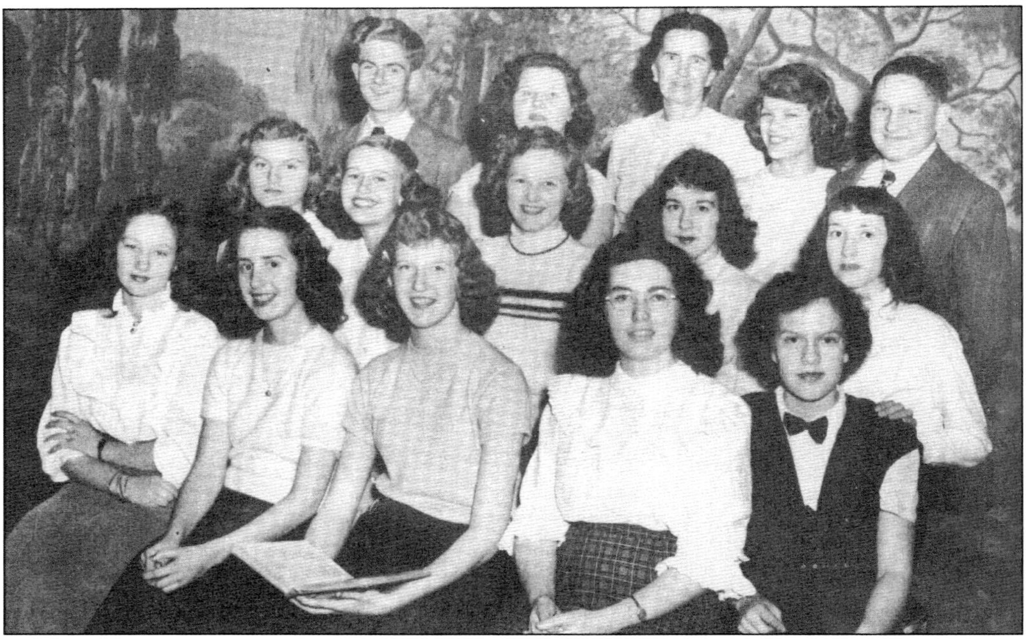

Students conversing in the French Club strengthened their foreign language skills under the guidance of advisor Bernice Ross. Club members are, from left to right, (first row) Eleanor Tise, Ruth Scott, Betty Jo Conrad, Sally Huffman, and Catherine Prince; (second row) Margaret Reich, Pat Jones, Eva Nelle Harper, Betty Potts, and Romelia Fulton; (third row) Lewis Craft, Rosa Bodsford, Bernice Ross, Iris Goin, and David Hicks. (LHS.)

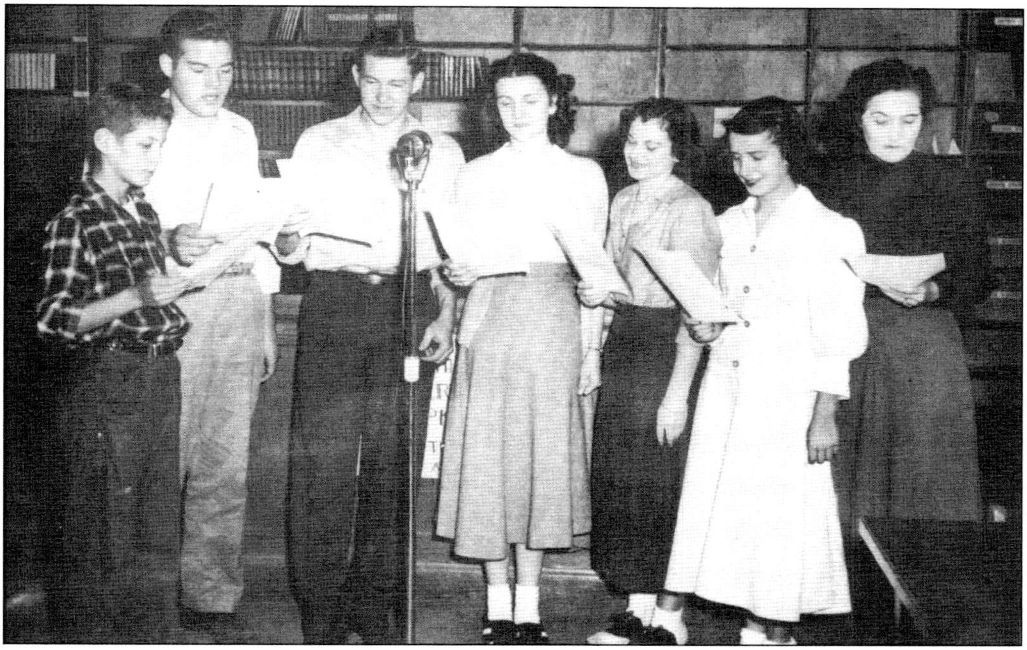

Members of the Lewisville Radio Council participated in a Forsyth County group which gave programs on the air for 10 weeks. The 1948–1949 students representing Lewisville School were, from left to right, David Holder, Ned Moser, Lloyd Caudle, Julia Ann Mock, Anna Jones, Ruth Scott, and their sponsor Inez Campbell. (LHS.)

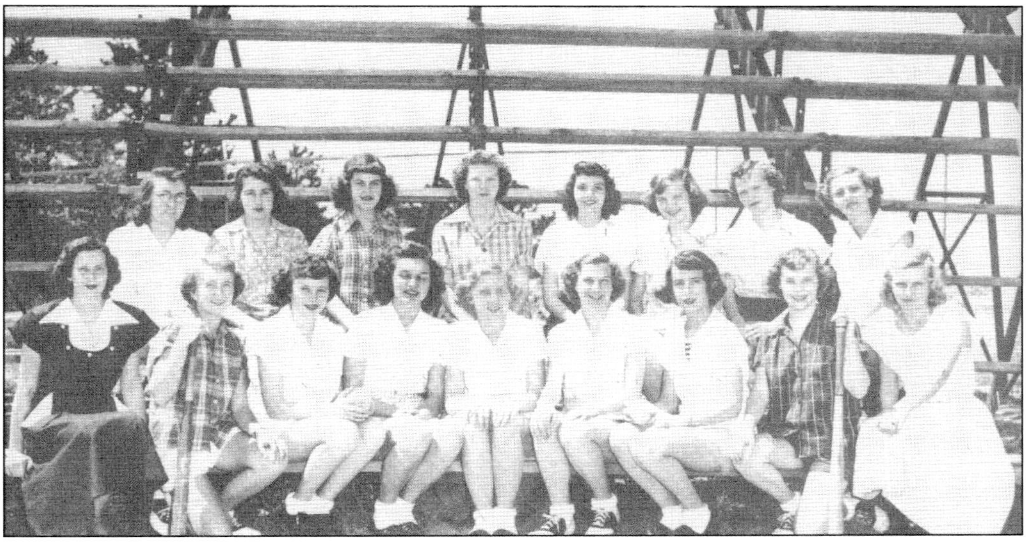

The 1950 girls' softball team was coached by Marjorie Holcombe. Seated on bleachers in the sports field are, from left to right, (first row) Coach Holcombe, Dot Moser, Delmas Mendenhall, Eunice Craft, Sarah Ruth Mock, Nancy Hauser, Ruth Scott, Carolyn Sprinkle, and manager Nancy Dull; (second row) Ward Huffman, Bettie Potts, Jean Bowen, Grace Jennings, Alda Blevins, Leota Harper, Eva Nelle Harper, and Martha Nifong. (LHS.)

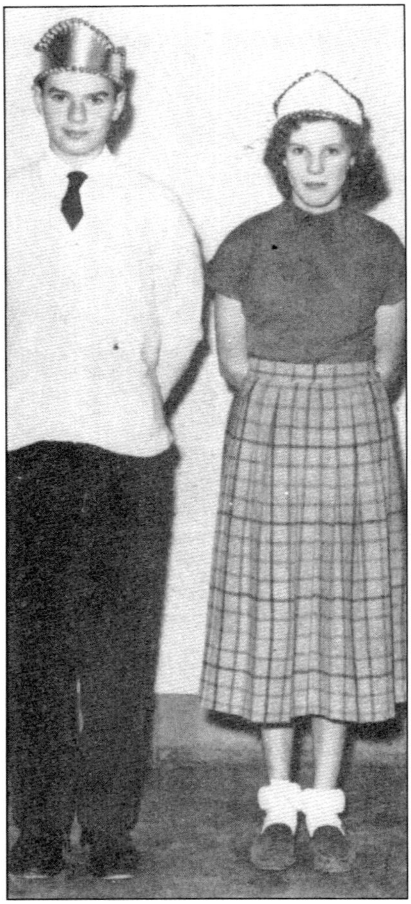

The Fall Festival was a popular annual event held in Lewisville with a parade, carnival, and activities in the school and community. Beginning in 1947, the festival was a fund-raiser sponsored by the Lewisville School PTA and often held in December. Students were selected for the "Royal Court," including a king, queen, prince, princess, duke, and duchess. In 1953, "King" Dicky Reynolds and "Queen" Barbara Sprinkle (Moser) ruled over the Fall Festival court and events. In 1954, the Lewisville Volunteer Fire Department began cosponsoring the event with the PTA. (LHS.)

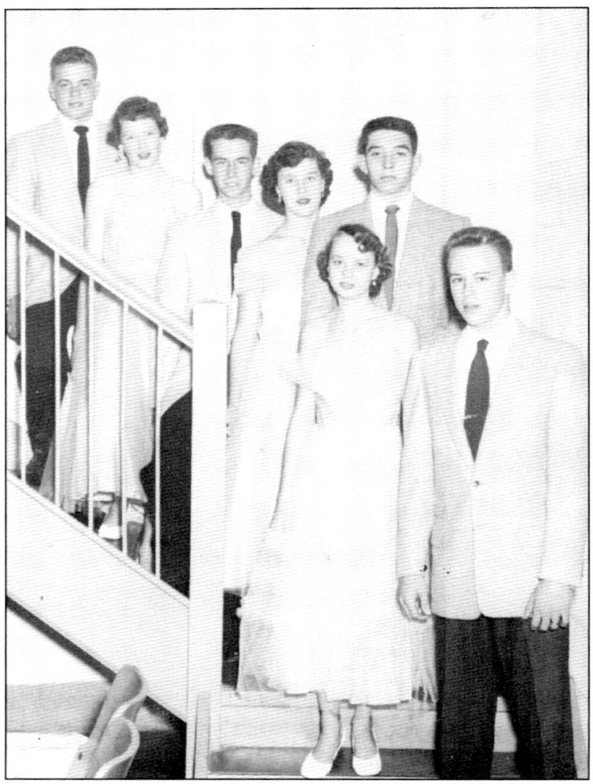

Junior classmates traditionally sponsored the Junior-Senior Banquet each year and assisted with the senior graduation ceremonies. The 1955 Junior Marshalls standing on the staircase included, from left to right, Kenneth Hauser, Libby Bowen, Allen Harbin, Carolyn Jarvis, Henry Pearce, Pat Willis, and Reginald Koontz (chief). (LHS.)

Four

Work and Prosperity

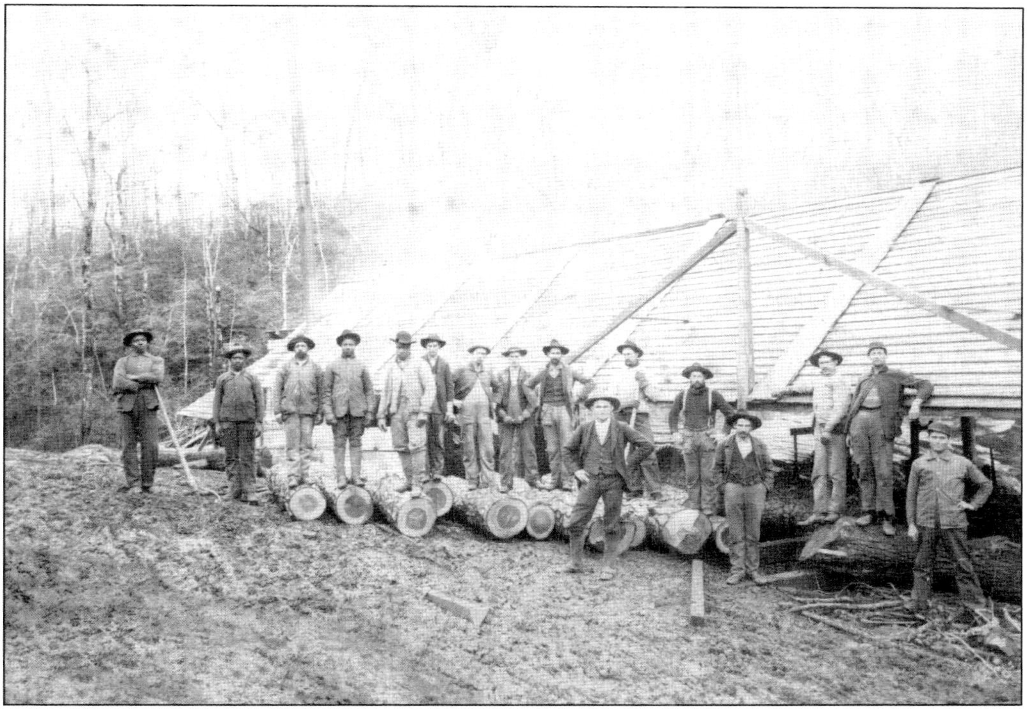

Oral tradition identifies this business as the Laugenour-Nissen Sawmill in Lewisville or the Frederick Ziglar Sawmill in the Vienna community. The Laugenour-Nissen Sawmill operated in the later 1800s on Shallowford Road at the present-day site of the Lewisville Town Square. Owned and operated by brother-in-laws Lewis Laugenour and George Nissen, their sawmill was the largest commercial enterprise in Lewisville during this time. Timber was sawed and transported many places, including lumber for building sturdy wagons in the George E. Nissen Wagon Works in the Waughtown area of Forsyth County. (LHS.)

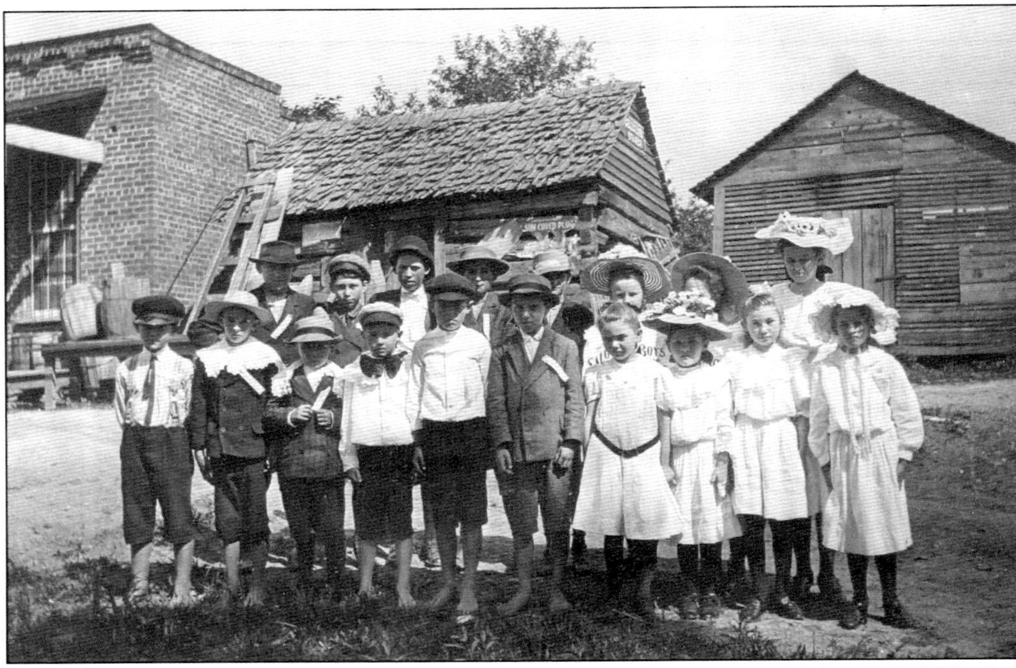

Established in the late 1800s, business thrived for many years at Eugene Harley "E. H." Wright's store, located on Shallowford Road near Styers Street. He sold tools for working, ammunition for hunting, shoes and clothing, fabrics and notions for sewing, and food and beverages for families. Wright took skins bartered with trappers and hunters to Winston to exchange for the variety of goods carried in his store. Sometimes called a trading post, Wright's Store was an early location of the post office and offered the first telephone in Lewisville. Children pose at the side of Wright's store following the Prohibition Rally around 1908. (LCH.)

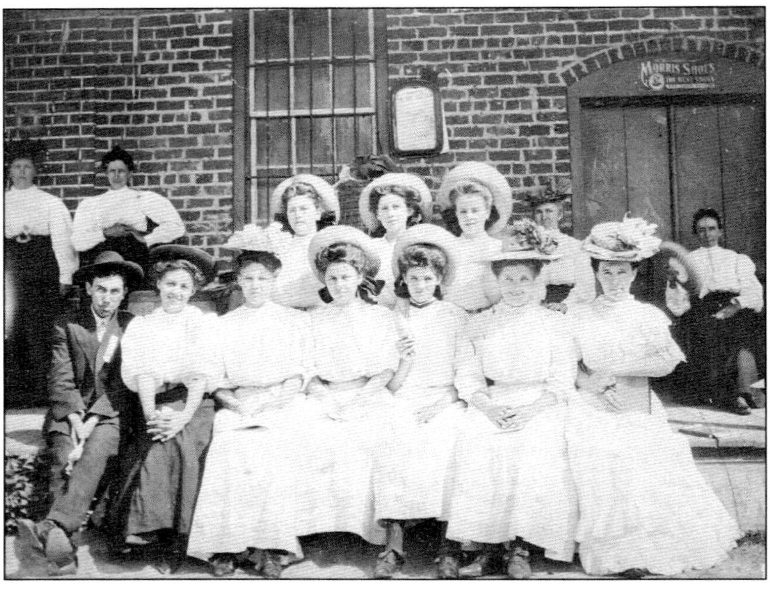

Teenage girls pose with friends at Wright's Store following the Prohibition Rally in the early 1900s. From left to right are (seated) Lee Hauser, Blanche Spaugh, Bett Hart, unidentified, Florence Holder, Mae Wallace, and Susie Tuttle; (standing) Ethel Spaugh, Elsie Doub, and Fannie Fulk. Alma Spaugh is the woman behind Fannie wearing a hat. (LHS.)

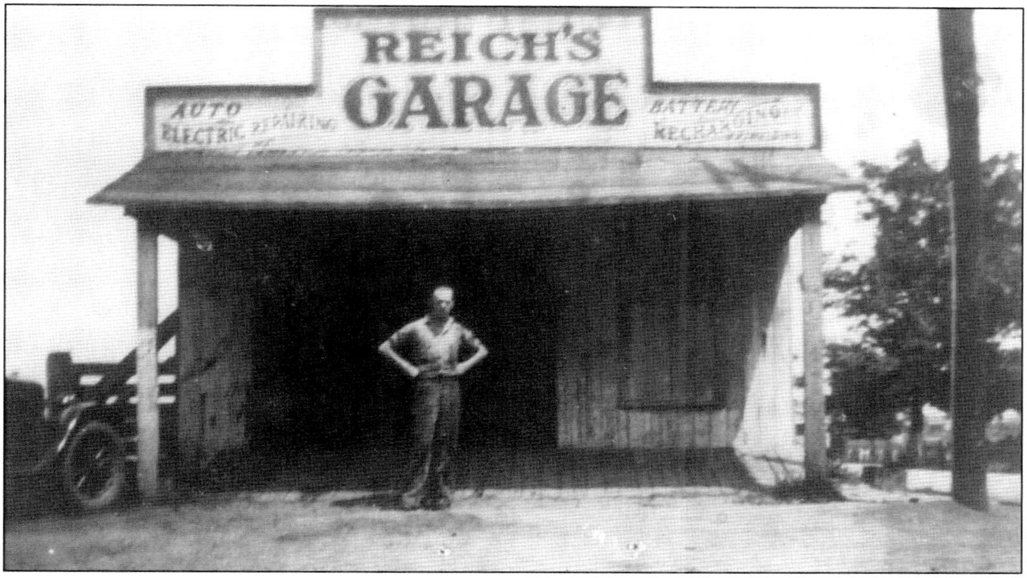

In 1929, William Spencer Reich stands in front of his first garage building. It was rented property, located on the corner of Shallowford and Lewisville-Vienna Roads. In his career, Reich worked for 25 years as an automotive electrician for the Atlantic Greyhound Company and as an automobile mechanic at Twin City Motors, Hoffman Motor Services, and Disher Chevrolet before beginning his own business. (MRB.)

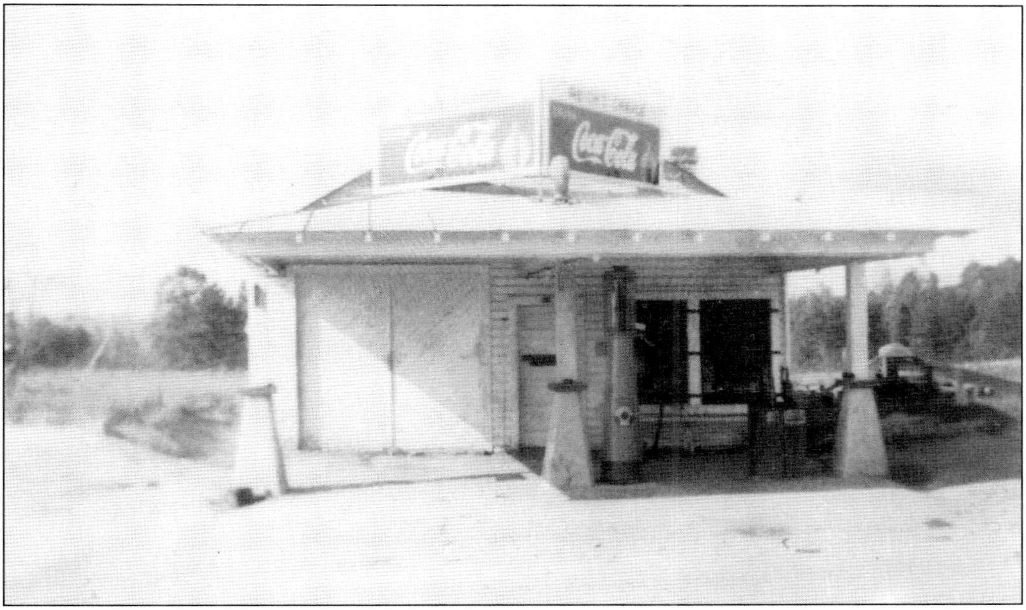

This Reich's Garage building was constructed about 1935 by Spencer Reich on the site of Black's School, a one-room schoolhouse, on Williams Road. He used the wood from the old school to build this structure and moved his family next door in 1938. In 1945, Reich moved his business back to Shallowford Road in Lewisville. Today the business operates as Lewisville Automotive Service in the fourth building site on Shallowford owned and operated by members of the Reich family. (MRB.)

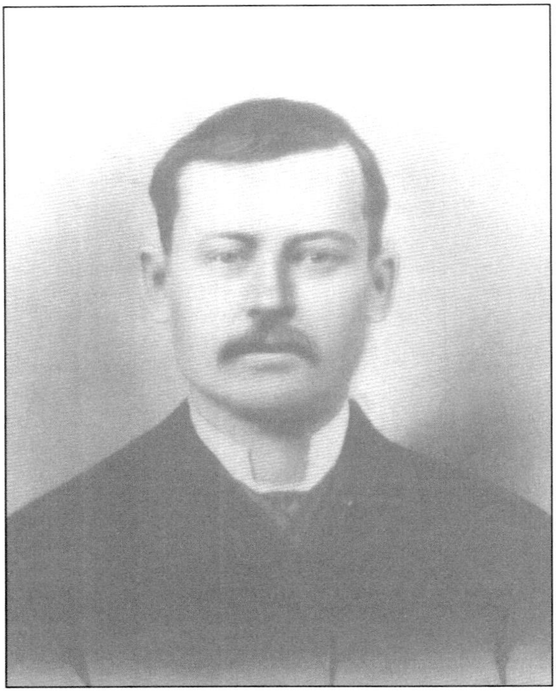

Thomas William Fulk apprenticed his blacksmith trade in Old Town with his uncle Andrew Fulk. Thomas and Mary Fulk raised nine children, and his home and blacksmith shop were located across from E. H. Wright's Store on Shallowford Road. Even on days when business was brisk, he always had time to stop and fix a broken toy for a child. (LCH, MAFW.)

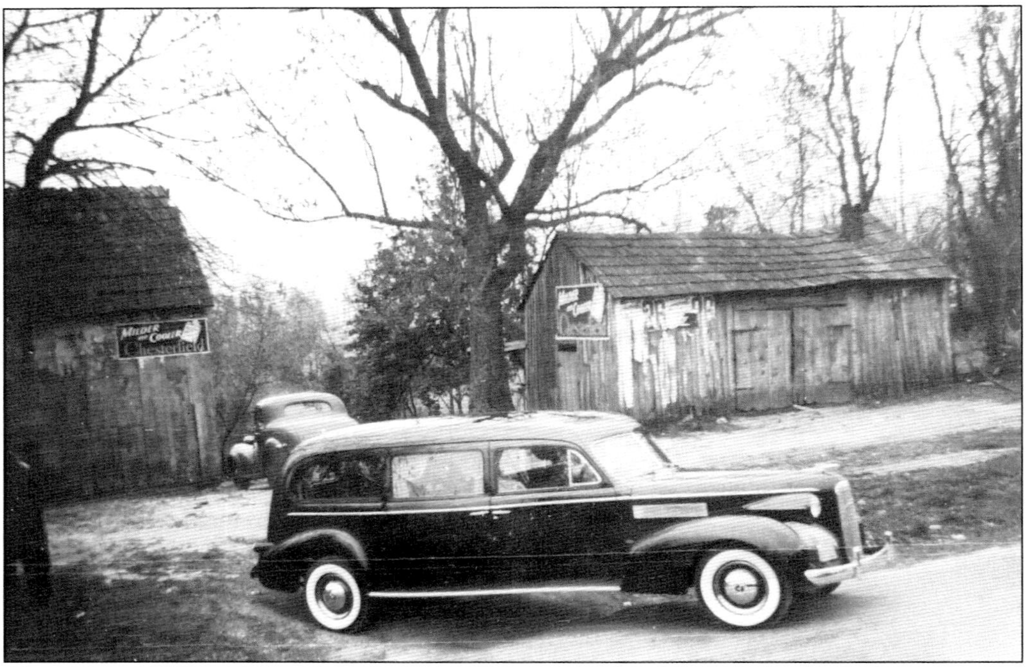

Thomas Fulk's Blacksmith Shop was a thriving business from the 1880s into the 20th century. E. H. Wright invited Fulk to relocate his business "uptown" in Lewisville, leaving his original shop on Lewisville-Vienna Road. T. W. Fulk's funeral procession in April 1940 is departing his home place, with the woodworking shop at left and blacksmith shop at right. The blacksmith shop stood at the site of the former Lewisville Furniture Store building. (MAFW.)

Mary Elizabeth Millis Fulk grew up in the Quaker community of Guilford County. She worked as a postmistress in Old Town before moving to Lewisville with her husband. Mary and her daughters, Fannie Fulk (Conrad) and Lela Fulk (Burke), operated the first telephone switchboard in their home on Shallowford Road, serving customers in southwestern Forsyth County. The phone system operated from 1911 to 1937 in the Fulk home place. (LCH, MAFW.)

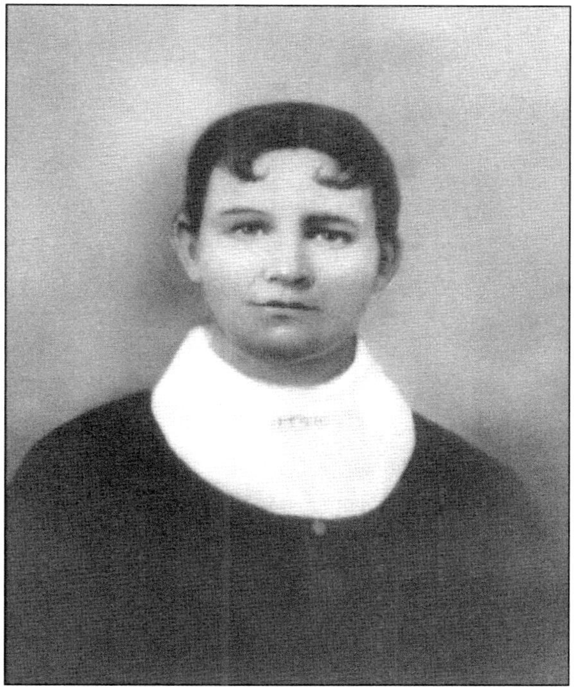

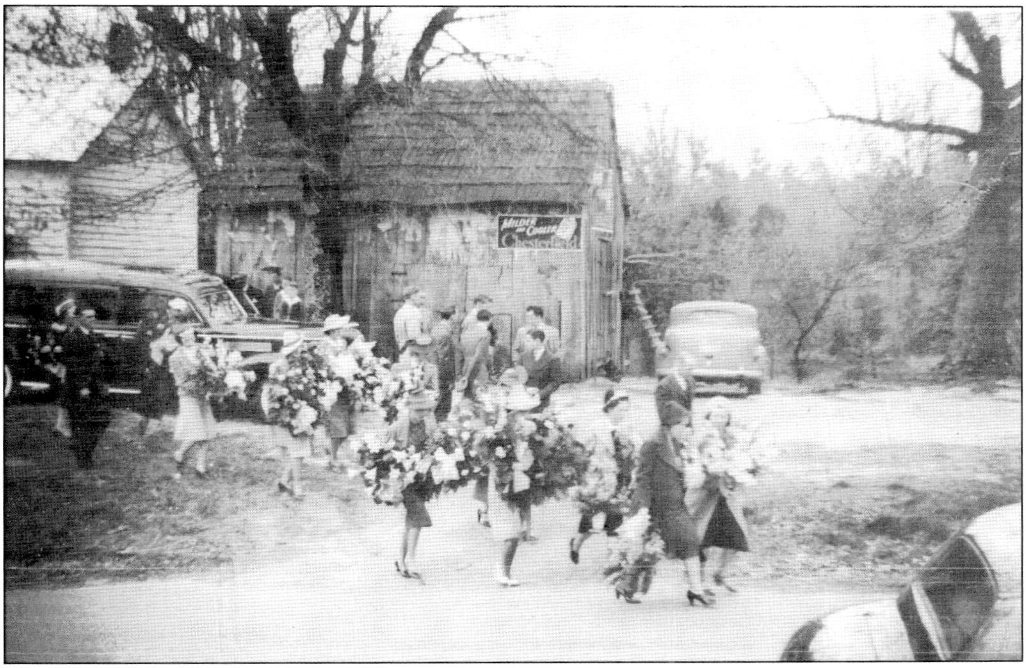

In earlier decades, funeral services were held in the home of the deceased, with funeral processions following to the church and cemetery. Family and friends carry flowers for T. W. Fulk's funeral procession in April 1940, walking from his home on Shallowford Road to Lewisville Baptist Church for his burial. The woodworking shop stood beside his home place. A commercial building for small businesses and former furniture store sit on the site of the home place today. (MAFW.)

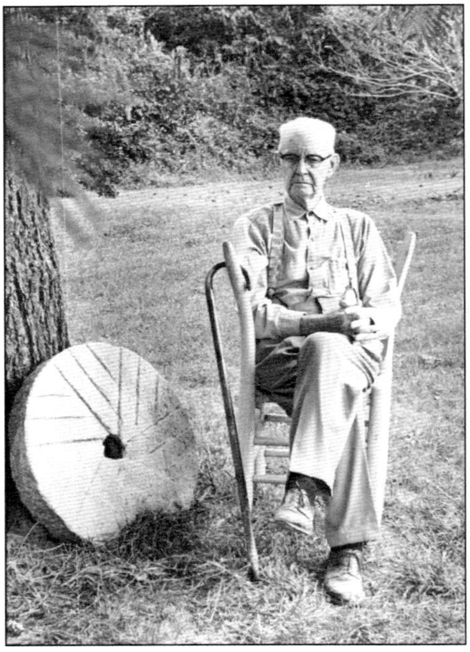

Fielden Hale "F. H." Jennings sits with a millstone beside his chair. In 1925, he moved from Galax, Virginia, to acquire the roller mill in Lewisville from the Sprinkle family. When the Jennings family took over operation of the mill, the name changed from Fairview Roller Mill to Lewisville Roller Mills. It was owned and operated for nearly 60 years by the Jennings family. (RJ)

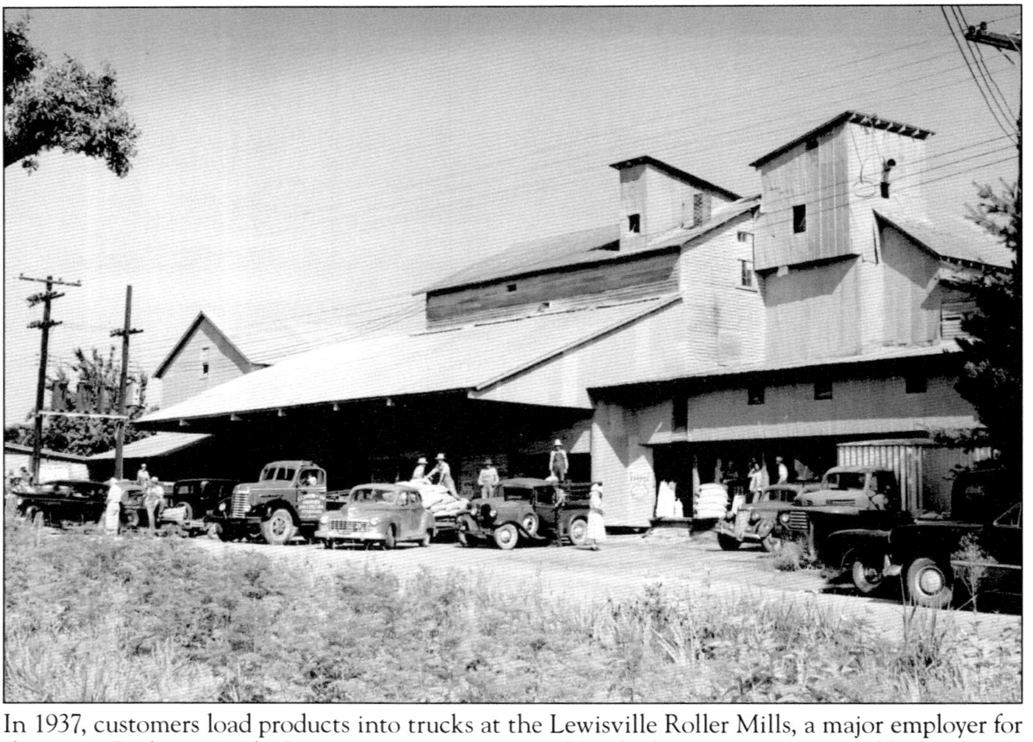

In 1937, customers load products into trucks at the Lewisville Roller Mills, a major employer for the town. Built in 1910 by James Pearson "J. P." Sprinkle, the business was operated by his family for 15 years as Fairview Roller Mill. The Jennings family operated the enterprise until 1984. The Lewisville cornmeal mix and flour can still be found in some area stores, manufactured by another mill. (RJ.)

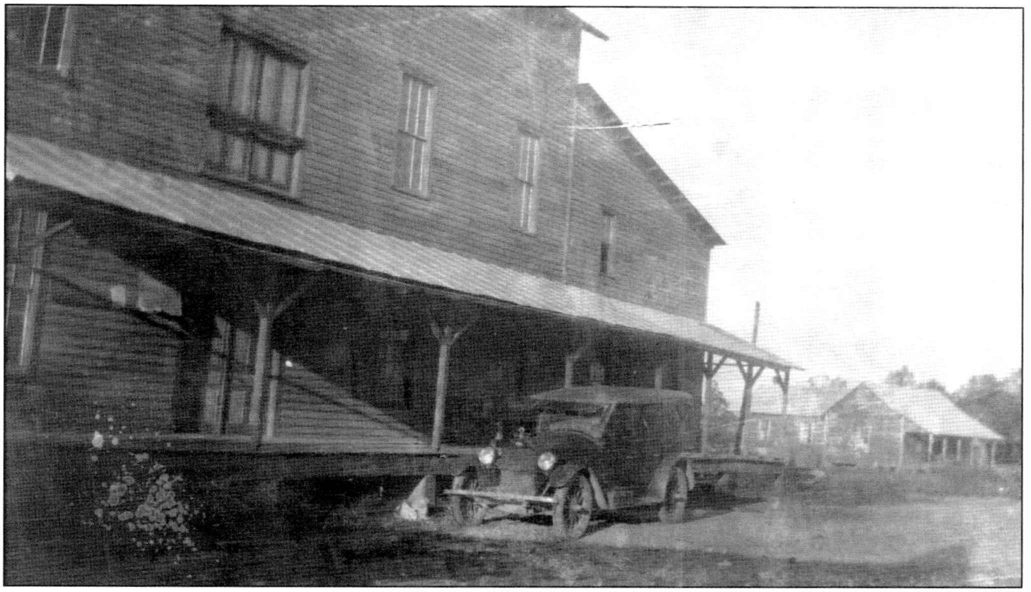

The cottage in view beside the Lewisville Roller Mills was the first home of the Jennings family when they moved to Lewisville in 1925. Today both the mill and cottage are restored with business enterprises housed in both structures. (DP.)

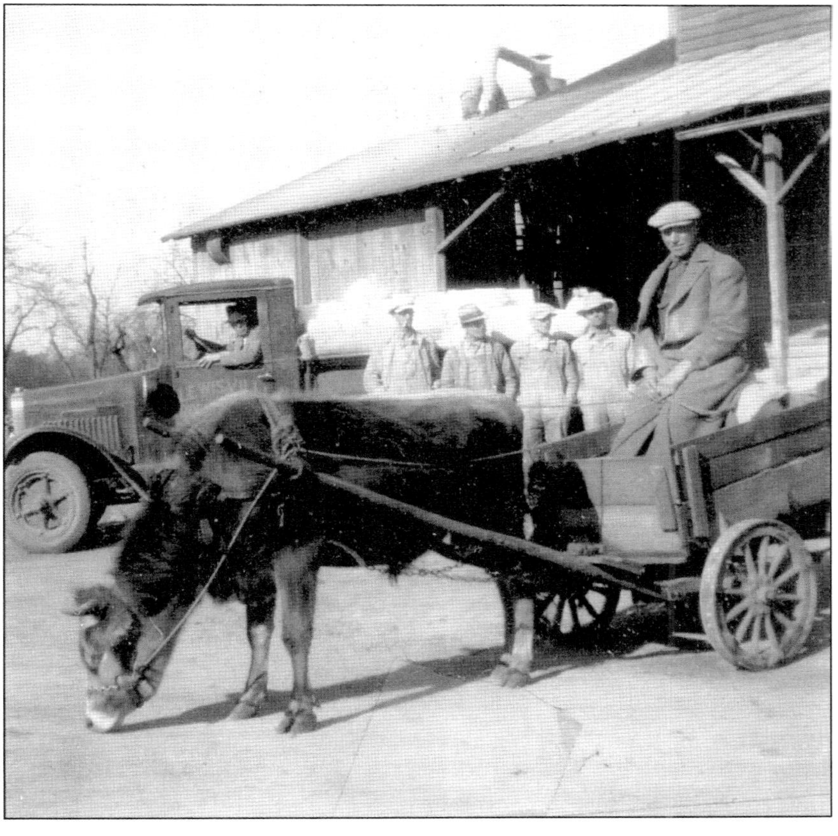

An ox-drawn cart is picking up products at the Lewisville Roller Mills on Shallowford Road. Owner Fielden Jennings is driving the company pickup truck loaded with bags of cornmeal and flour products for delivery. (RJ.)

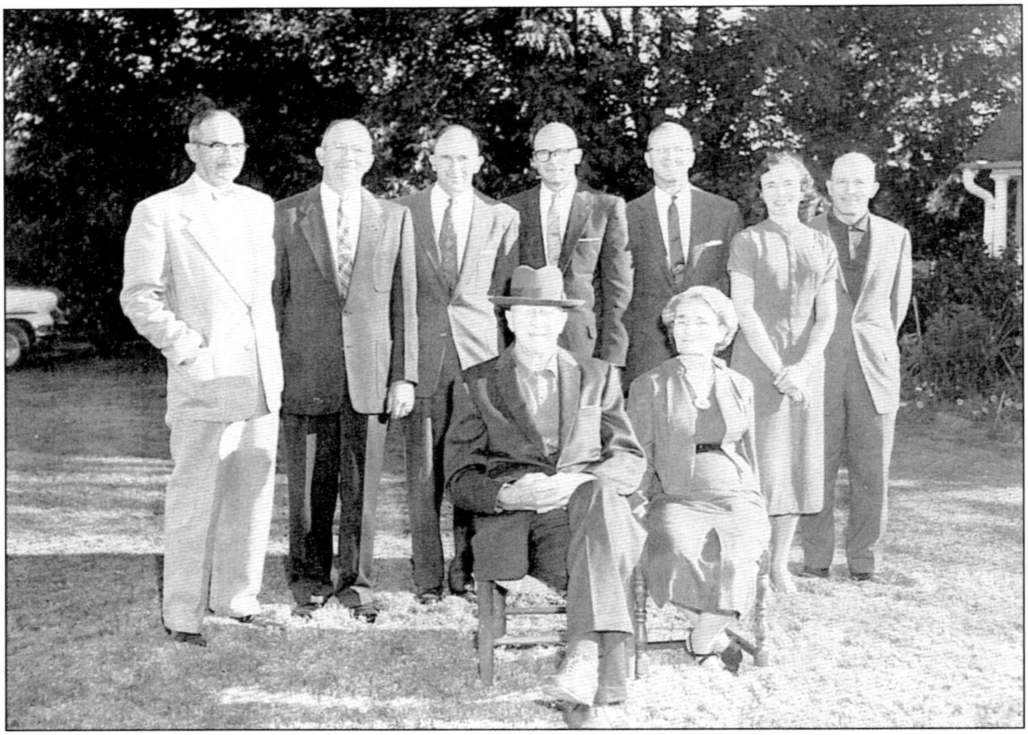

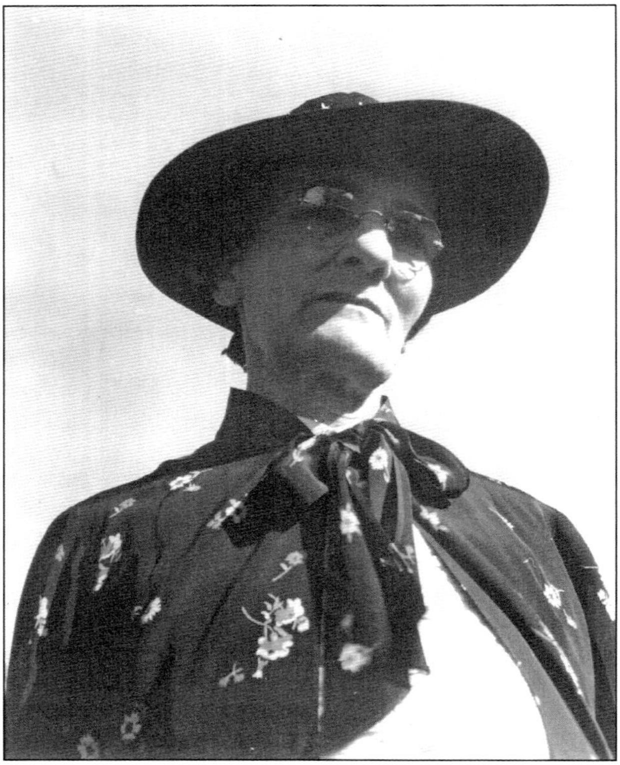

The Lamb Archibald Reynolds family poses in the yard of their home. Seated are L. A. and Bessie Binkley Reynolds. Their children standing are, from left to right, Glen Galloway, Frank Taylor, Thomas Archibald, Porter Graves, Daniel Ferdinand, Ruth Naomi, and Herbert Reynolds. (RRH, SL.)

Bessie Binkley Reynolds grew the flowers in the family business for the younger sons to sell. She is the daughter of Daniel and Laura Jarvis Binkley. (RRH.)

Lamb Archibald "L. A." Reynolds established L. A. Reynolds Nursery in 1914 on his property located on Reynolds Road. In 1917, he moved the business to a location in Winston-Salem, later moving back to the home place in Lewisville in 1924. He and his sons also owned and operated other business enterprises. L. A. Reynolds became a leading nurseryman in the area during his career. Today the business he created still bears his name. He was the son of Ferdinand L. and Henrietta Spaugh Reynolds. (RRH.)

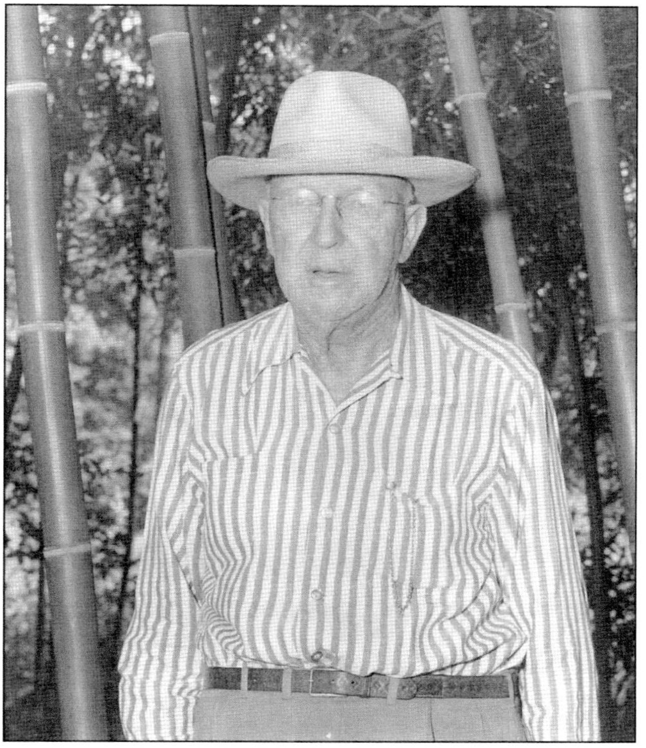

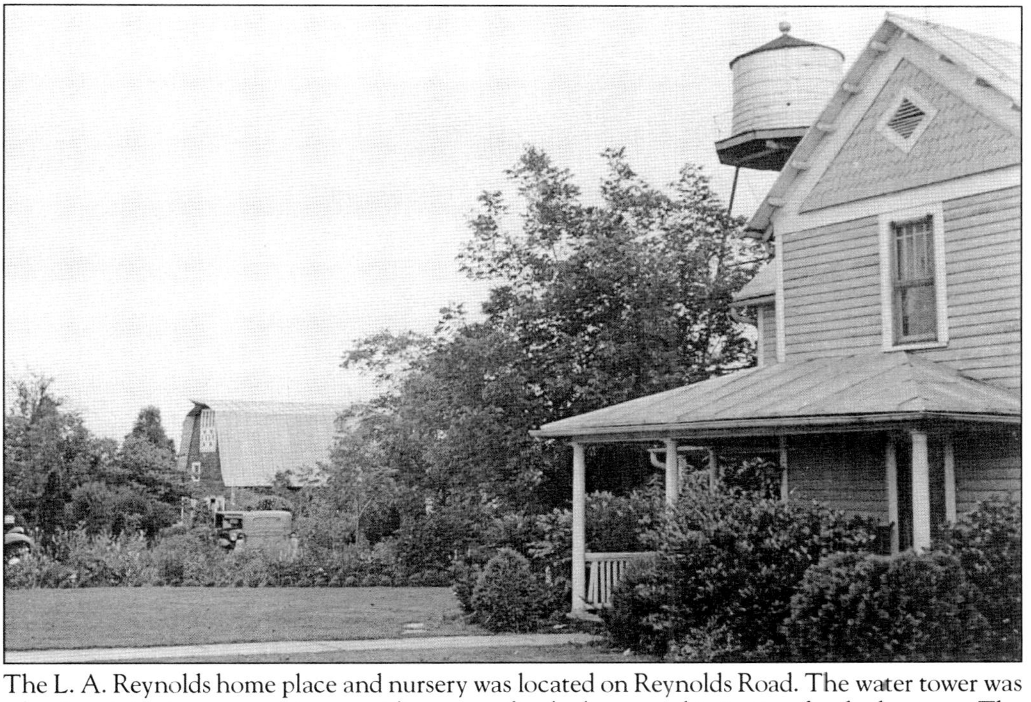

The L. A. Reynolds home place and nursery was located on Reynolds Road. The water tower was a landmark in the community, providing water for the home and irrigation for the business. The L. A. Reynolds home remains a private residence. (RRH.)

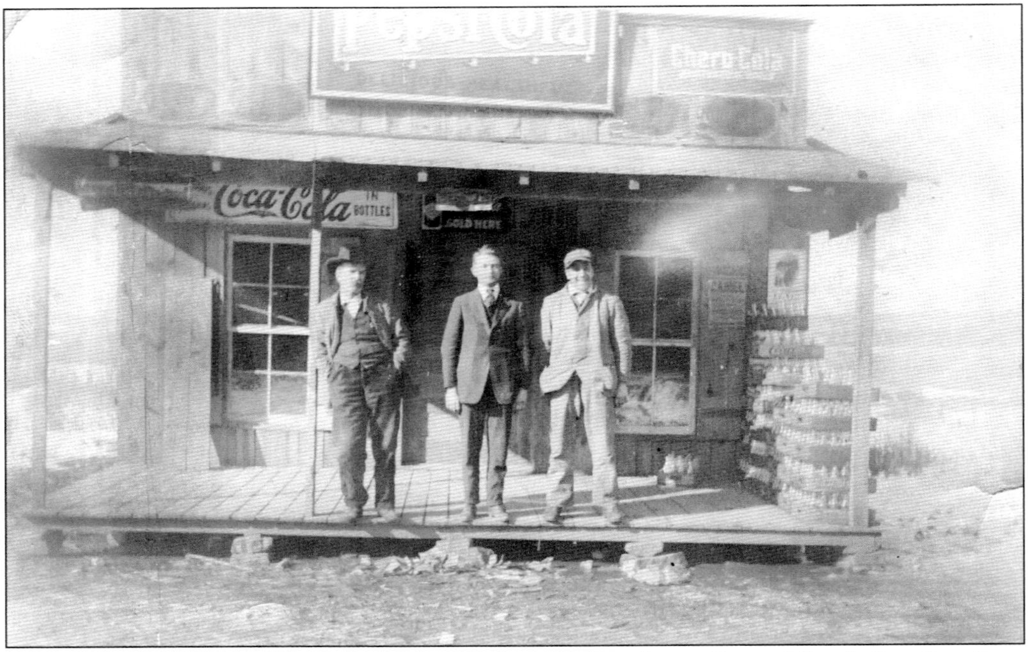

In 1918, Wake Fulk's store was located on Yadkinville Road near Conrad Road. Standing from left to right are Bud Conrad, Wake Fulk, and Will Conrad. (MAFW.)

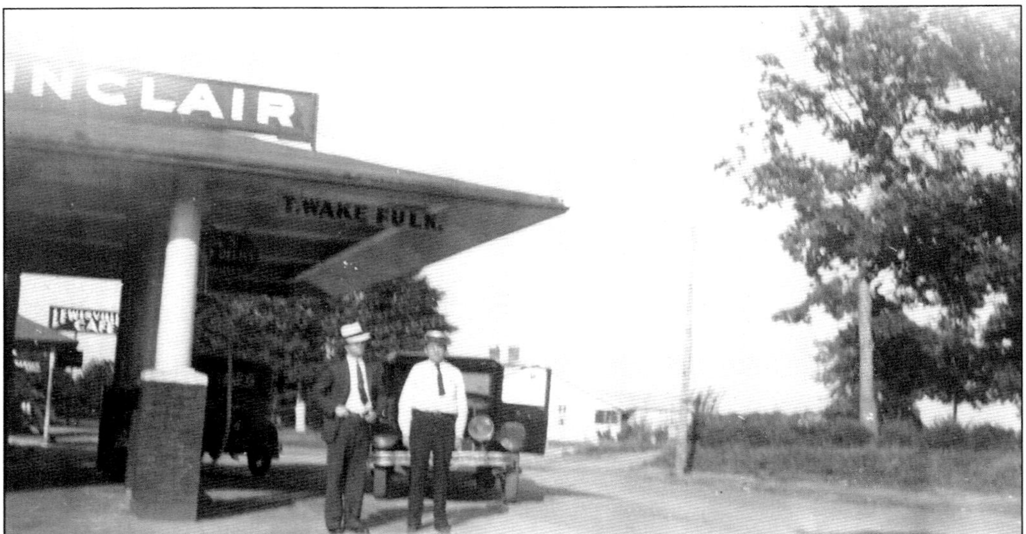

Wake Fulk stands at right with a customer in front of his store at the intersection of Shallowford and Lewisville-Vienna Roads. Foods, merchandise, and gasoline were sold, and the post office was located here from 1923 to 1934 when Mr. Fulk was postmaster. The Lewisville Café sign is visible next door. Jacob Hicks operated the cafe, which stood across the road from his home on Shallowford Road. Today the Jennings Building sits on this business site. (MAFW.)

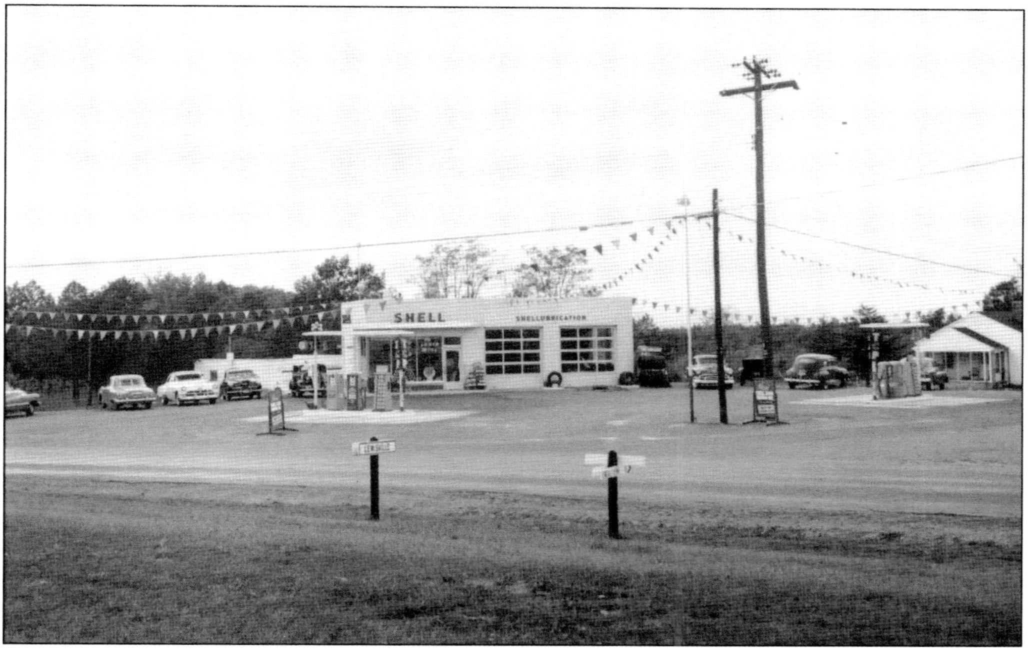

Quality Oil Company operated a Shell gasoline station at the corner of Shallowford and Lewisville-Vienna Roads. Later the building was rented for other commercial uses before it was torn down. (FCPL.)

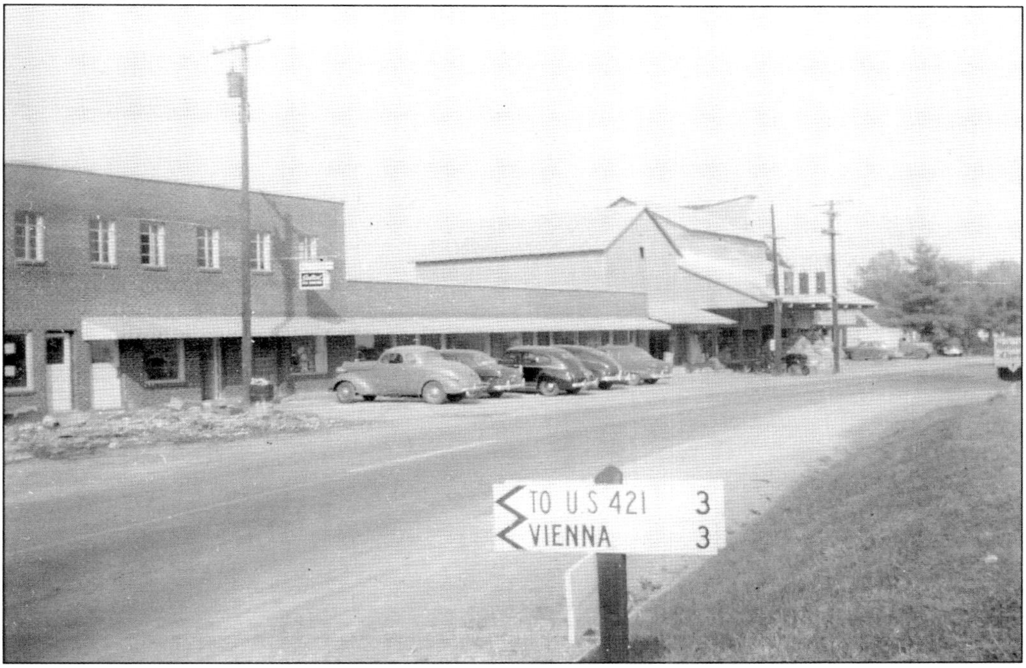

Here is Shallowford Road looking east with the Jennings Building and Lewisville Roller Mills in view. (LHS.)

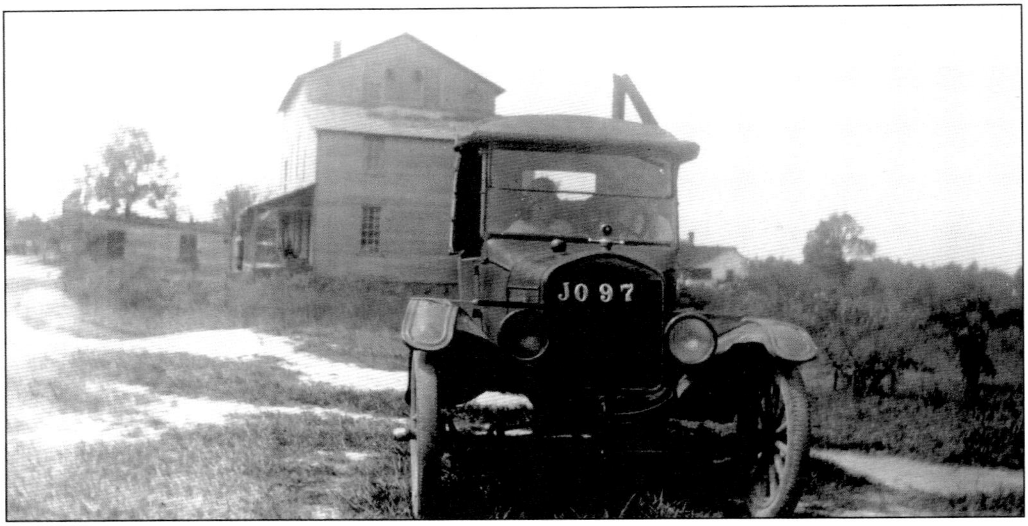

An unidentified couple is driving a vintage automobile across the yard to the Fielden Jennings home. The Lewisville Roller Mills stands on Shallowford Road, surrounded by an open landscape area in the late 1920s. (DP.)

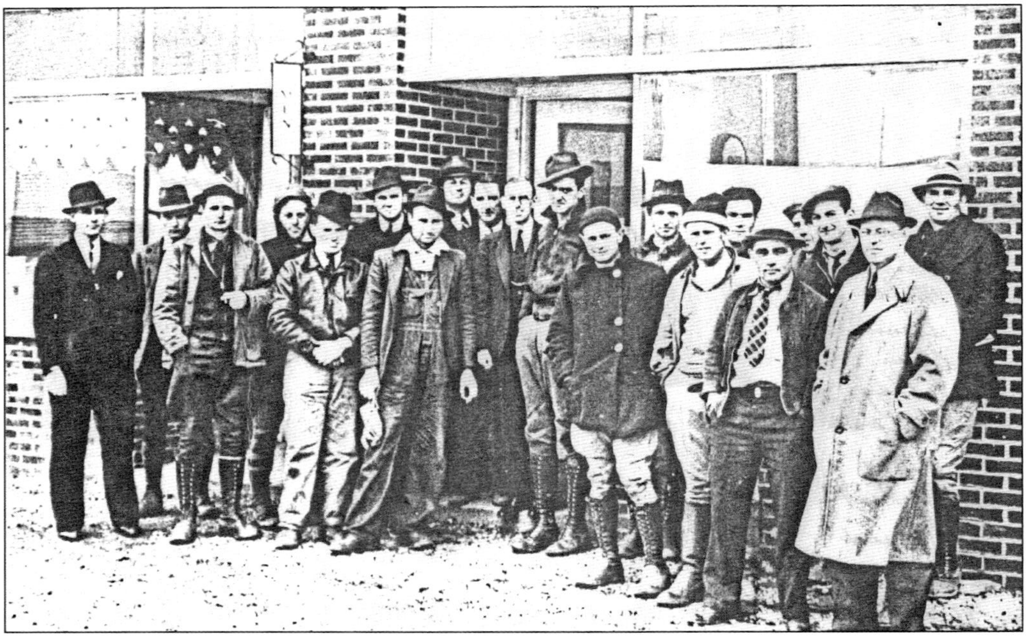

Several Lewisville men worked on survey crews in the winter of 1938 for the proposed High Point Hydro-Electric Project, which would have been located on Styers Ferry Road at the Yadkin River. The cancellation of the dam was a disappointment to some people in Lewisville. Standing, from left to right, are ? Kinnard, Henry Hooper, Tom Mitcheal, Pledger Parker, Joe Perkins, Porter Reynolds, Clyde Davis, Horace Wilcox, J. B. Skinner, K. K. Kelsey, ? Lilley, Studie Clark, Clyde Nifong, Bill Copeland, Kermit Essex, ? Scales, Bud Chamblin, W. S. Kiger Jr., George Rothrock, and Frank Reynolds. The men gather at a location in Winston-Salem. (RRH.)

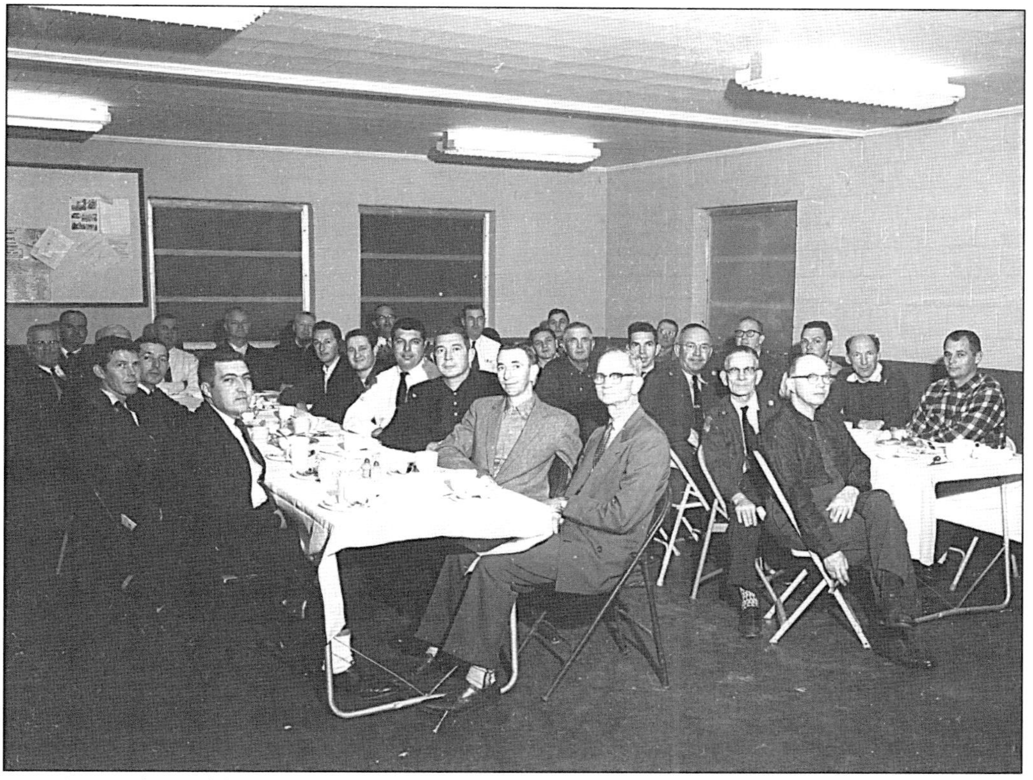

In 1959, members of the Lewisville Civic Club and Lewisville Volunteer Fire Department collected $1,000 on Donation Day in the Lewisville community. These funds were used to purchase a new fire truck for the Lewisville Volunteer Fire Department. The men volunteering their time for these organizations were leaders in the business and agricultural communities of Lewisville. (MV.)

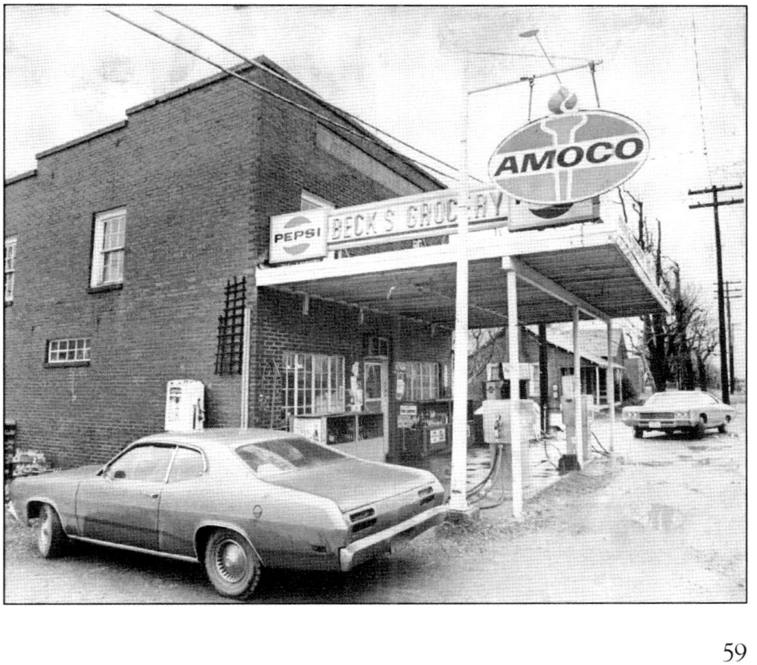

John Beck's Grocery Store operated in the 1970s, located at the intersection of Lewisville-Clemmons and Shallowford Roads. The brick store was built by Jacob Robert "J. R." Whitman after his original store burned in 1922. Whitman operated his store from the late 1800s until his death in 1937. Other proprietors include Ray Lasley, Frank Reynolds, Tom Trivette, and Wiley Gunter. A bank sits on the property today. (LHS.)

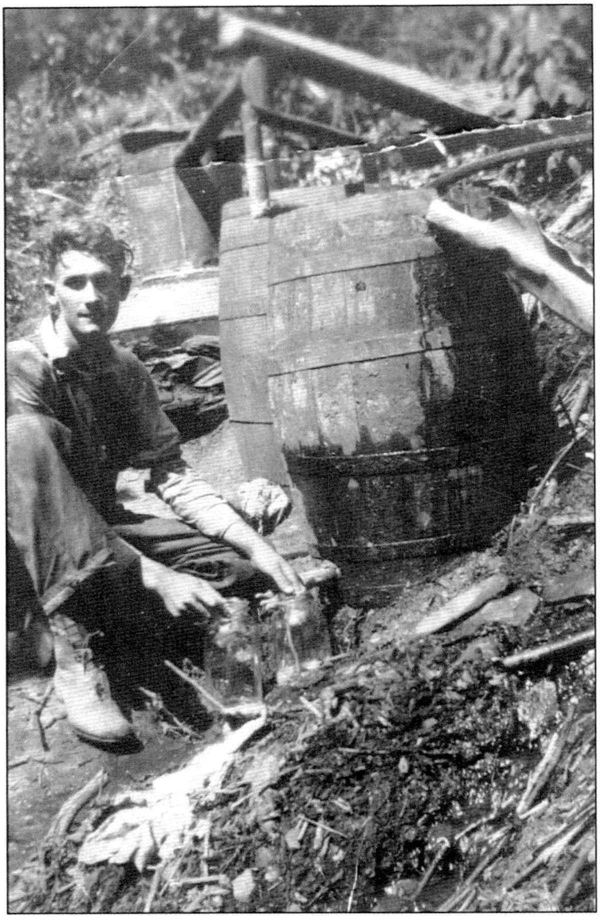

Old Yadkin Rectifier of Spirits and Wholesale Liquor Dealer 5th District NC operated in the late 1800s in a log building on Williams Road. Albert William Jones and Bob Daniels owned and operated the business. Jones family members identify Casper Newton Jones posing with a whiskey still on the family property. Today the Old Yadkin Rectifier building is an outbuilding located near an early 20th century farmhouse. (SJ.)

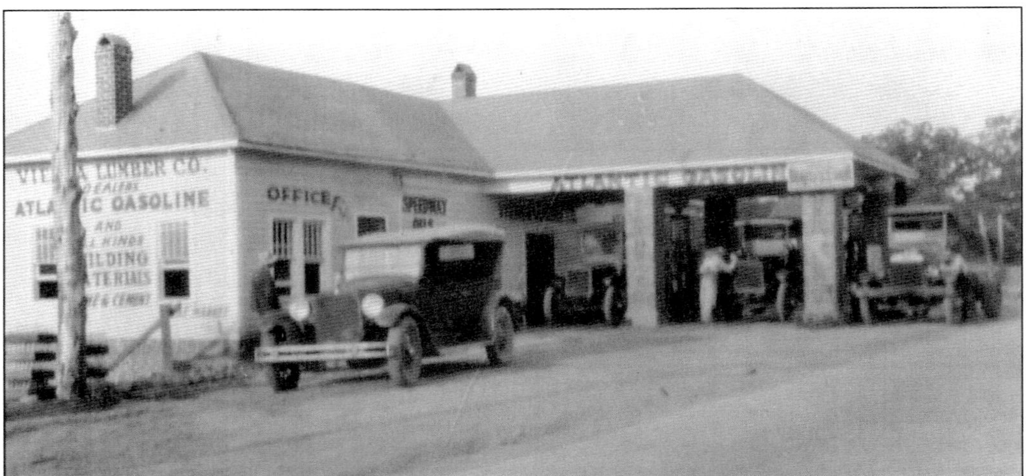

Vienna Lumber Company stood on the corner of Lewisville-Vienna and Yadkinville Roads on the eastern side of Brookstown United Methodist Church. Victor Beroth and his son, Elbert, owned and operated the business. The Beroths also operated a store and gas station in this building. (JL.)

Lula Rucker gathered sticks, roots, and leaves in the countryside around her home in Lewisville and sold them for many years at the City Market in Winston-Salem. The "Herb Woman" sold a variety of natural items such as spring tonic, yaller root, hunt leaf, Adam and Eve root, rats bane, calamus root, and mullen leaves to prevent and cure a variety of ailments. (FCPL.)

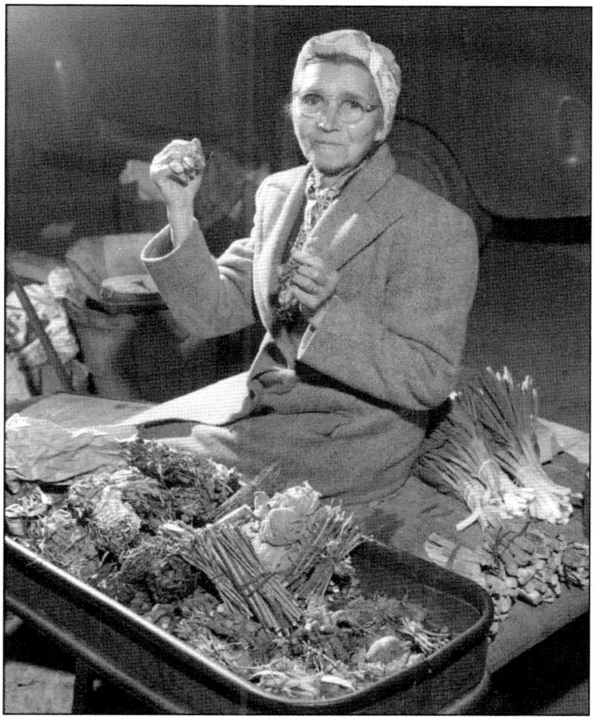

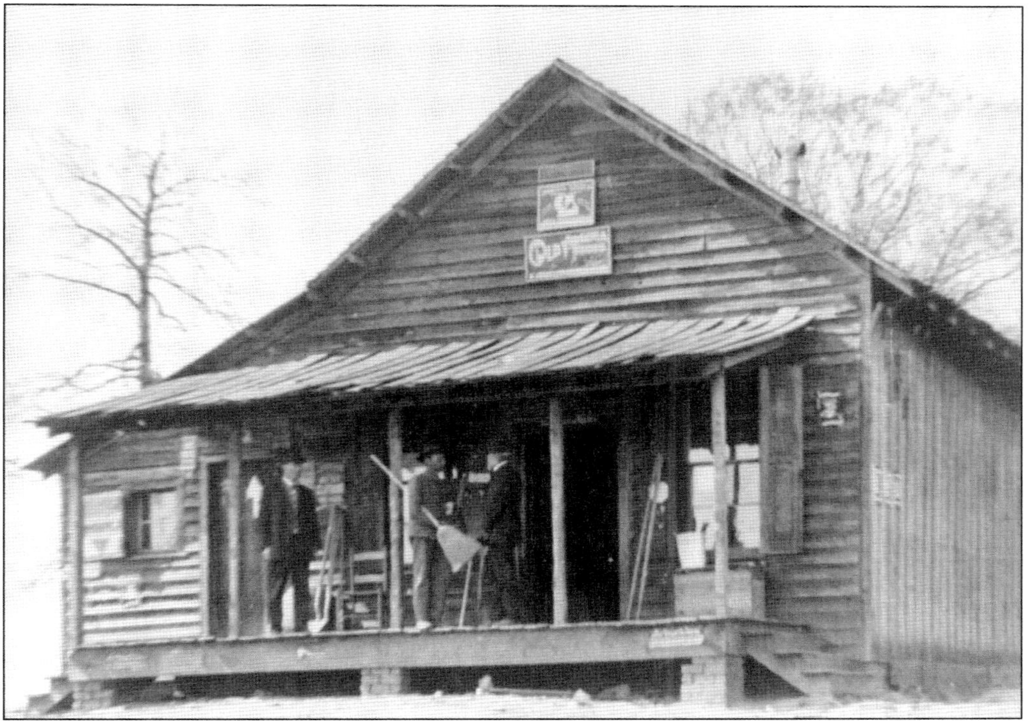

The Mickle Store stood at the intersection of Lewisville-Vienna and Yadkinville Roads near Brookstown United Methodist Church, owned and operated by Columbus F. Mickle. (JL.)

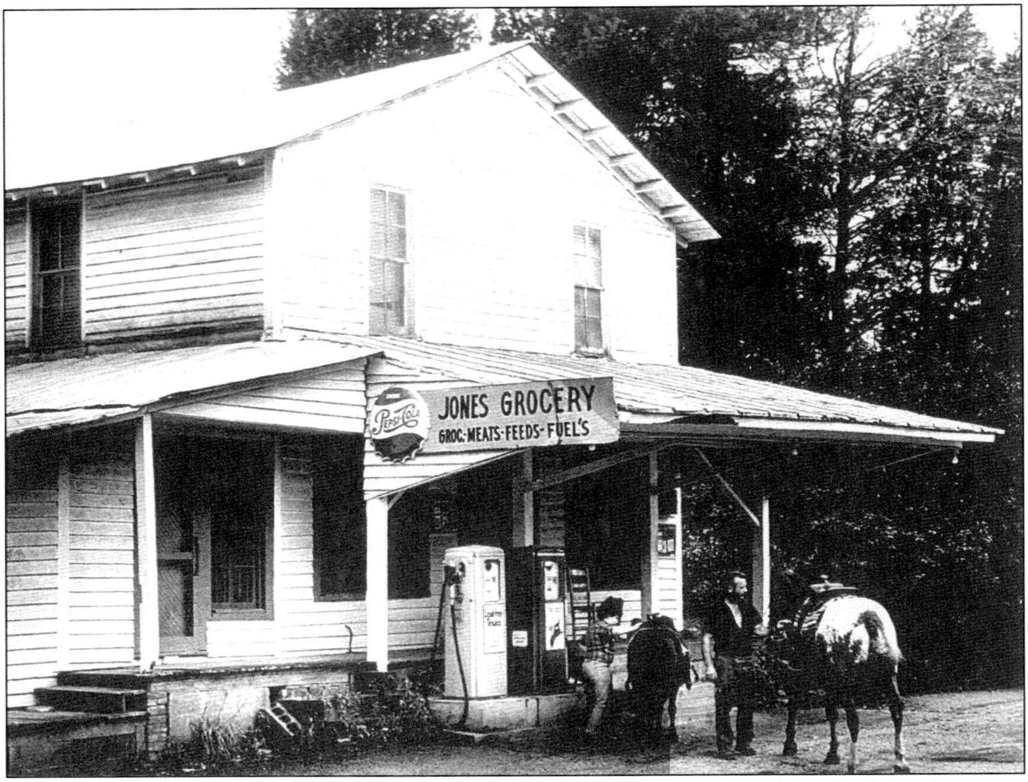

Jones Store in West Bend was a favorite stopping place. Joseph Spurgeon Jones built his first store in 1875 on the corner of Nading Ferry Road (now Scott Road) and Shallowford Road in the West Bend community. In 1914, Will A. Jones moved the store across the road near the present structure. After a robbery in 1926, the old building was torn down and a new one was built consisting of two stories, including a residence. In this 1977 photograph, Herman and Chris Allgood rode to the store on horse Nick and pony Doll. (LHS.)

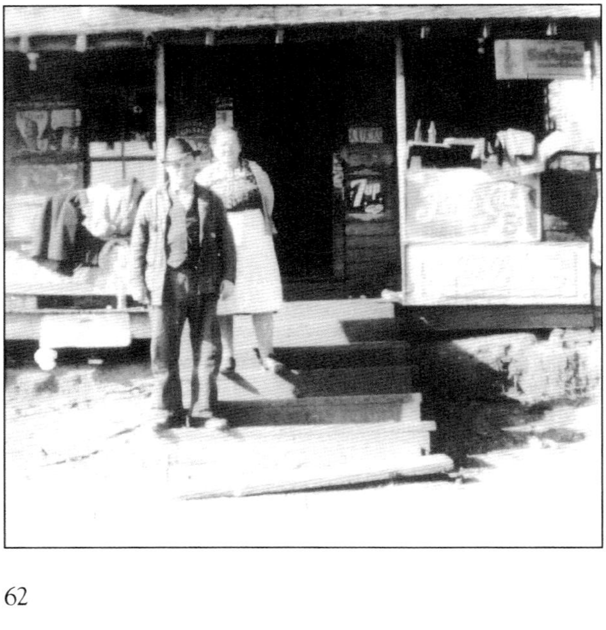

Ephraim G. Davis operated a thriving business at his store on Yadkinville Road. He and his wife stand on the steps in front of his store in the Brookstown community. (JL.)

Five

On the Home Place

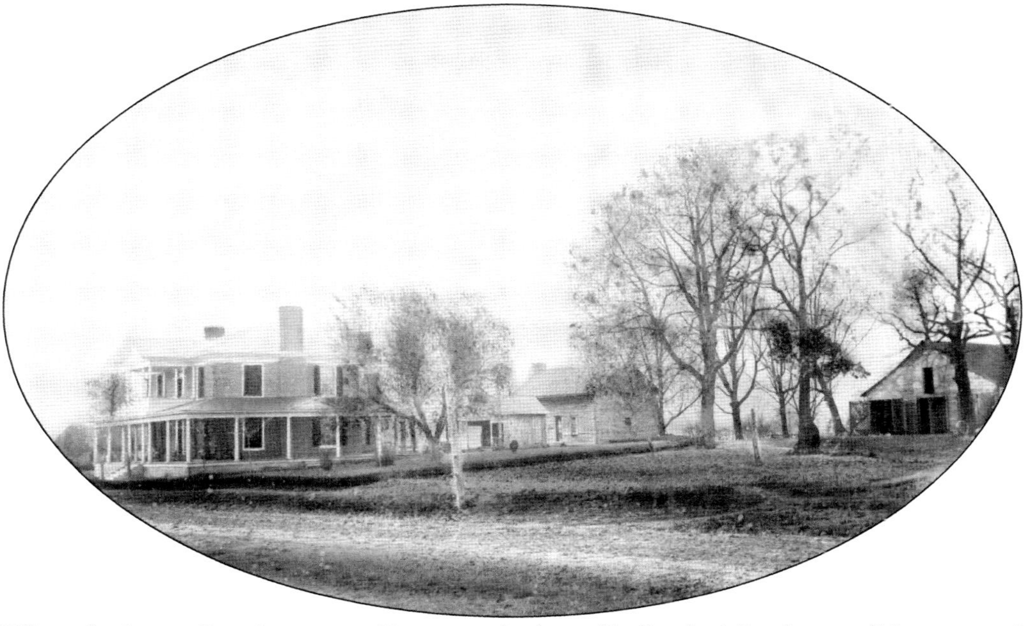

When the Lewis Case Laugenour House was built on Shallowford Road, a small house stood behind it and a granary farther back on the property. Oral tradition has indicated the newlywed Laugenours may have lived in the small house until their new home was finished. This view of the house shows the wraparound porches added in 1921 by the Sprinkle family during their ownership. (DCH.)

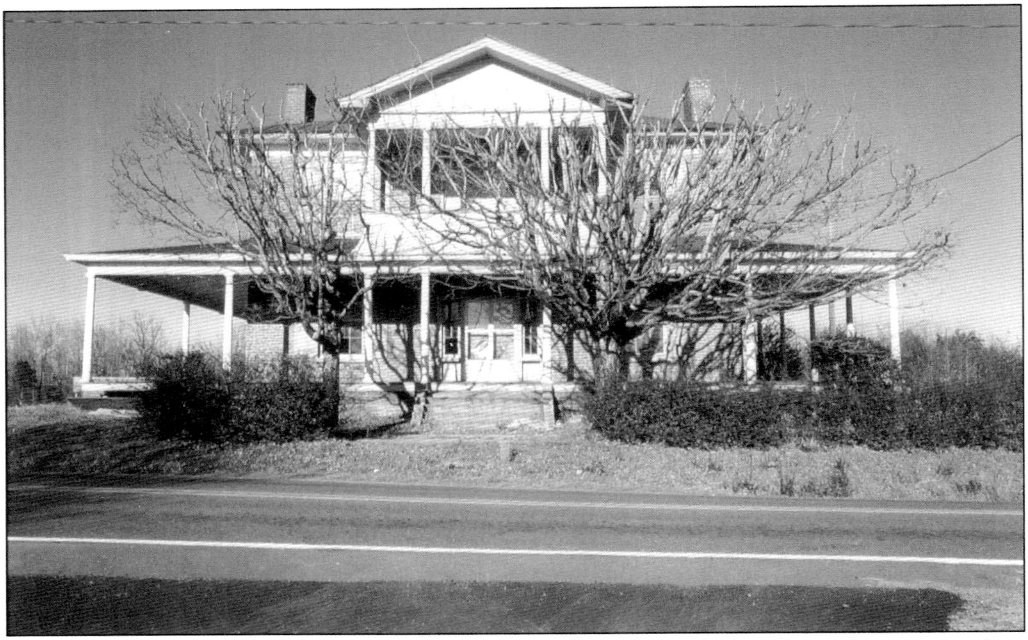

The Laugenour House is pictured on Shallowford Road as it looked with porches surrounding the house. Charles Oliver "C. O." Sprinkle bought the house in 1914. He built the porches, and when he was confined to a wheelchair in his later years, he could easily move around and visit with his neighbors. After Sprinkle's death, his daughter Nell ran the house as a "teacherage" where Lewisville School teachers could live across from the school. (GST.)

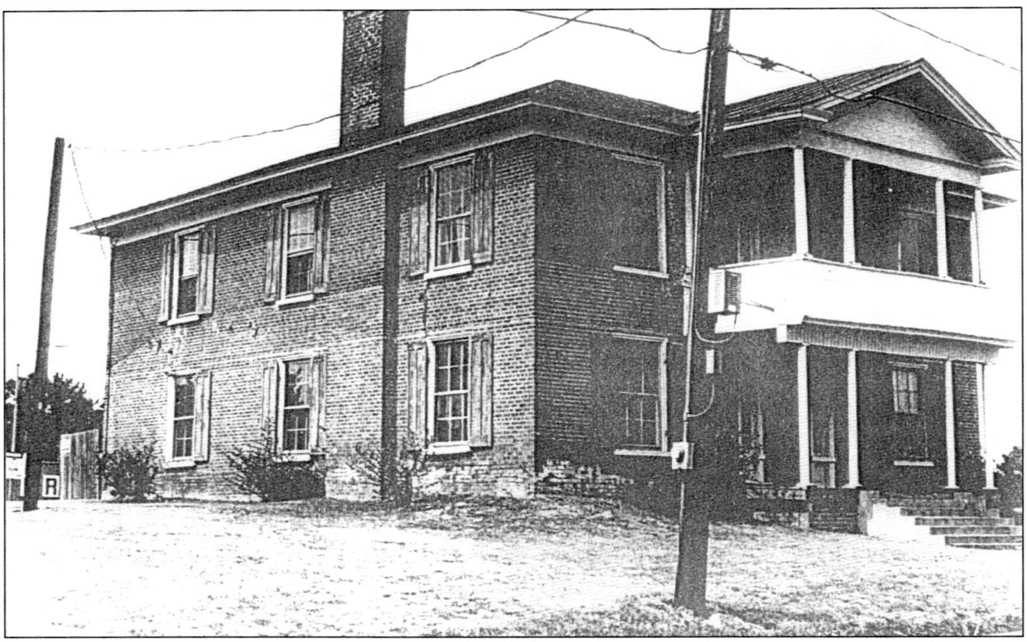

In the 1970s, the porches were removed from the Laugenour House, restoring it to a more original appearance. Loiterers were using the porches during a time of vacancy. Over the years, the house has been used as apartments, an antique shop, and offices for lawyers and other businesses. (LHS.)

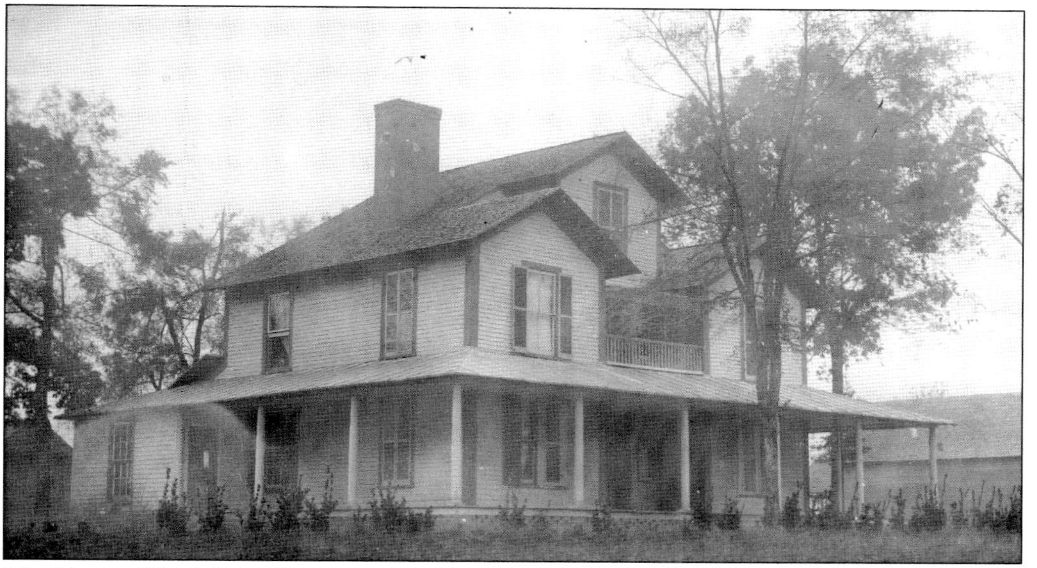

The George Elias Nissen House as it appeared in 1909 on Shallowford Road when it was owned by Dr. John D. Williams. Many families and individuals have owned the home: Nissen, Conrad, Kiger, Williams, Sheets, Reece, Roselli, Dampier, Browder, and Liner. Teachers boarded at the house in earlier decades, and businesses such as a doctor's office and a bakery served the community in this house. The Lewisville Historical Society relocated the house from its original location at 6570 Shallowford Road to 213 Arrowleaf Drive on January 1, 2009. (LHS.)

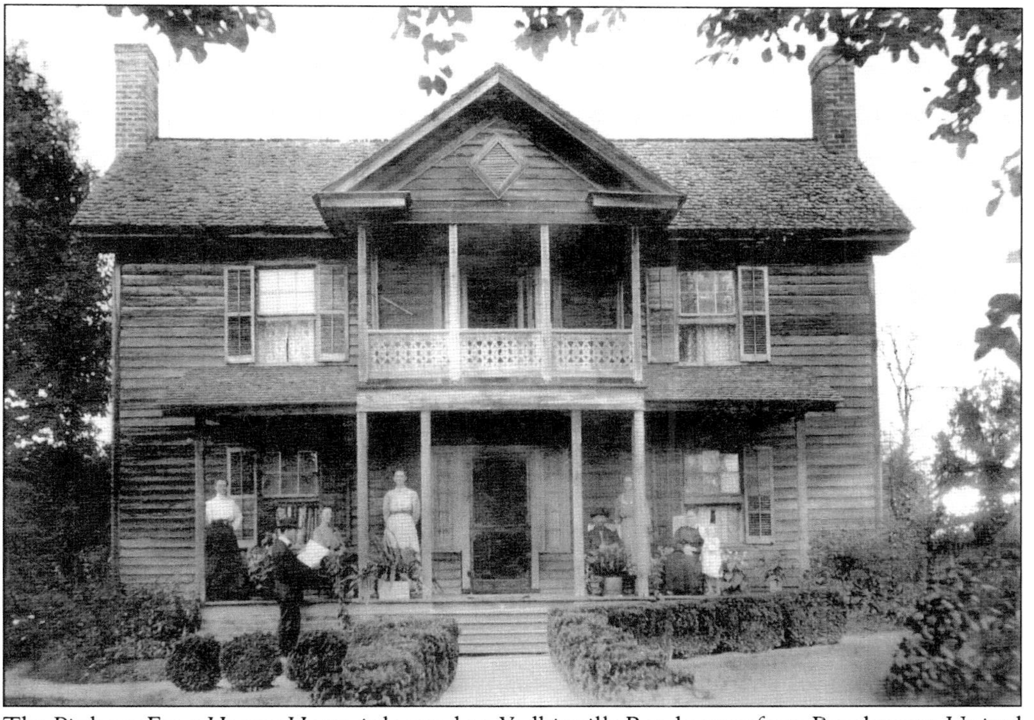

The Pinkney Evan Hauser House is located on Yadkinville Road across from Brookstown United Methodist Church. (JL.)

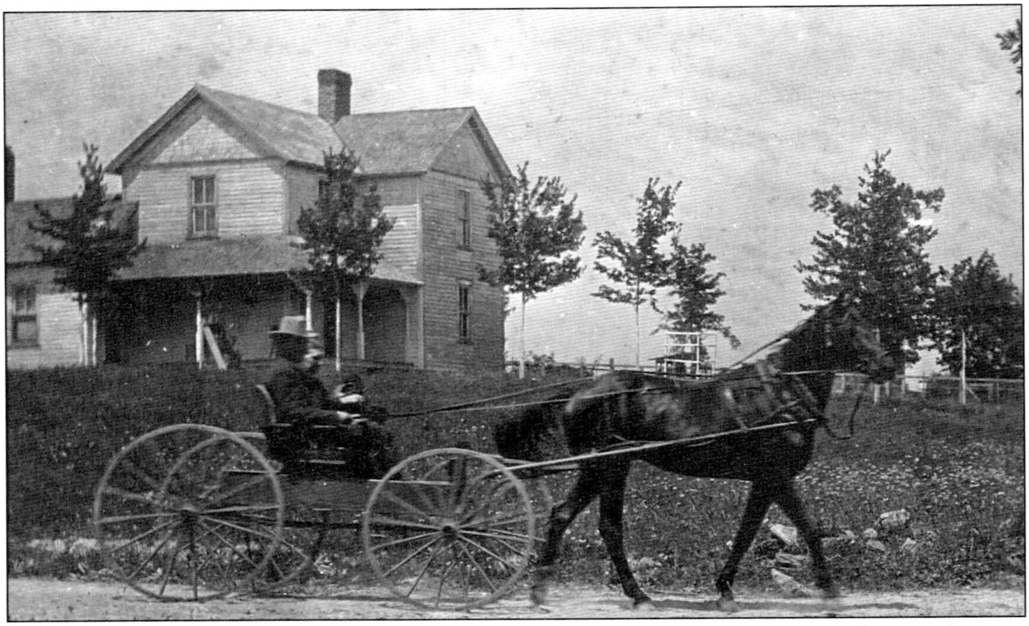

Built around 1900, the Charles L. Spaugh house is located on Shallowford Road. Spaugh was a civic leader who built this house with lumber from the Spaugh family sawmill, where he worked with his father, Bennett, and brother Lewis. The Spaughs are descendants of Adam Spach of the Moravian settlement at Friedberg. (LHS.)

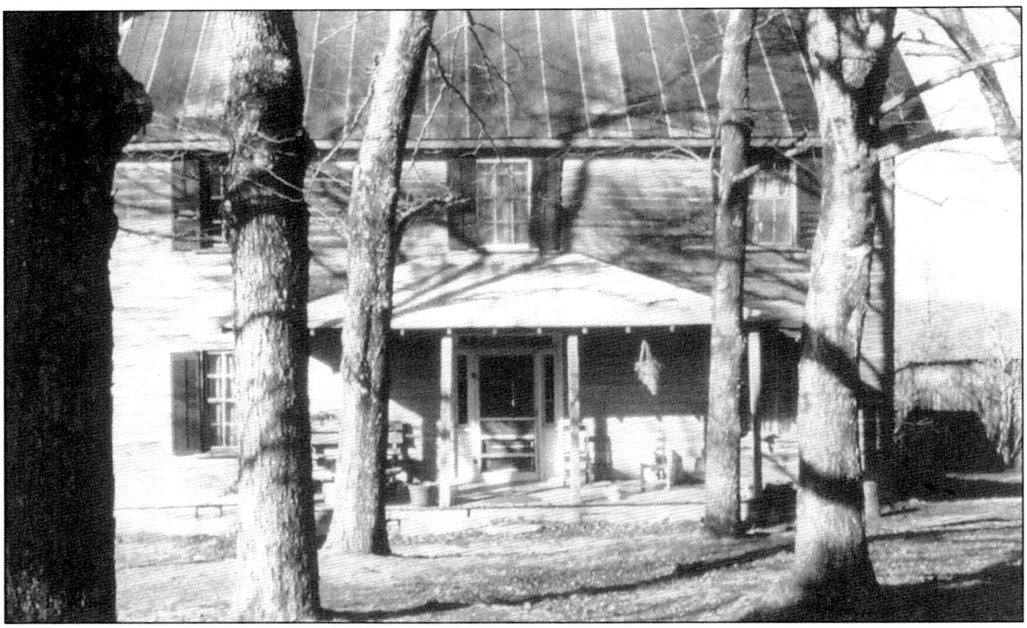

The Jack Kiger House located on Williams Road was built around 1900. Located on a large acreage of land farmed by the Kiger family, the house and outbuildings stood until the late 1990s at this site. (GST.)

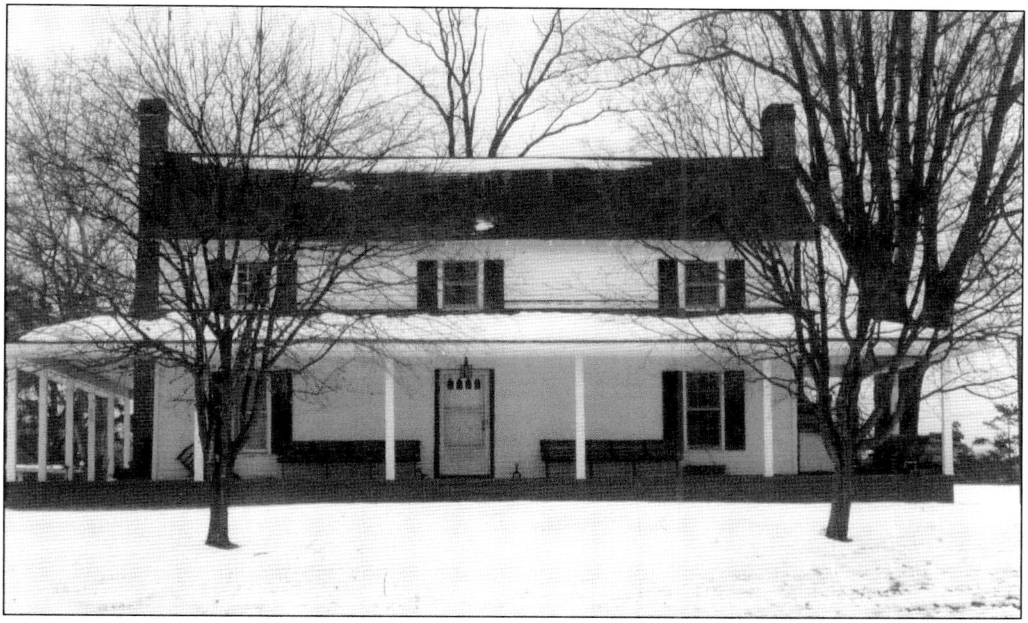

The Finch-Kimel House located on Concord Church Road was built around 1900. Jerome Holloway Finch and his wife, Ida Jane Miller Doub Finch, were early landowners and residents of this house. In 1914, Walter J. and Mary E. Kimel, who were active community leaders, purchased the house. Following the Kimels, the house had several owners including the former mayor of Winston-Salem, M. C. Benton Jr. Some of the original log structure remains inside. (GST.)

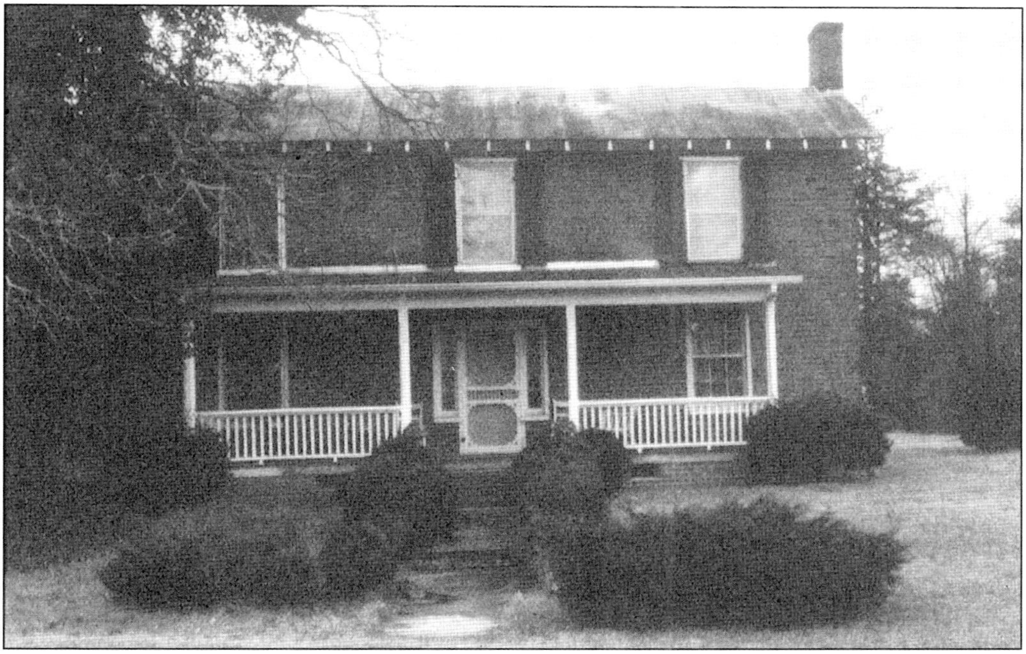

The Shore House on Grapevine Road was built around 1876. The words "Centennial 1876" were painted on the second-story facade. Owners have included Eli Mullican, William Stedman Kiger, and Gene Hege. (GST.)

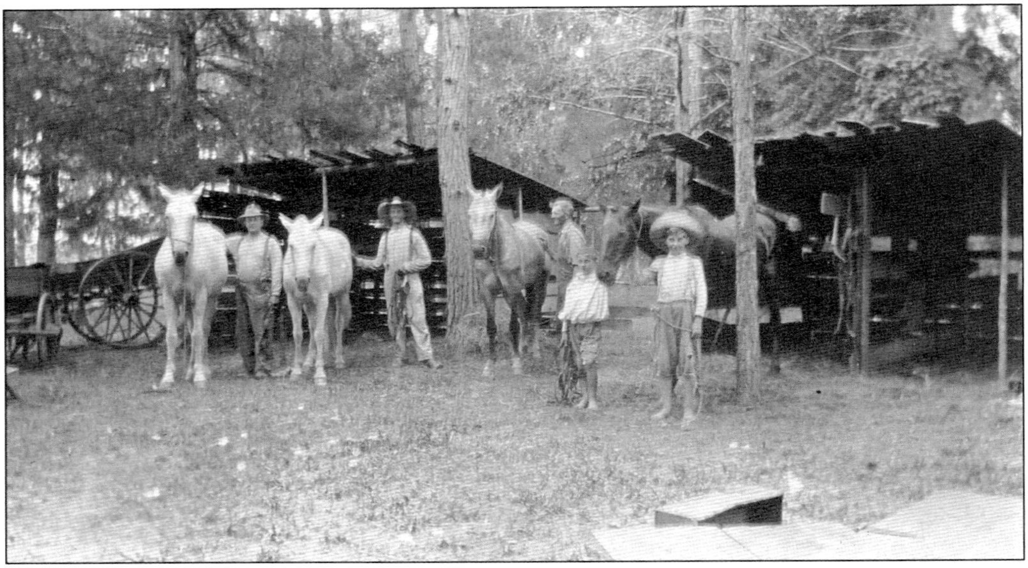

Walter Martin's family lived in their home place on Shallowford Road. The Martins and their Hauser family relatives farmed at camps on the bottomlands of the Yadkin River in the West Bend area. Standing with their horses are, from left to right, John Hauser, Arch Hauser, and Tom Hauser, with two unidentified young boys. (NGC.)

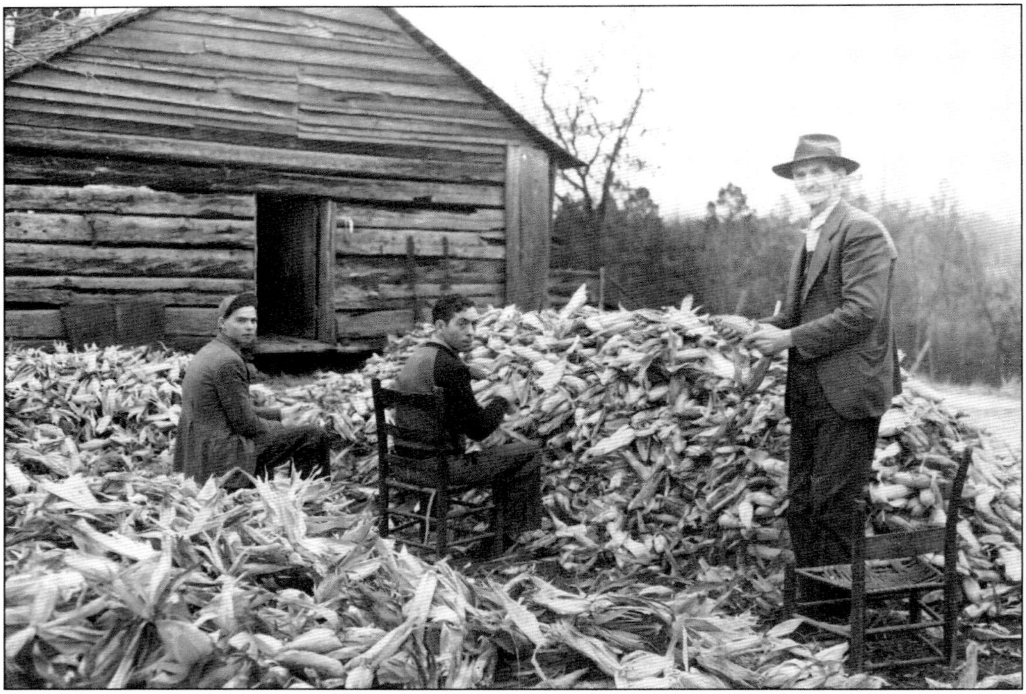

Near a cabin site in the Lewisville area, the Aldridge family works together shucking corn in the 1940s. From left to right are Francis, Walter, and Sydney Aldridge. Corn shucks were family and community affairs with men, women, and children participating. Often a chicken stew accompanied these gatherings. (FCPL.)

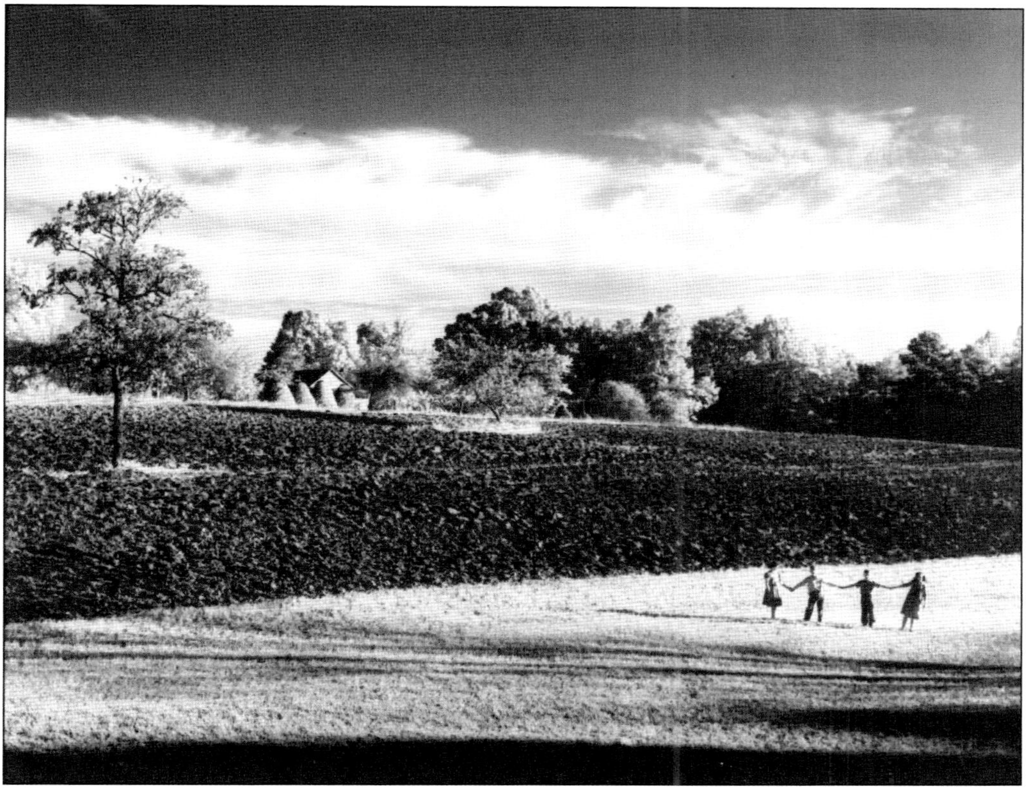

The landscape of the J. G. Blackburn Farm in 1952 delights children, from left to right, Tona Jennings, Tommy Cumby, Sammy Strupe, and Mary Lou Perryman as they run and play together. (FCPL.)

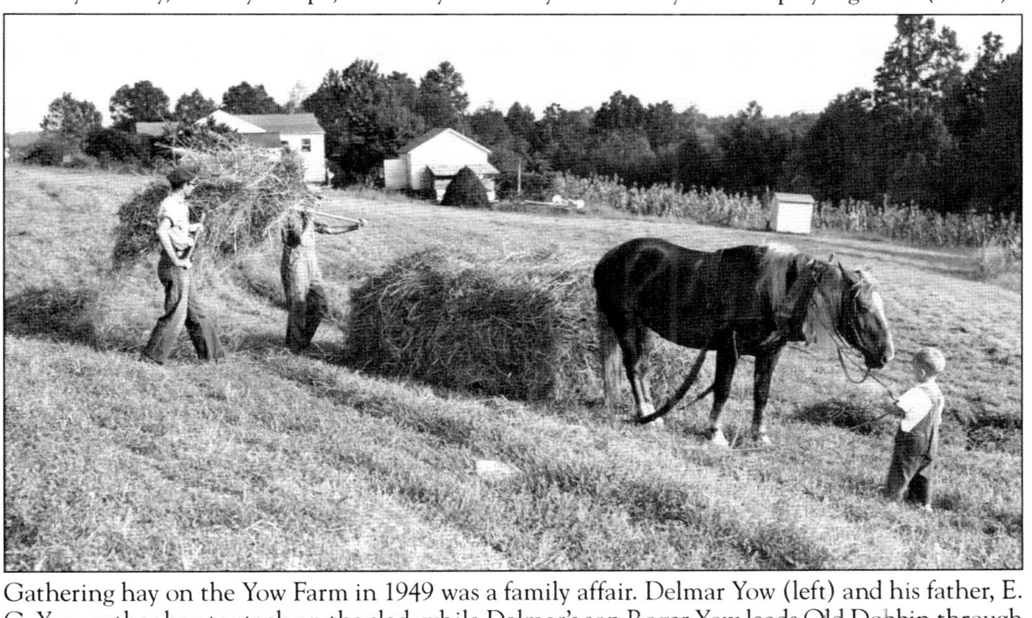

Gathering hay on the Yow Farm in 1949 was a family affair. Delmar Yow (left) and his father, E. G. Yow, gather hay to stack on the sled, while Delmar's son Roger Yow leads Old Dobbin through the fields. (FCPL.)

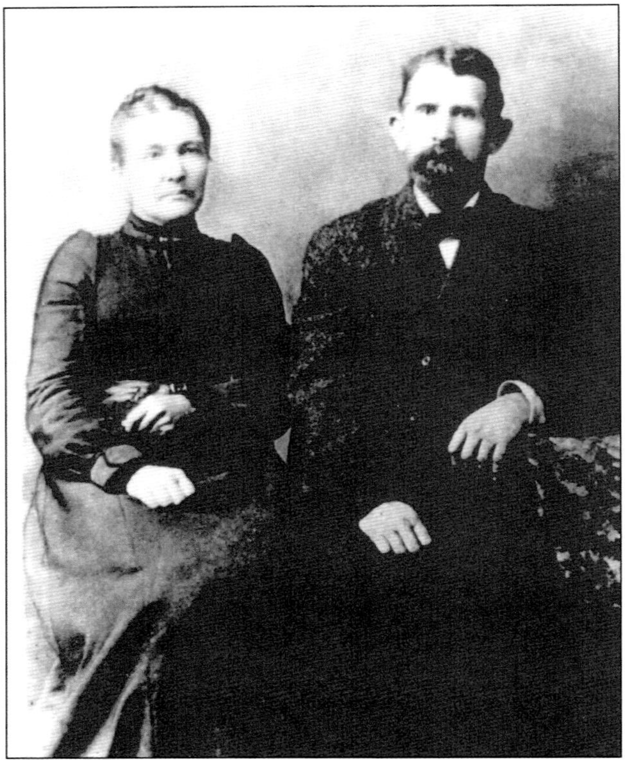

George and Adeline Shouse Mock resided in the eastern portion of the Lewisville community on Shallowford Road. George Mock built his house about 1879. The family left the Brookstown United Methodist Church congregation with other members to establish Lewisville United Methodist Church, which was organized in 1878. (LHS.)

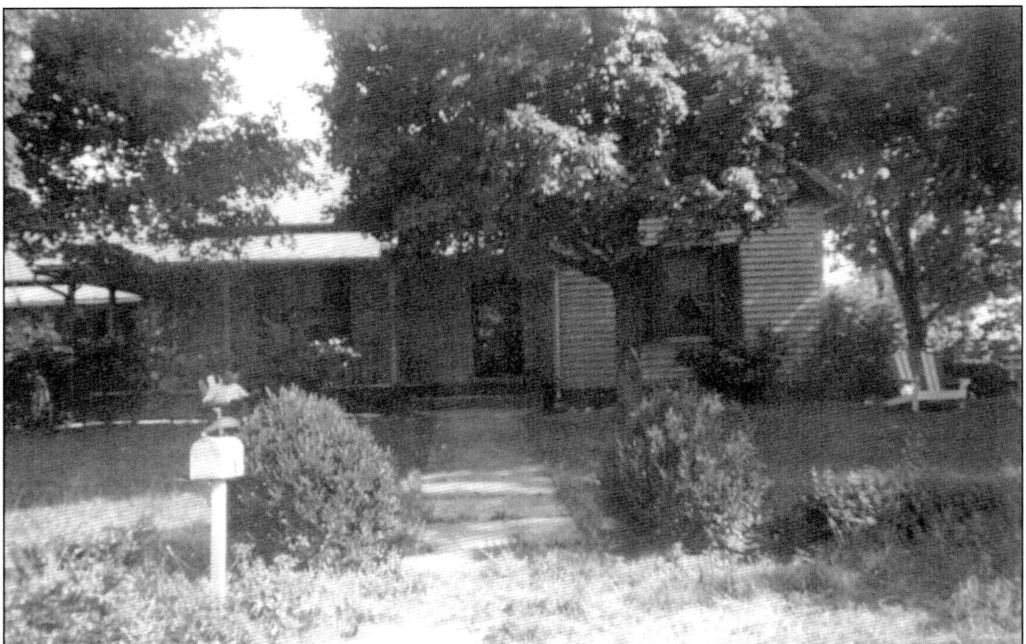

In 1943, the George Mock House on Shallowford Road had a walkway leading straight to the road and mailbox. (LHS.)

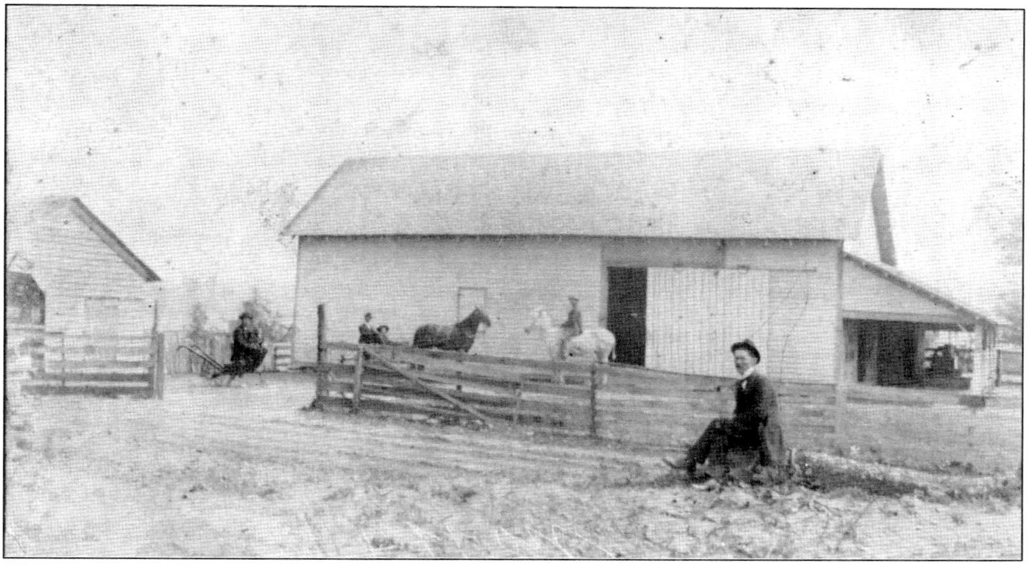

This scene on the George Mock farm shows several large structures for sheltering animals, equipment, and storage of crops. (LHS.)

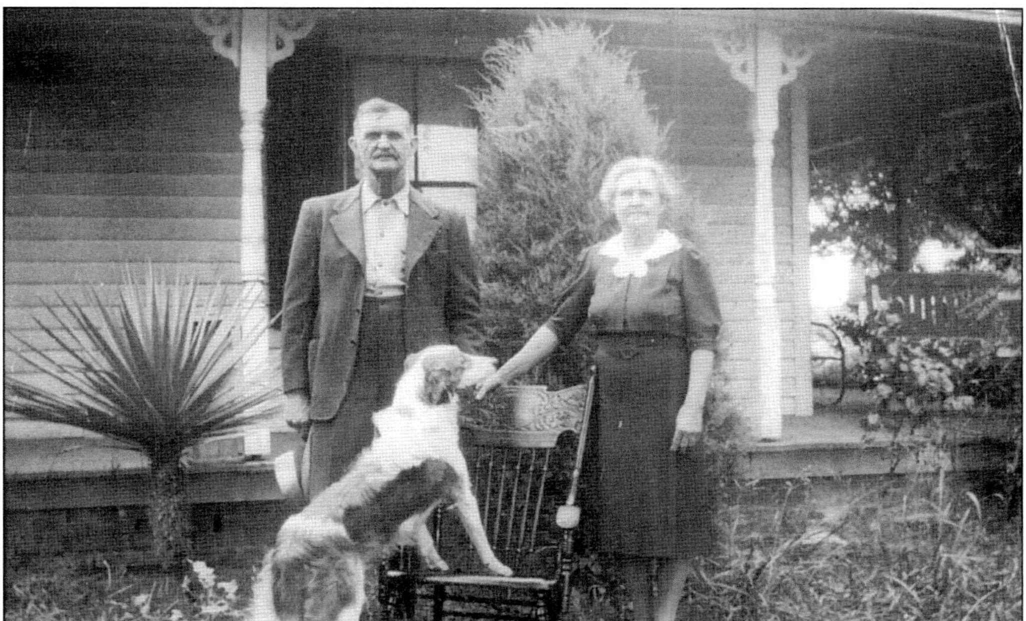

Marvin Henry Mock and his wife, Lillie Apperson Mock, pose with their dog in front of the Mock home built by his father, George Mock. (LHS.)

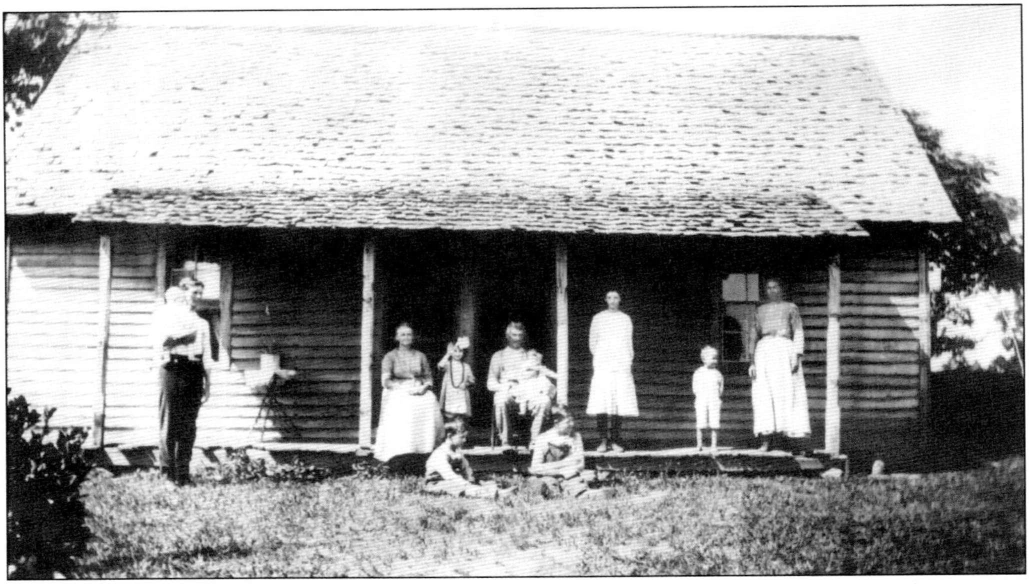

The former Blackburn's School was relocated for use as a home by the Leon Reid Jones family on Styers Ferry Road. The school was located near Harmony Grove United Methodist Church. (SJ.)

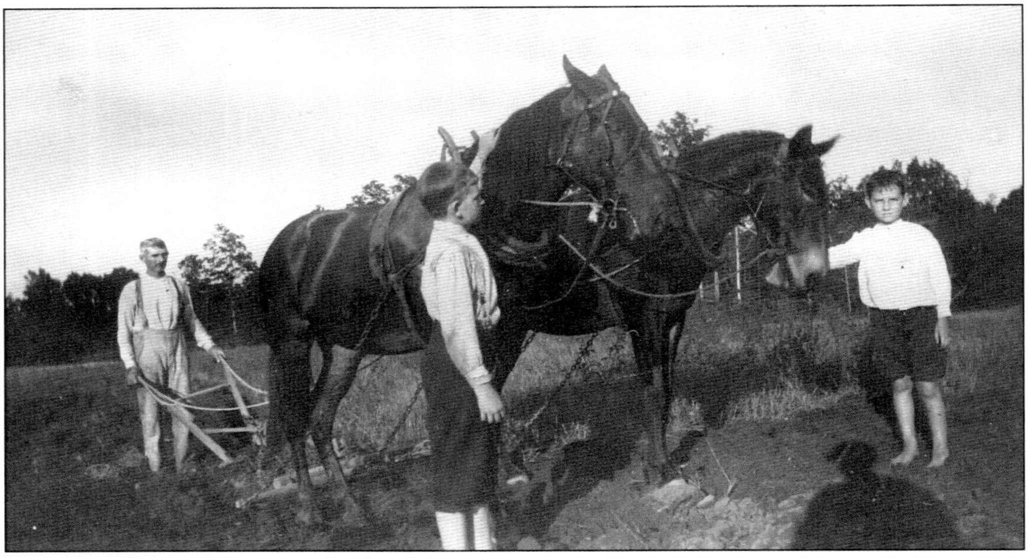

Leon Reid Jones is plowing a field with his youngest child of 10, Ferdinand Jones (left), and his oldest grandchild, Spenser Jones, around 1913. The family farm was located on Styers Ferry Road and is still in the Jones family. (SJ.)

Joseph Elias Binkley and his wife, Addie Bolen Binkley, farmed and raised their family on Reynolds Road. They were members of Warner's Chapel Church of Christ. (HJH.)

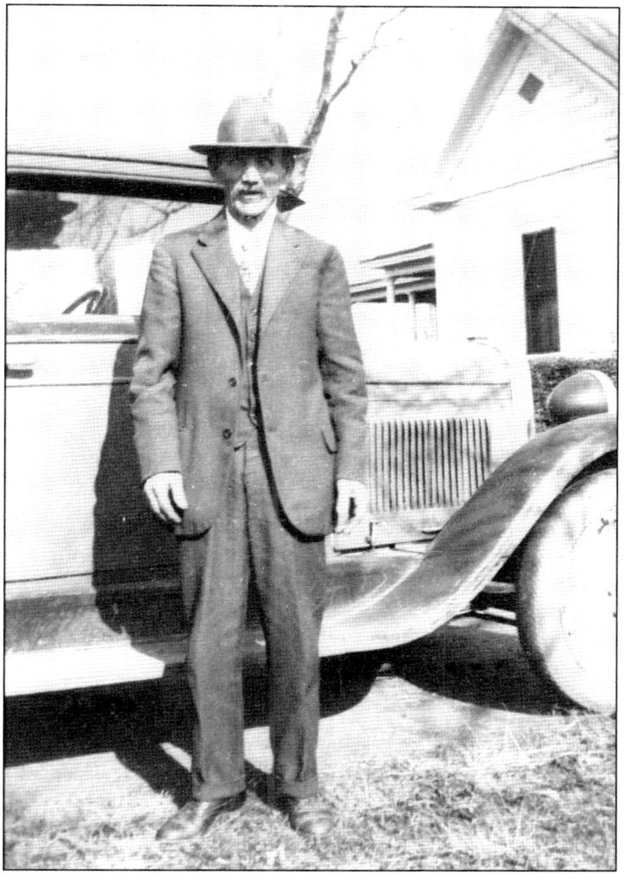

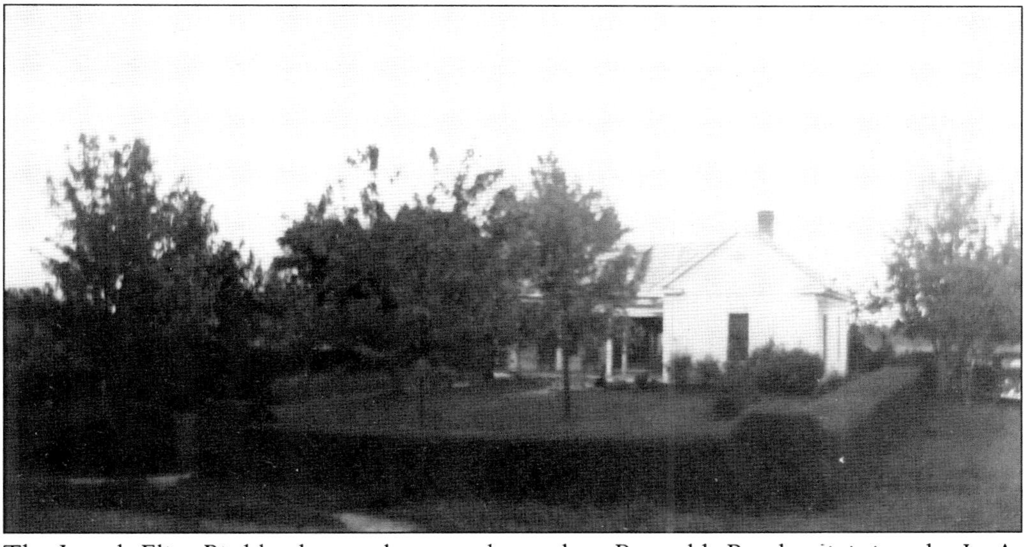

The Joseph Elias Binkley home place was located on Reynolds Road, adjoining the L. A. Reynolds property. The house no longer stands, as Highway 421 was built running through this property. (HJH.)

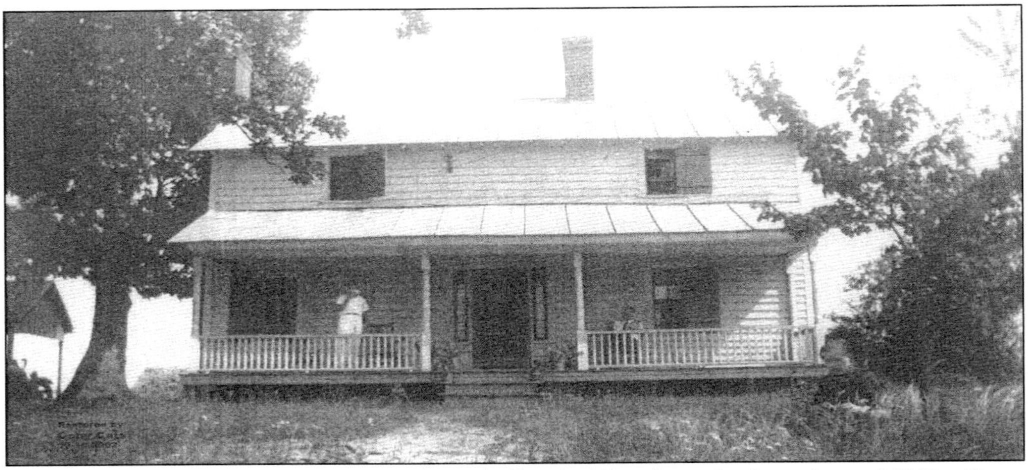

The Omer Conrad home place, located on Shallowford Road, was built in the mid-1850s. Omer and Fannie Conrad farmed and raised their family on this property. Today a business operates in the house. (LCH.)

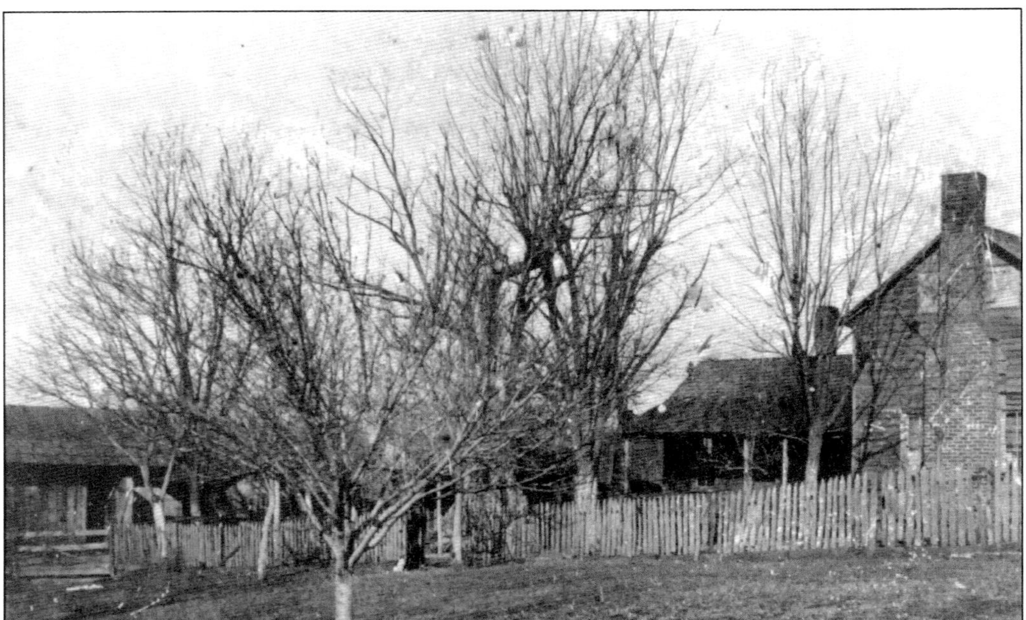

The George A. Hauser home place on Hauser Road included outbuildings spread around the farm. When the property was developed, a cabin was relocated to the Dixie Classic Fairgrounds historic village area. (LCH, NGC.)

William H. "Bud" Dull and wife Sarah "Sallie" Dull farmed in the Lewisville community, where they resided on Concord Church Road. They attended Lewisville Baptist Church with their family. (KDB.)

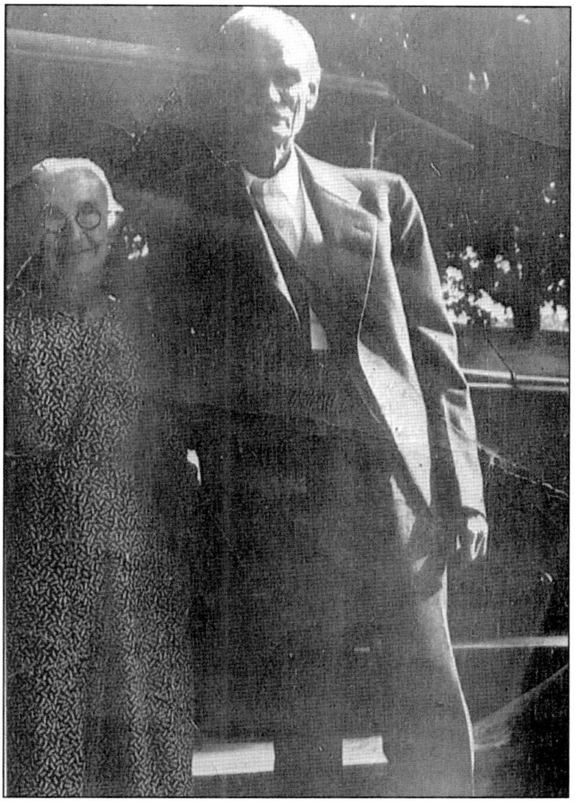

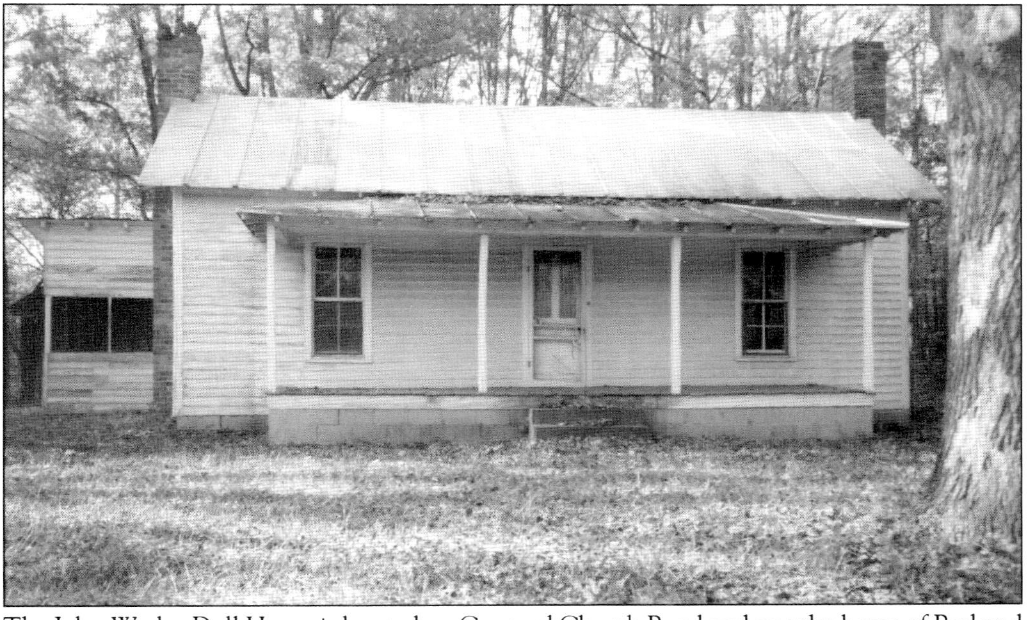

The John Wesley Dull House is located on Concord Church Road and was the home of Bud and Sallie Dull. The house was extensively remodeled with additional rooms built in the late 1970s by Sadie Hunt Henning. (KDB.)

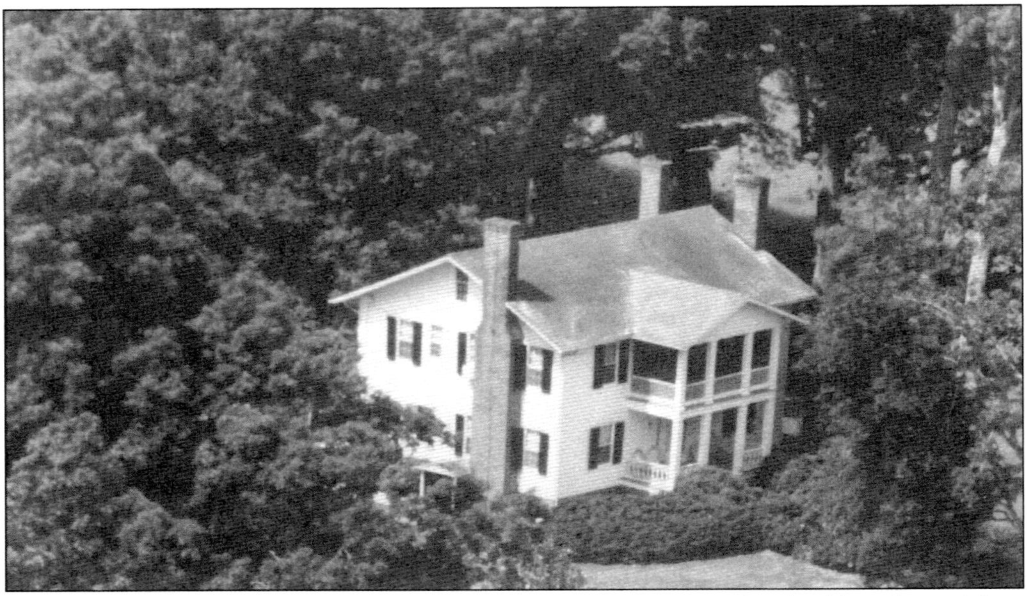

Hilltop House was built in the mid-1850s by Augustine Eugene Conrad on land he inherited from his grandfather, "River John" Conrad. Located in a beautiful setting atop a hill at the intersection of Conrad and Grapevine Roads, the house and surrounding land have been in the Conrad family for over 140 years. (GGR.)

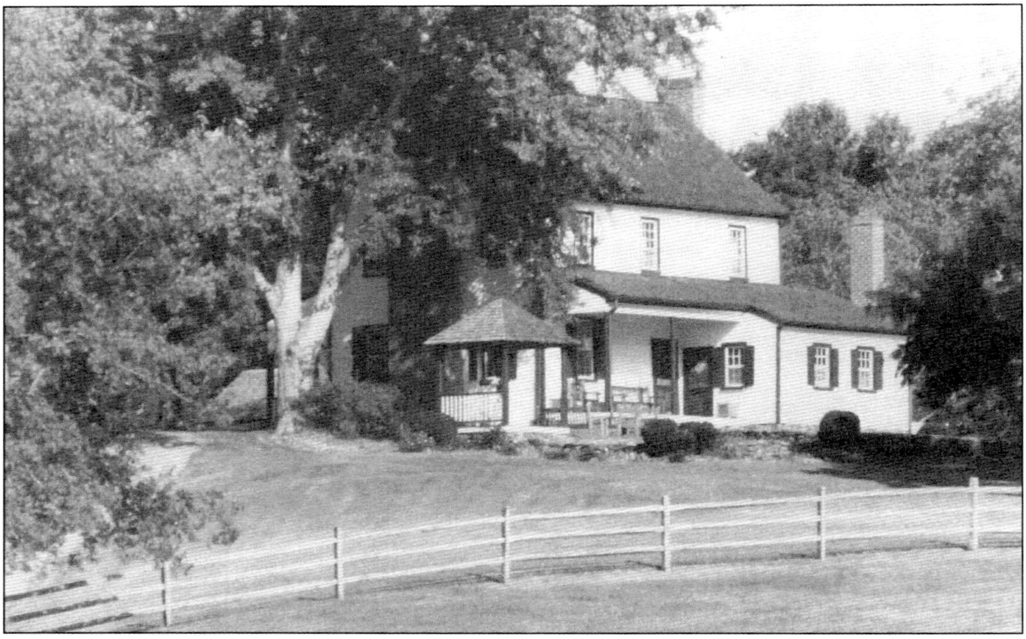

River View House sits on the banks of the Yadkin River off Conrad Road. Built in 1805, it was the home of "River John" Conrad, who operated Conrad's Ferry on the Yadkin River nearby. A well sits beside the house in this view of the backside of the Conrad home place. (GGR.)

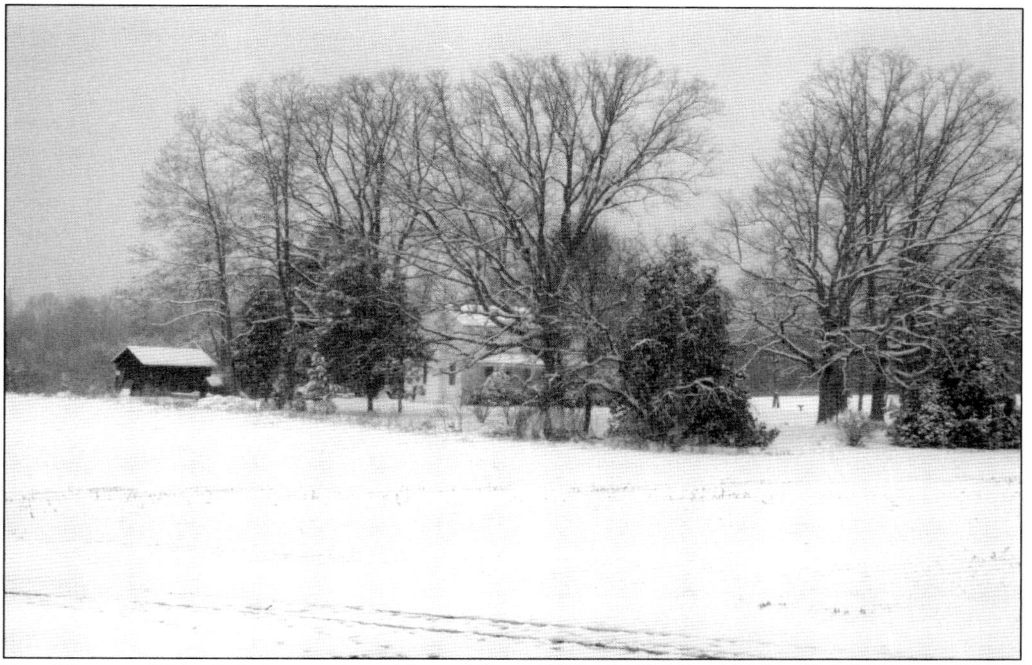

The Thomas Wake Fulk home place is located on Lewisville-Clemmons Road. Sid Lawrence built the house around 1900. Other residents included the Moore and Bailey families. Today a portion of this property is Jack Warren Park. (MAFW.)

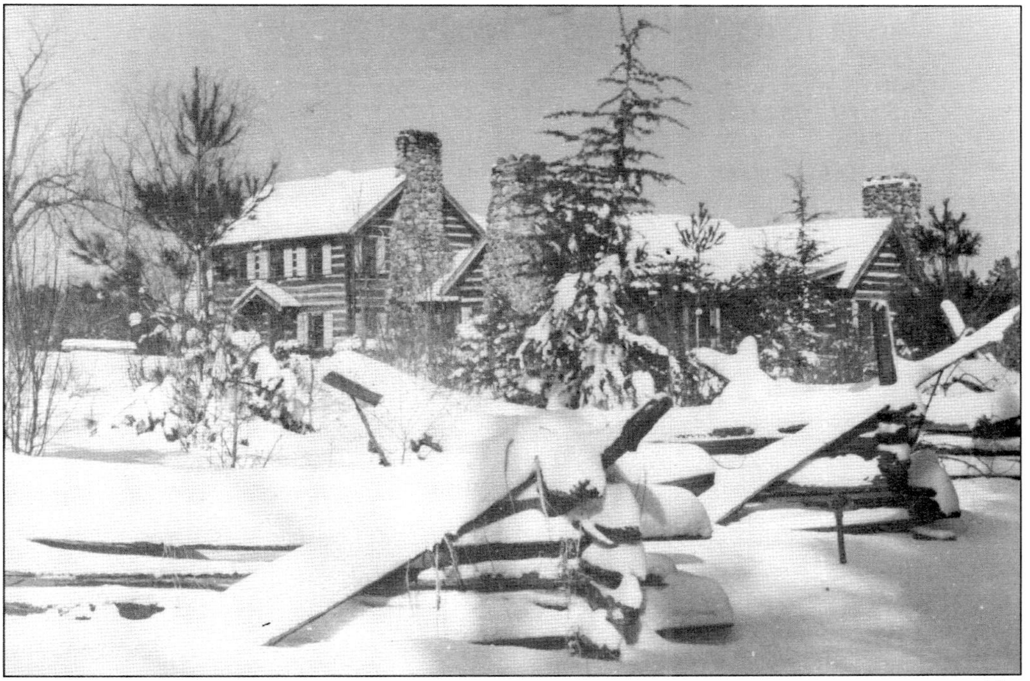

The Henderson Dull House on Dull Road was built in about 1860. The property was restored by M. A. Braswell in the 1930s. (MAFW.)

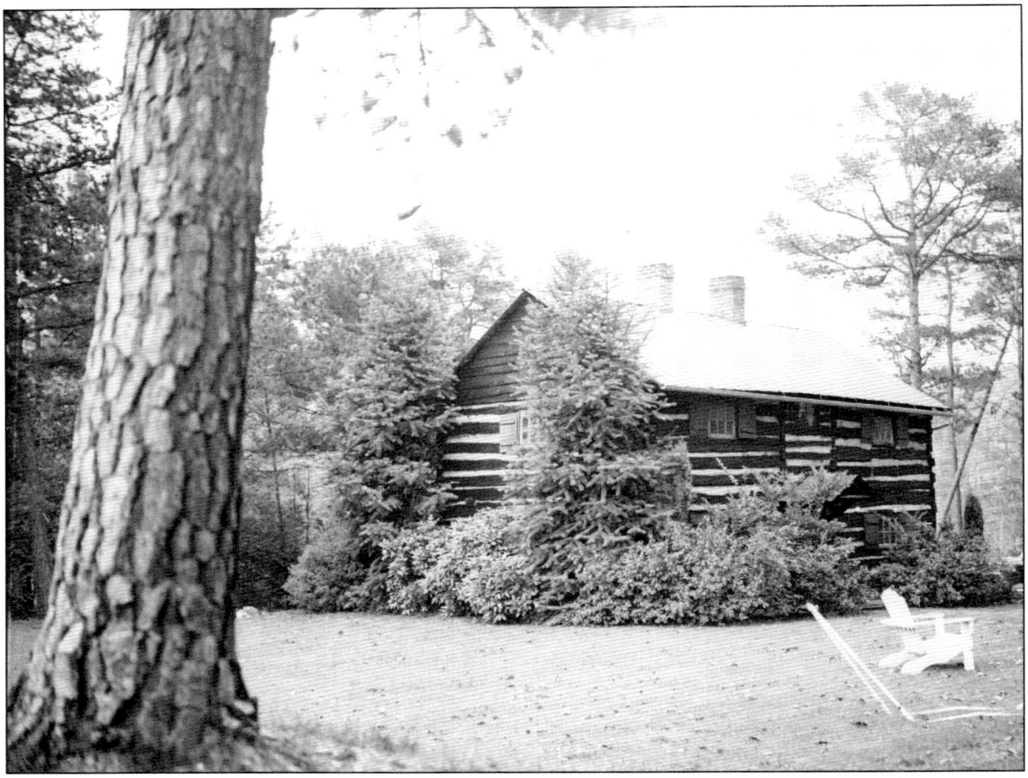

The Transou cabin is known as the Wagner cabin today, located off Reynolds Road. Built with logs from the original Concord United Methodist Church building, the four-room cabin was home to members of the Binkley and Reynolds family. (FCPL.)

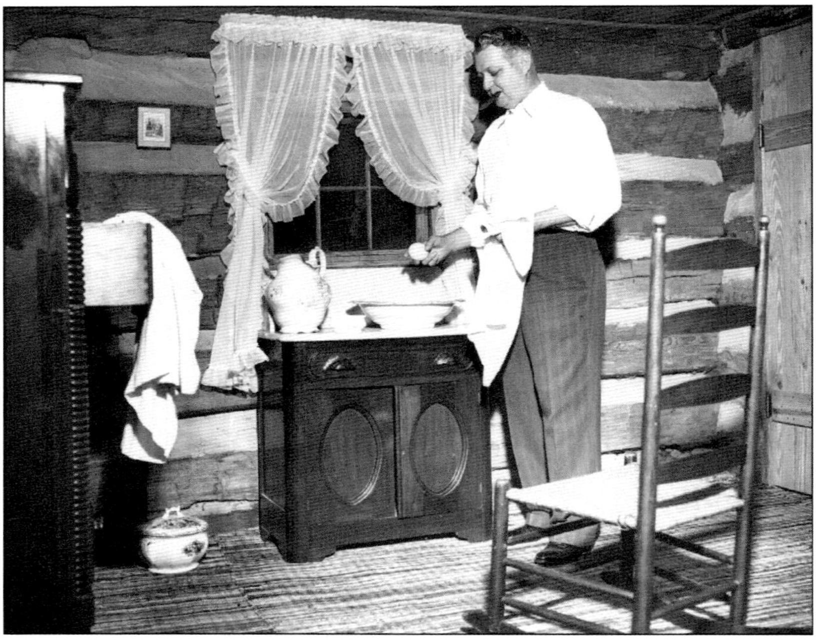

Dr. Paul Transou and his wife filled their cabin with family antiques and heirlooms. The Transous used their cabin as a country getaway from Winston-Salem. (FCPL.)

Six

Lewisville Citizens

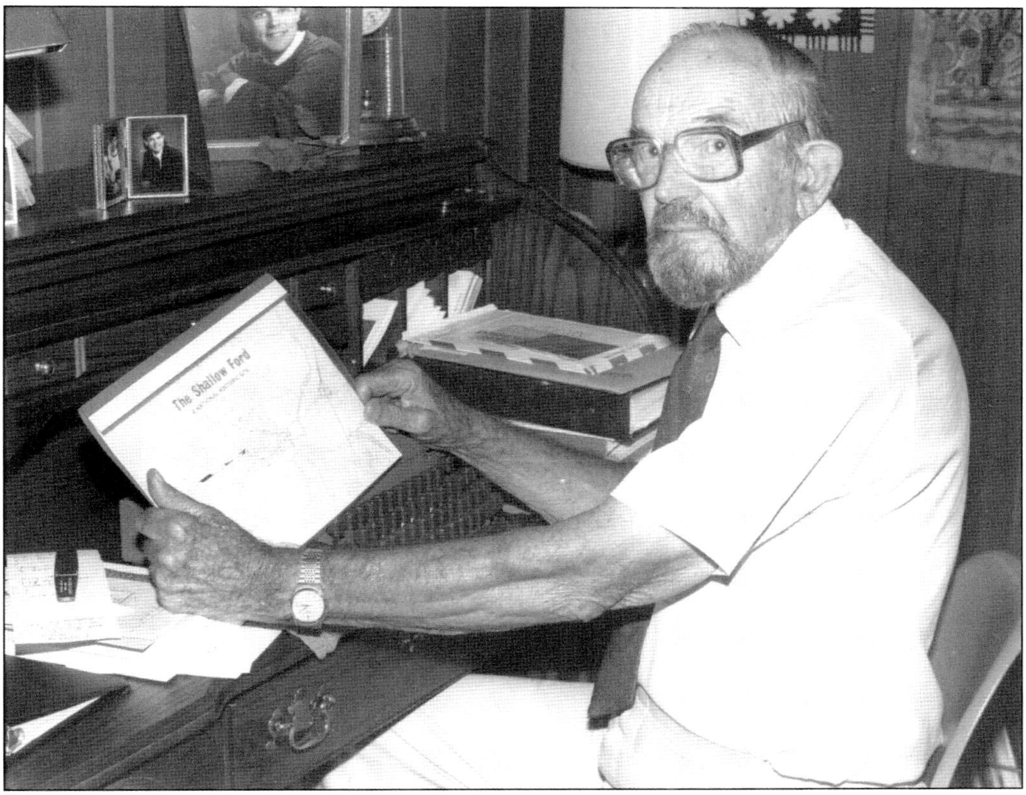

Glen Galloway "Buck" Reynolds was a well-known civic leader and local historian, recording oral history and capturing photographic images of the community. He co-edited the publication the *Lewisville Citizen*, which was published from 1948 until the early 1960s, when the *Clemmons Courier* began publication and featured news about Lewisville. His writings and photographs were published in a book titled *Shallow Ford Country*. (MV.)

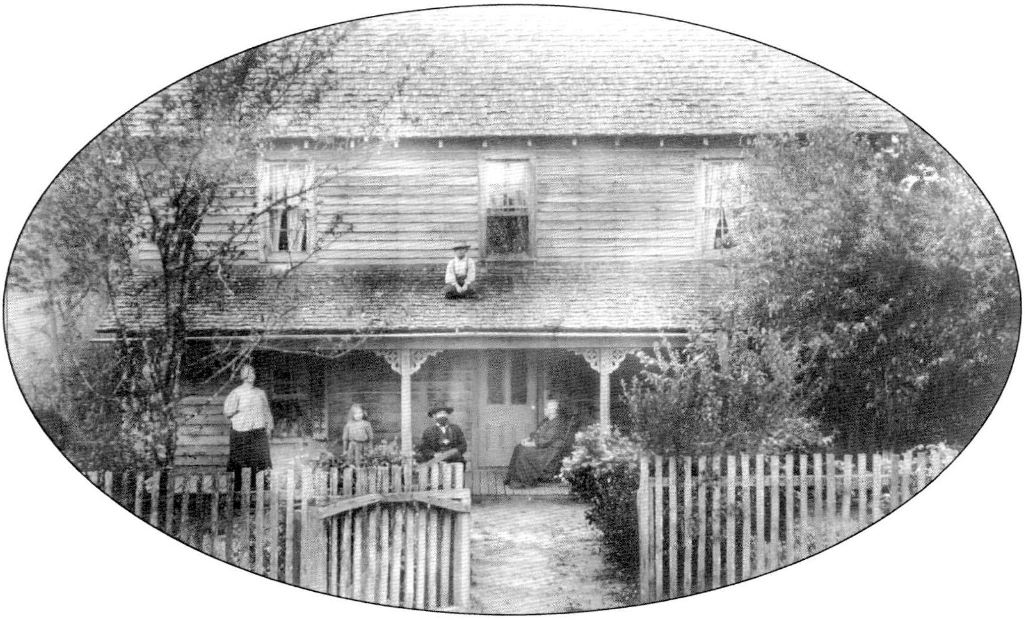

The family home of Philip Turner and Ellen Thomasson Mock was located on Lewisville-Clemmons Road. Family members standing in front of the house are, from left to right, Ellen, daughter Josephine Mock, Philip, and Virginia Cuthrell Thomasson. Sitting on the roof is son Newsome Mock. The home place sat off the road on a large farm where the Joanie Moser Park is located today. (FPC.)

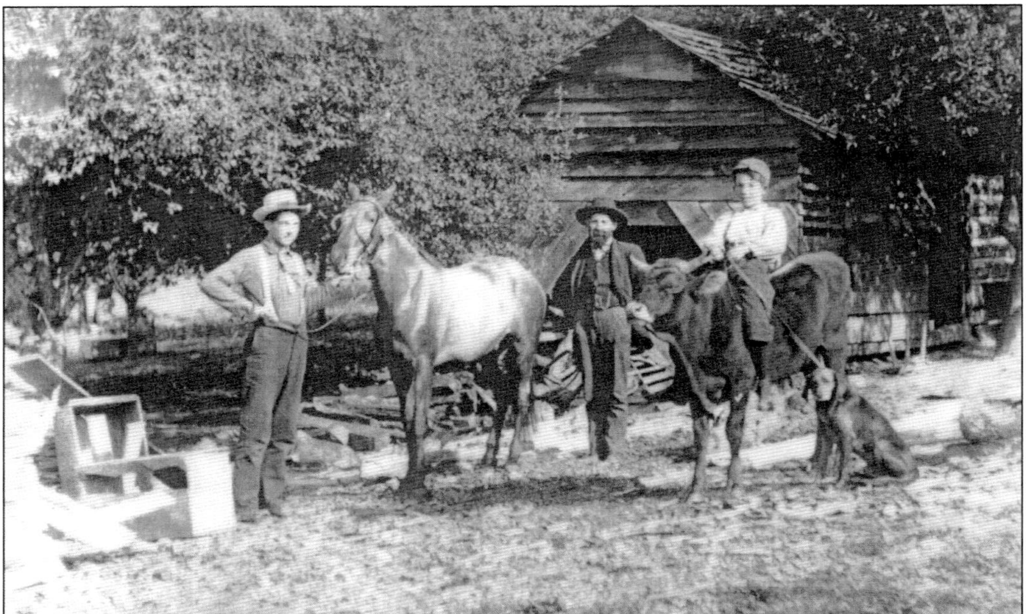

The Philip Turner Mock farm spread over a vast acreage of land. Sons Jasper Mock (left) and Newsome Mock (riding the bull) worked with their father to manage crops and livestock. (FPC.)

In this portrait of the Philip Turner Mock family, daughter Josephine is standing between her parents, Philip and Ellen and son Newsome is beside his father. Children standing behind are, from left to right, Pearl, Carrie, Jasper Wiley, Dora, and Nina. (FPC.)

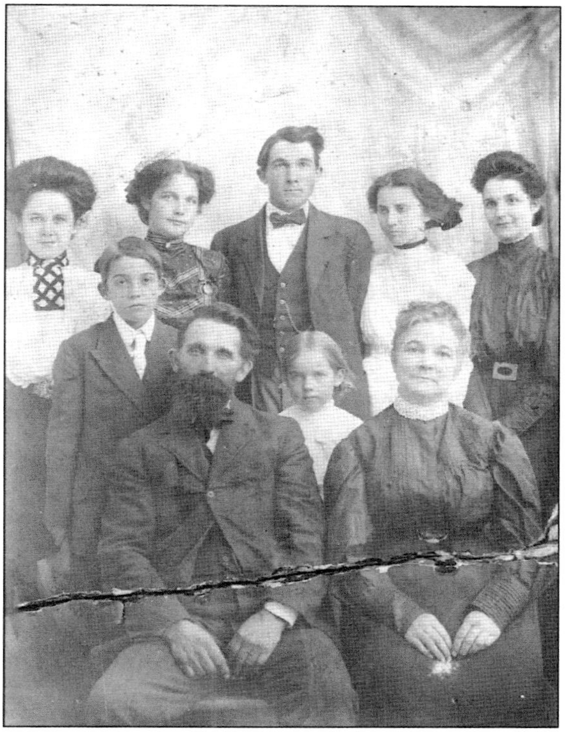

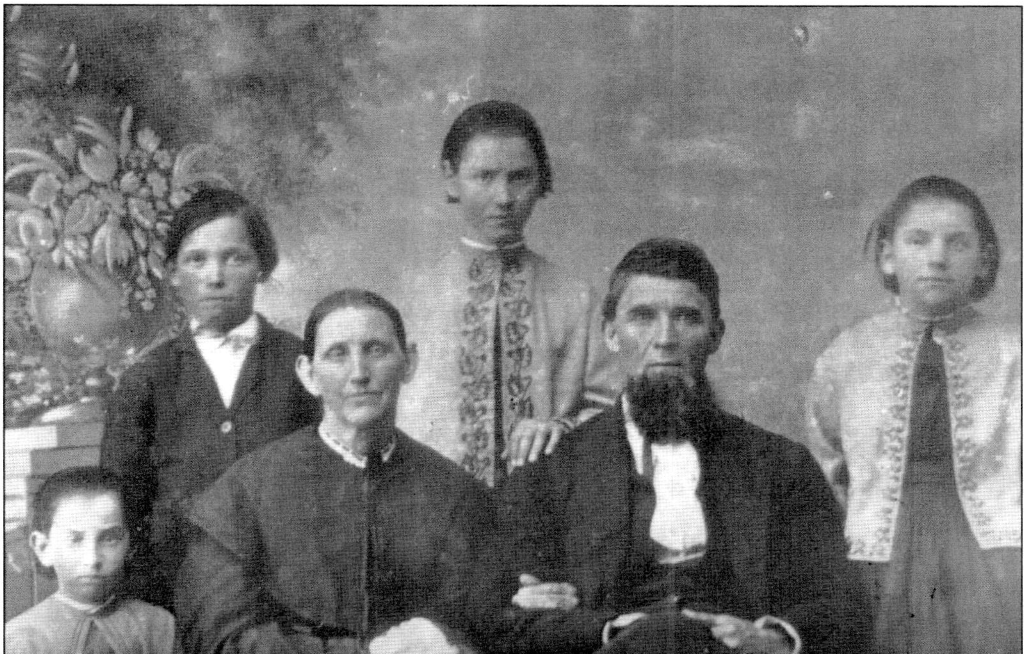

Philip Mock and his wife, Mary Newsome Mock, are seated with their children for this portrait. Posing with their parents are, from left to right, Sarah, Philip Turner, Mary Ellen, and Lenore Ann. (FPC.)

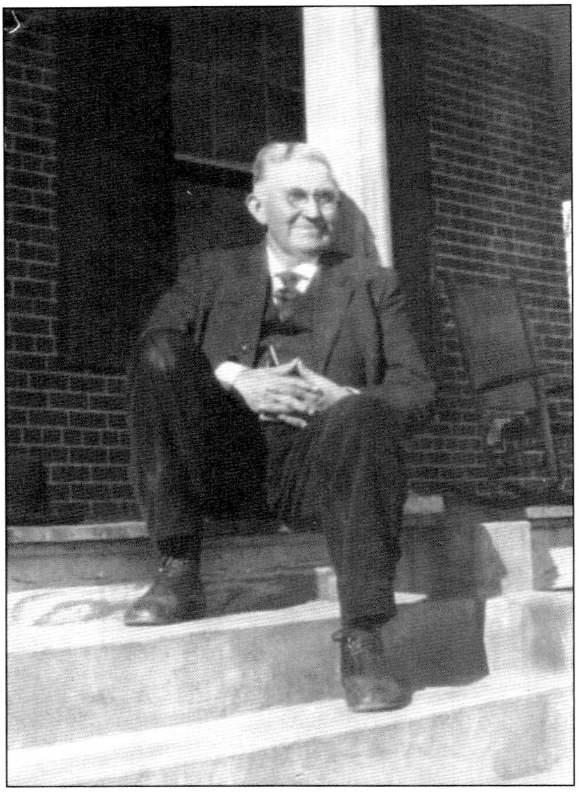

Charles Oliver "C. O." Sprinkle sits on the steps of the Laugenour House, which his family owned from 1914 to the late 1960s. He added wraparound porches in 1921 during his ownership to make it easy to navigate his wheelchair in his later years to talk to friends and neighbors. (DCH.)

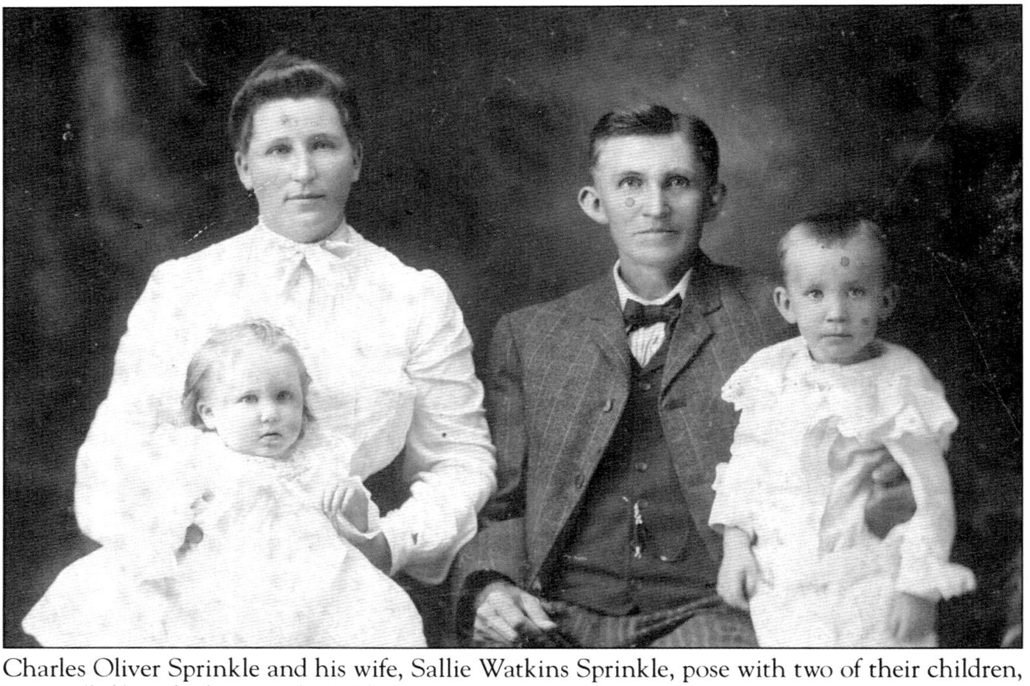

Charles Oliver Sprinkle and his wife, Sallie Watkins Sprinkle, pose with two of their children, Carrie (left) and Clunette. (DCH.)

Carrie Sprinkle (left) and Margaret Doub are standing in the yard beside the Laugenour House. Carrie was a teacher at Lewisville Academy. The shutters are closed on the windows. (DCH.)

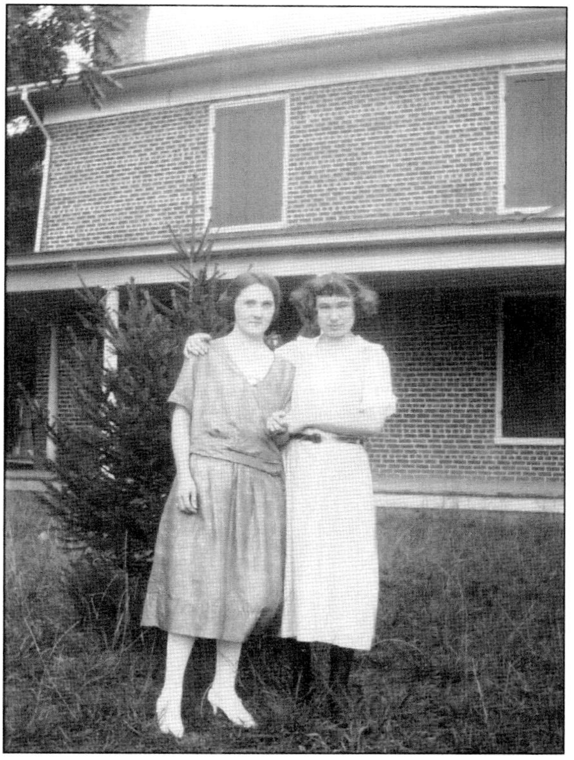

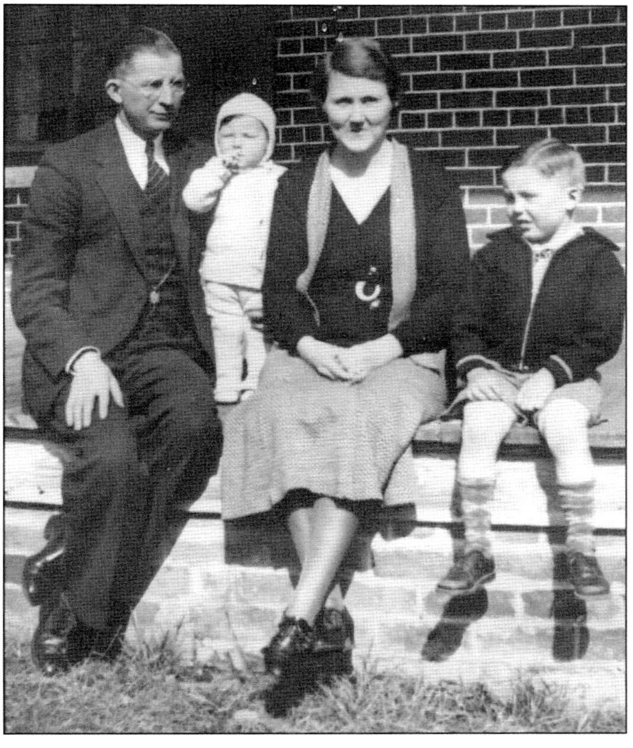

Floyd W. Hauser and his wife, Carrie Elizabeth Sprinkle Hauser, are sitting on the porch of the Laugenour House in 1926 with their children, Nancy, who is 13 months old, and Charles, age five. (DCH.)

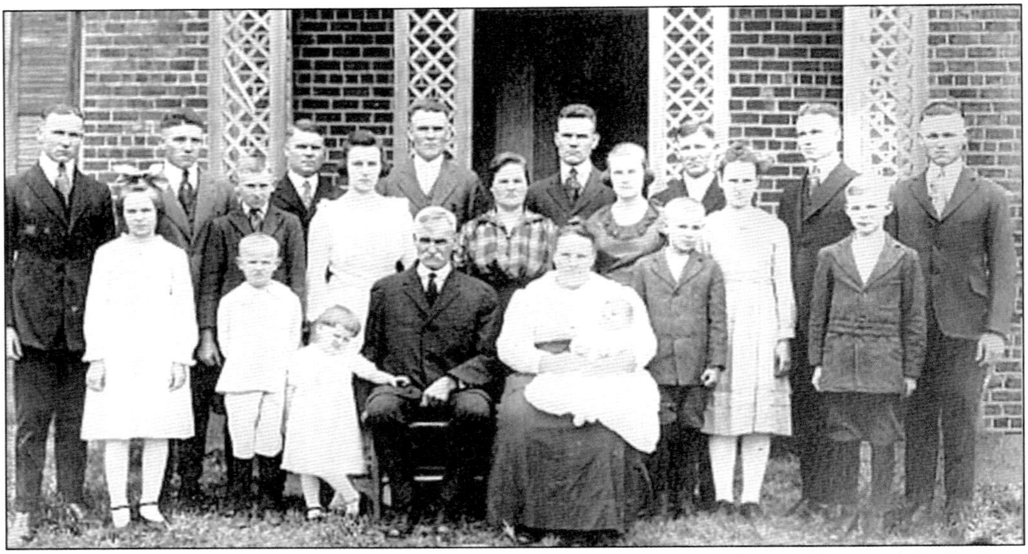

Charles P. and Ellen Kiger Bailey reared 19 children. From left to right are (first row) Della Sue, Charles and Ellen Bailey, baby John Edward, and Fred Warren; (second row) Mary Lucile, Walter Dalton, Robert Elwood, Lelia Gray, Stella May, Laura Cornish, Betty Almira, and Taft; (third row) Coy Eugene, Gilbert Tobias, Paul Cornelius, William Thomas, Lee Jackson, Oscar Costen, Charles Anderson, and Frank Tennyson. (FB.)

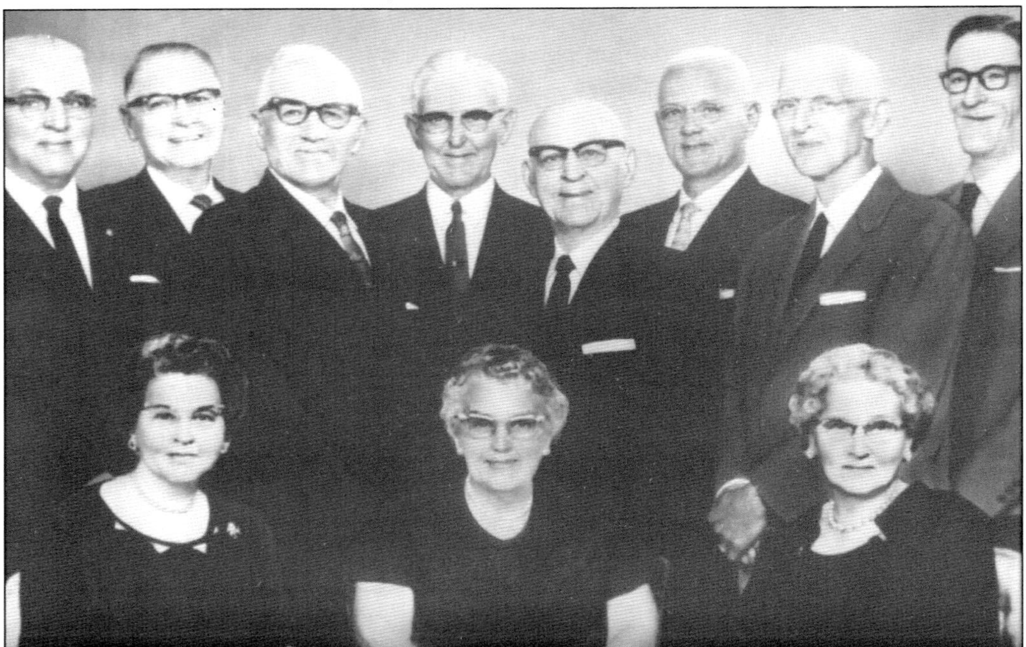

Edwin Alexander Conrad and his wife, Laura Rebecca Transou Conrad, raised 11 children in the Brookstown community. The Conrad siblings lived long lives and were active in the community. Posing together are sisters, from left to right, Ruby Conrad Pfaff, Lula Conrad Binkley, and Amy Conrad Needham. Brothers standing together are, from left to right, Harold, Howard, Omer, Luther, Walter, Fred, Everette, and Edwin Conrad. (LCH.)

Brothers Abraham Grant Clayton (left) and George Thomas Clayton resided in central Lewisville. Grant and his wife, Margaret Pfaff Clayton, lived on property at the corner of Shallowford and Lewisville-Clemmons Roads. Croquet games were popular recreation on their lawn, and he operated a garage across Shallowford Road. George farmed, and his wife, Della Millis Clayton, delivered many babies in the community. (LCH, NGC.)

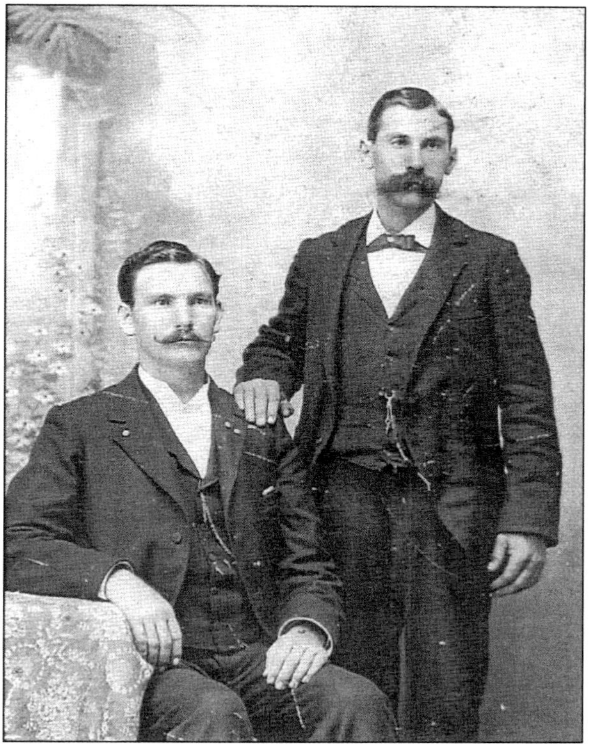

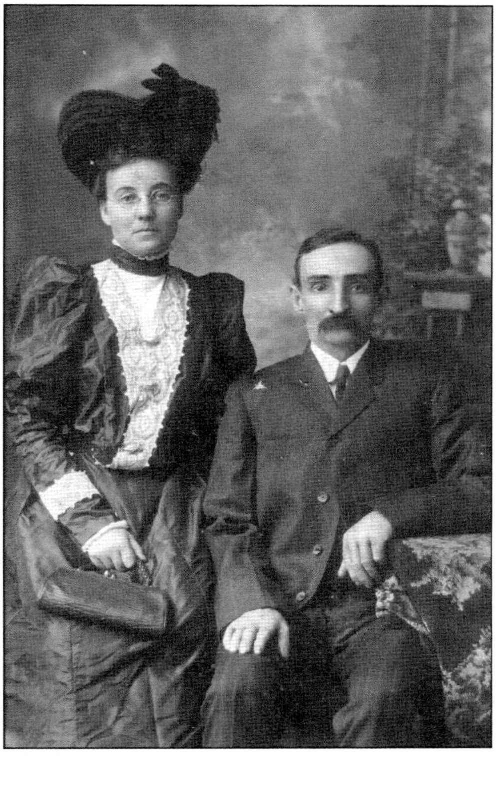

John Wesley Holder was a native of Lewisville. His wife, Sarah Millis Holder, grew up in the Quaker community in Guilford County. The Holders resided in Lewisville and later moved to the Waughtown area of Forsyth County where he worked for Nissen Wagon Works. (MAFW.)

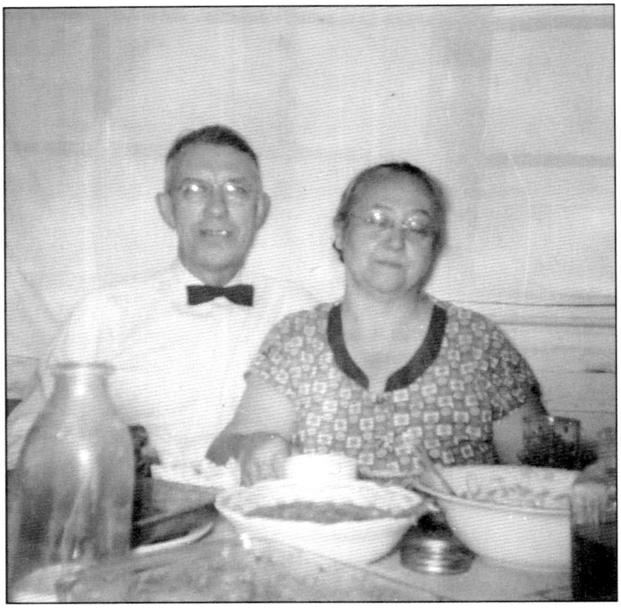

Gurney and Nola Craft, parents of the Craft Brothers quartet, nurtured their son's love of music in their home. Nola used her $300 inheritance from her mother to purchase matching brown pin-striped wool suits for her boys when they began performing. (JRC.)

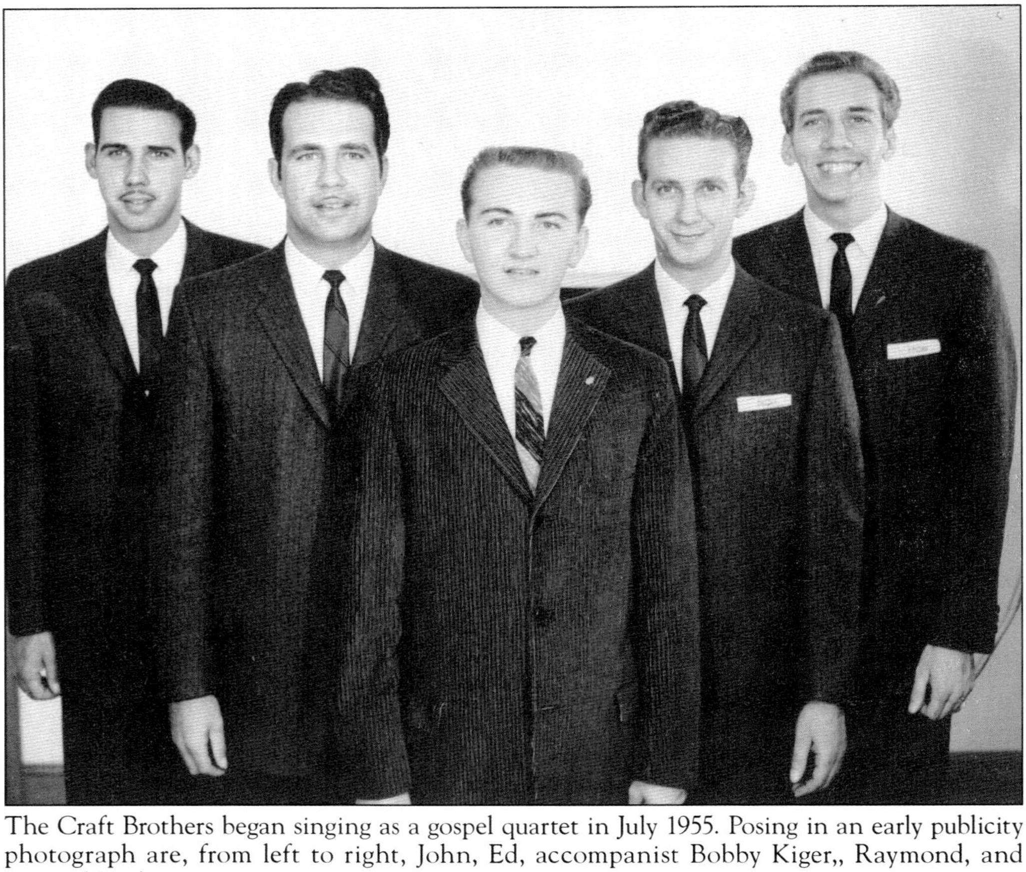

The Craft Brothers began singing as a gospel quartet in July 1955. Posing in an early publicity photograph are, from left to right, John, Ed, accompanist Bobby Kiger,, Raymond, and James. (JRC.)

The Craft Brothers as children grew up attending Harmony Grove United Methodist Church, where their father directed music. The boys standing together are, from left to right, (first row) John and James; (second row) Ed and Raymond. (JRC.)

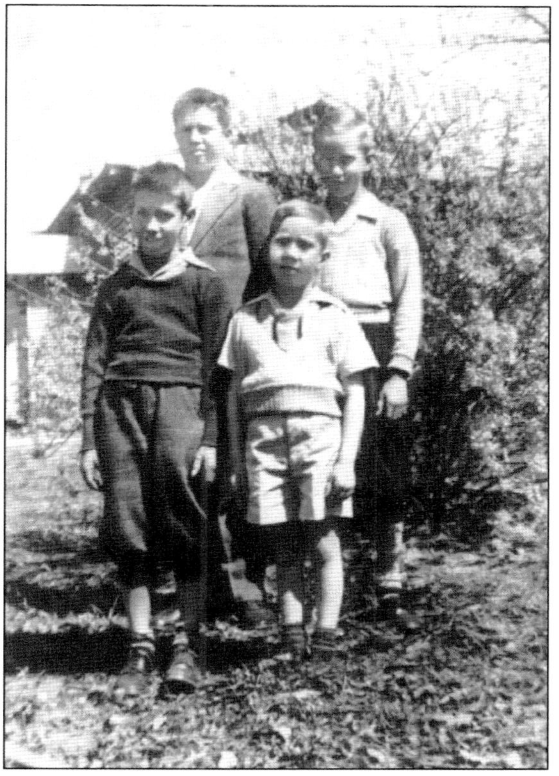

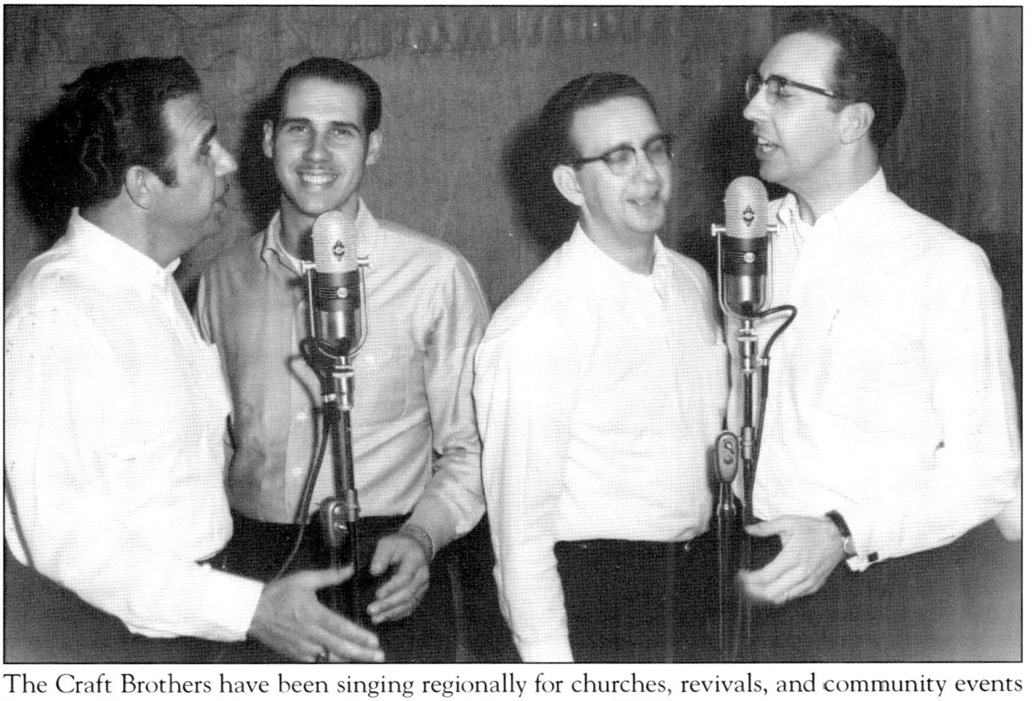

The Craft Brothers have been singing regionally for churches, revivals, and community events for over 50 years and have recorded some of their music. (JRC.)

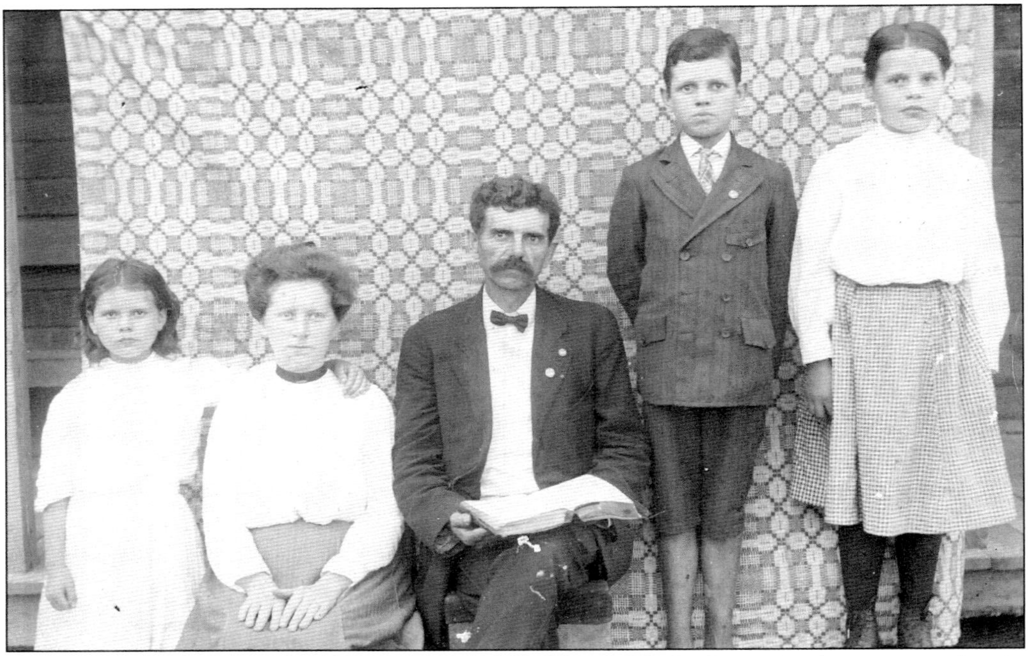

Quilts and coverlets were family treasures, and the Enoch Wesley Jones family poses together in 1911 with a decorative backdrop. Enoch was ordained in the Wesleyan Methodist Church in 1912. The family includes, from left to right, Myrtle Susan, wife Mary Patton Jones, Enoch Wesley, Malden Worth, and Lillian Vesta Jones. (SJ.)

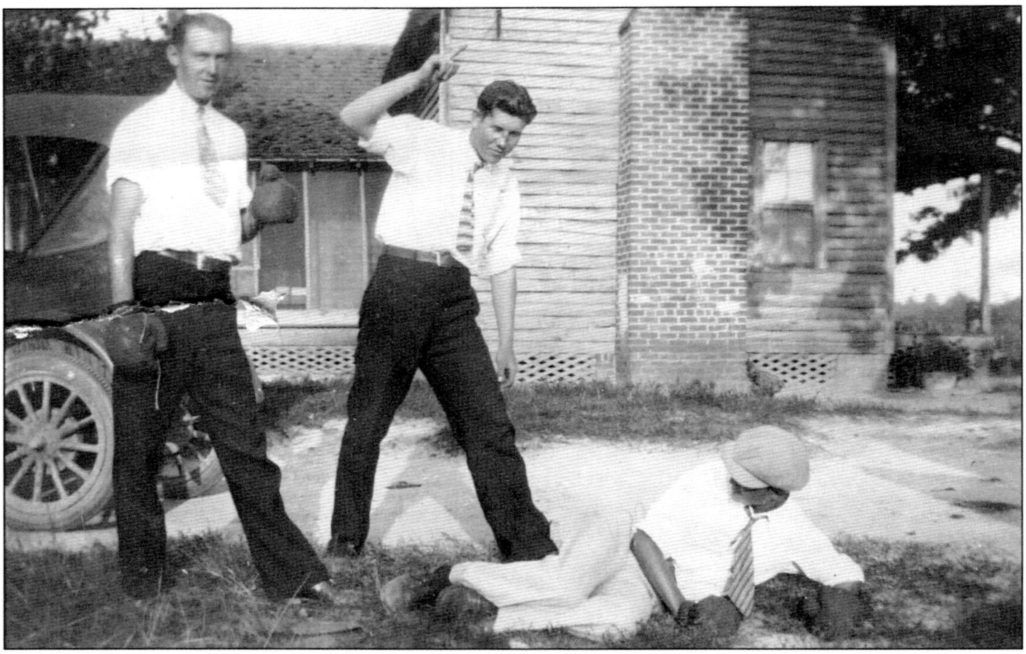

Young men enjoy a boxing match in the yard of the Fred and Margaret Black Reich home place on Concord Church Road. Spencer Reich stands at left, while an unidentified man counts the time as Gerald Casey remains on the ground. (MRB.)

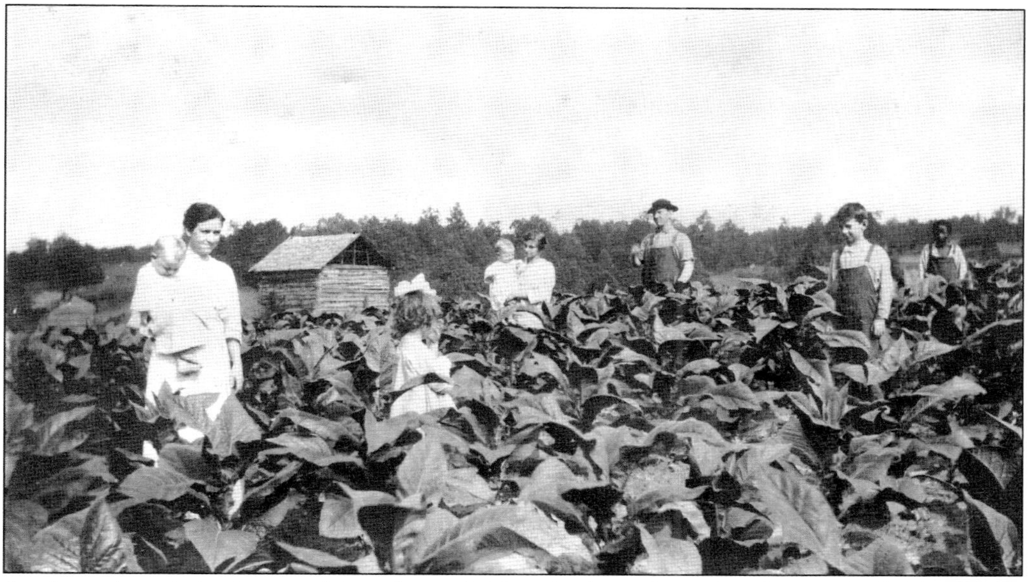

A tobacco barn is in view amid the tobacco field on the Jones farm. Standing in the field are, from left to right, Nannie Craft Jones, wife of Henry Jones, holding one of her twin sons Woodrow or Wilson; daughter Grace with her back to the camera, Mabel Jones holding the other twin boy, unknown man wearing hat, Ferdinand Jones; and unidentified young boy. (SJ.)

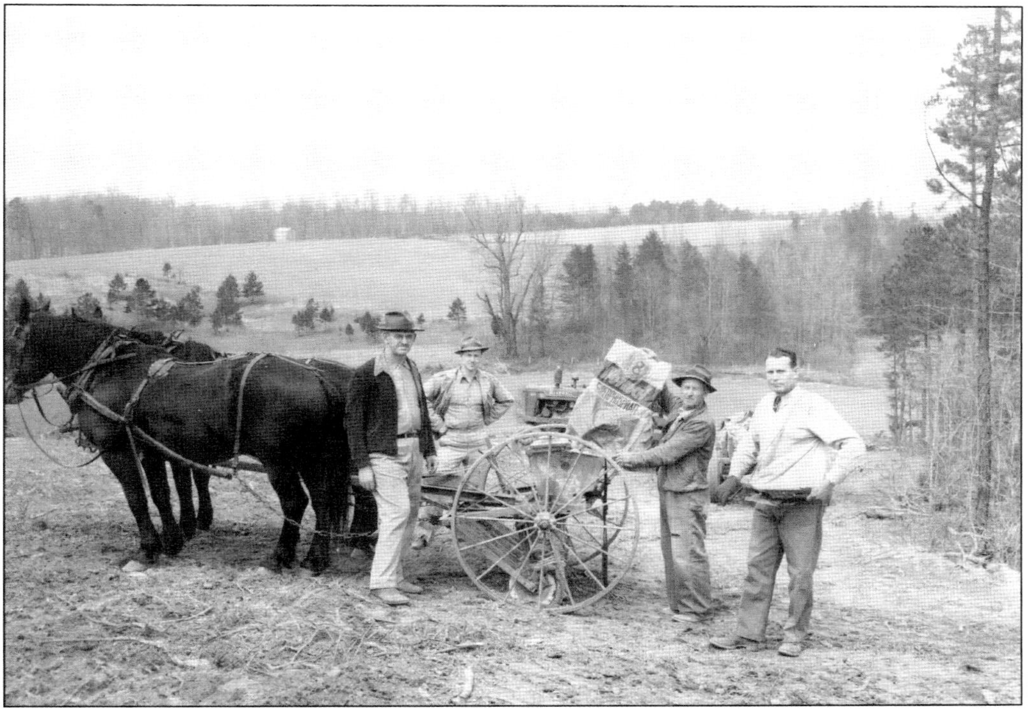

Ferdinand Jones stands at left as Errett Cline is putting fertilizer in a disk harrow for sowing the pasture on the farm.. The large field at the top left is developed as Bradford Place today. (SJ.)

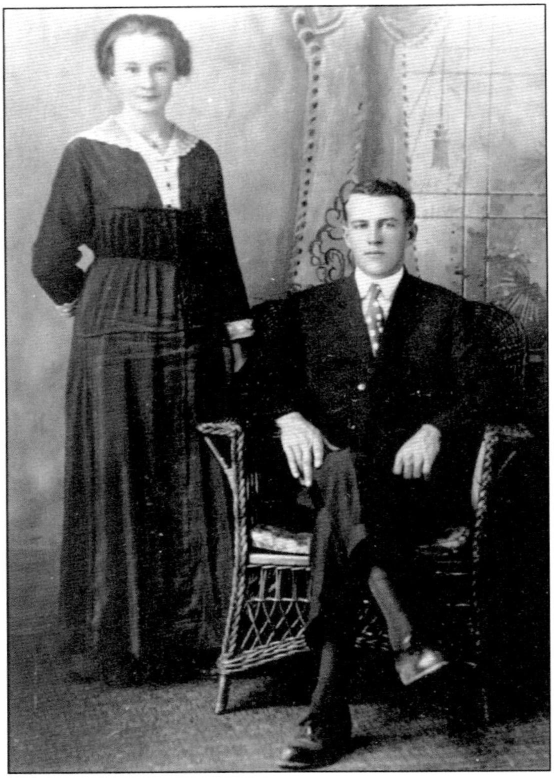

Lela Fulk Burke worked with her mother, Mary, and sister Fannie in operating the first telephone switchboard in the Fulk home, serving the southwestern area of Forsyth County. She married Aaron David Burke and moved to the South Fork community near his family's business. They raised 10 children, and Lela lived to 103 years of age. She was one of the oldest living members of Lewisville Baptist Church for many years. (DMJ.)

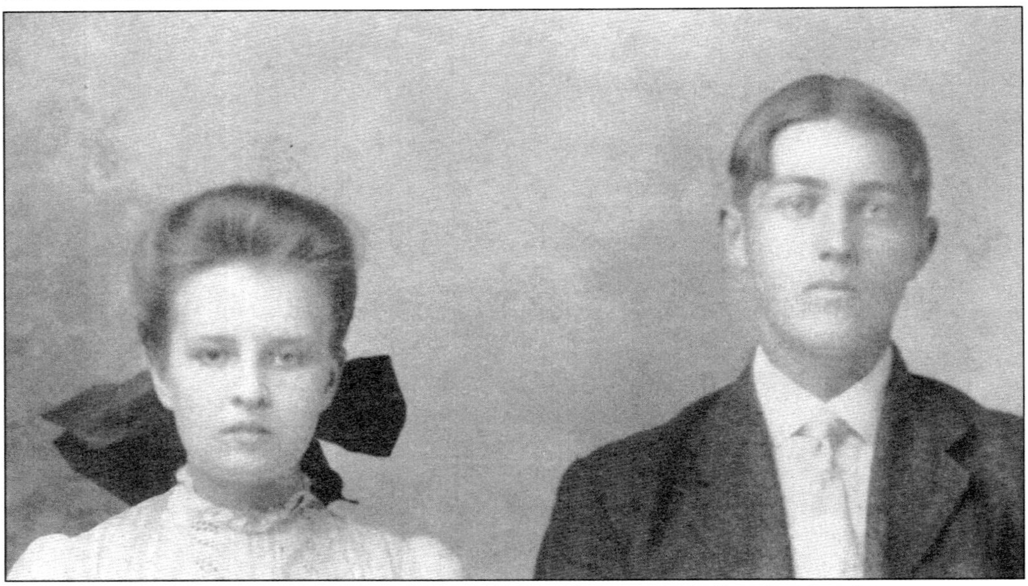

Omer Carless and Fannie Fulk Conrad were residents living on Shallowford Road for many years. Omer farmed, and Fannie managed the Lewisville School cafeteria and taught piano lessons. Before her marriage, Fannie established the first telephone switchboard in her parents' neighboring home, which was operated with her mother, Mary Fulk, and sister, Lela. Fannie was one of the longest living members of Lewisville Baptist Church, where she served as church pianist. (LCH.)

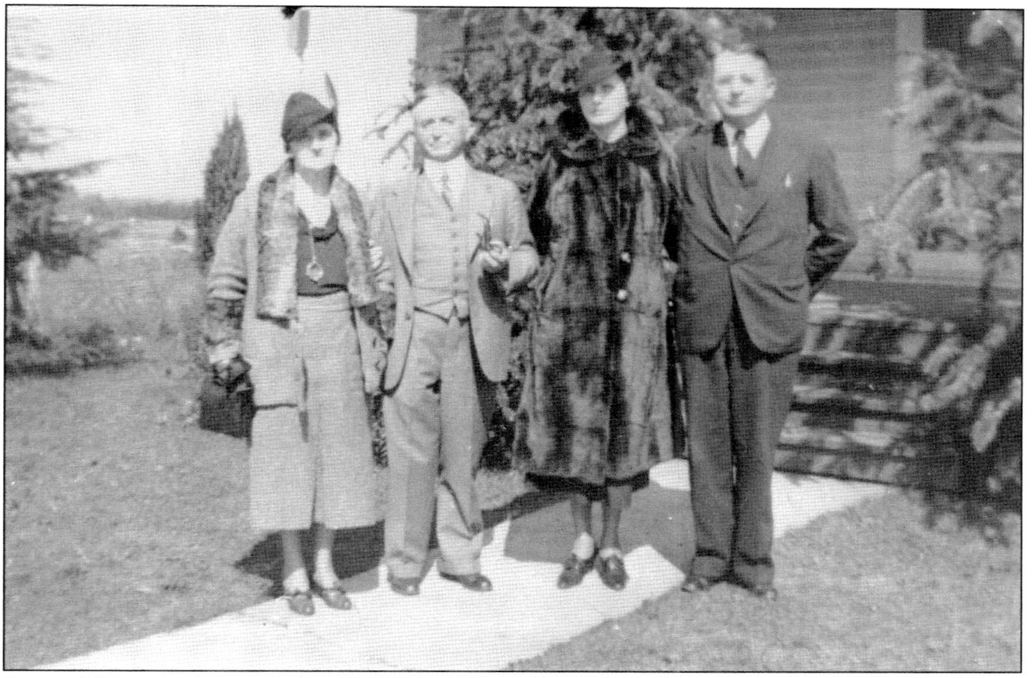

Dressed for an evening on the town are Nellie and Smith Williams (left) and Maude and Wake Fulk. They were leaving to attend a theater performance in Winston-Salem. (MAFW.)

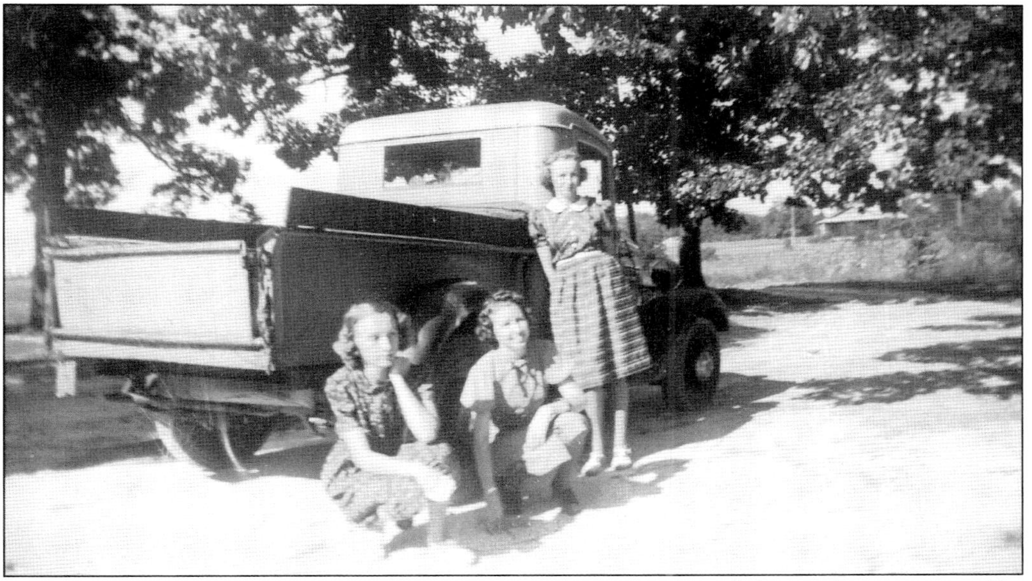

Lewisville School coeds enjoy a Sunday afternoon visit at the Wake Fulk home place on Lewisville-Clemmons Road. From left to right are Kathryn Burke (Morgan), Mary Alice Fulk (Warren), and Doris Burke (Todd). (MAFW.)

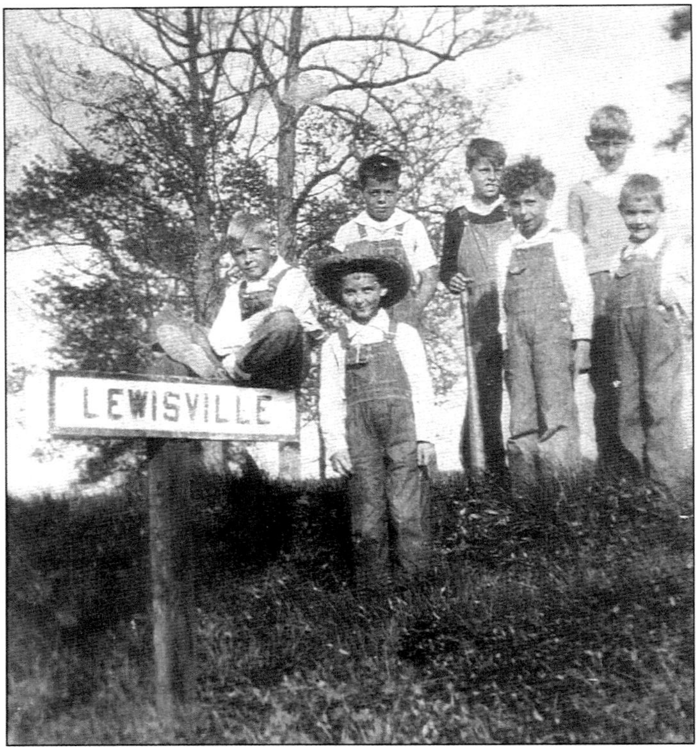

Neighborhood boys gather at the road sign on Shallowford Road at Lewisville United Methodist Church. Sitting on the sign is Sid Moser Jr. with his brothers Glenn Moser (wearing a hat) and Dick Moser (far right). The boys standing from left to right are Glenn Thrush, brothers Duran and Ronald Stimson, and Gray Fulk. (DS.)

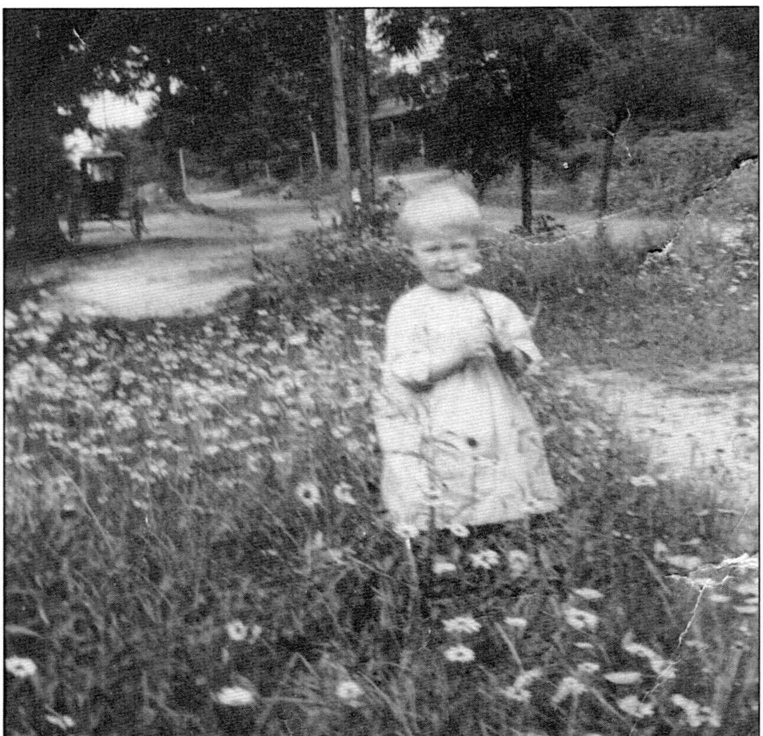

Laura Conrad (Huffman), daughter of Omer and Fannie Conrad, plays in the flowers at her home place on Shallowford Road in 1919. Wright's Store is visible in the trees, and a buggy is parked in front of Thomas Fulk's blacksmith shop. (LCH.)

William Spencer Reich poses with his tricycle at age four. He is the founder of Reich's Garage, today operating as Lewisville Automotive Service on Shallowford Road, which has been owned and operated by three generations of Reich family members for over 80 years. (MRB.)

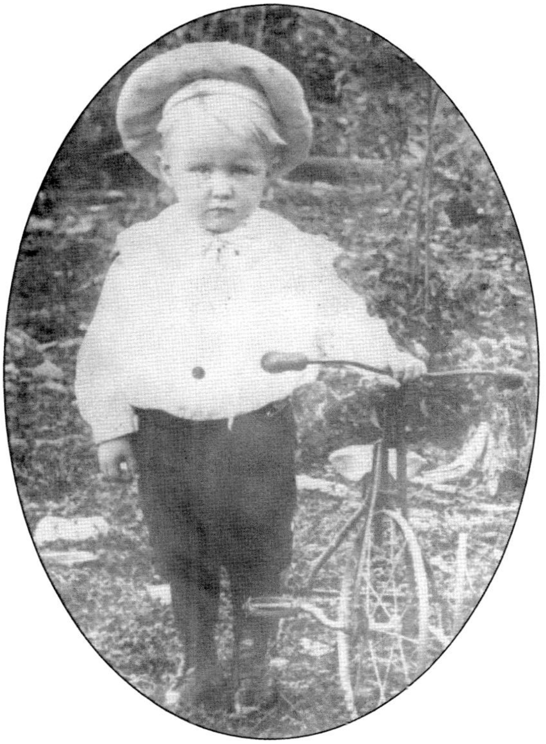

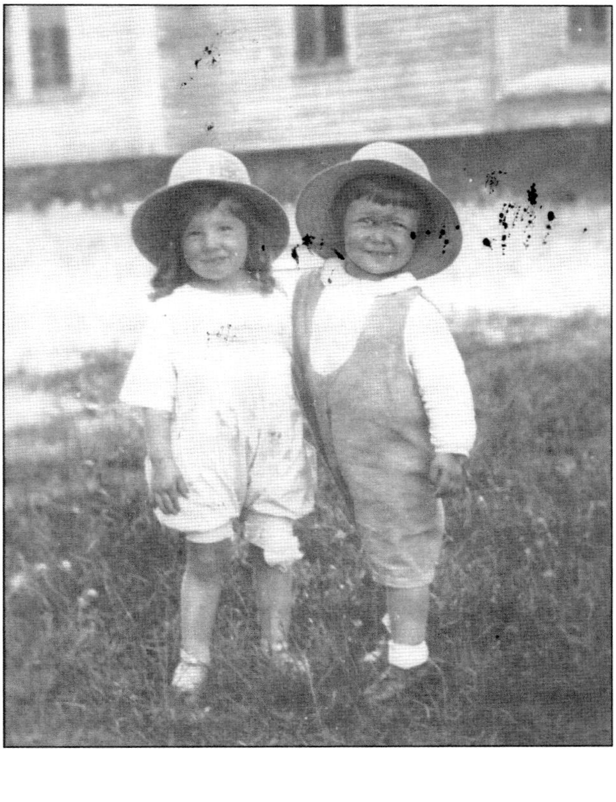

The three-year-old Martin girls pose together at the Martin home place located on Shallowford Road. At left, "Aunt" Ruth Jean Martin (Hurtt) and her "niece" Frances Martin (Todd) at right grew up playing together in Lewisville. (NGC.)

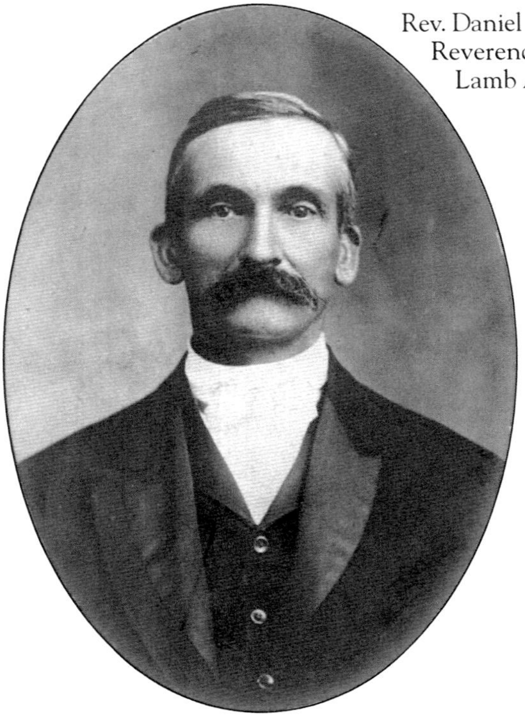

Rev. Daniel Alvin Binkley was a teacher at Warner's School. Reverend Binkley's daughter, Bessie Binkley, married Lamb Archibald Reynolds. (RRH.)

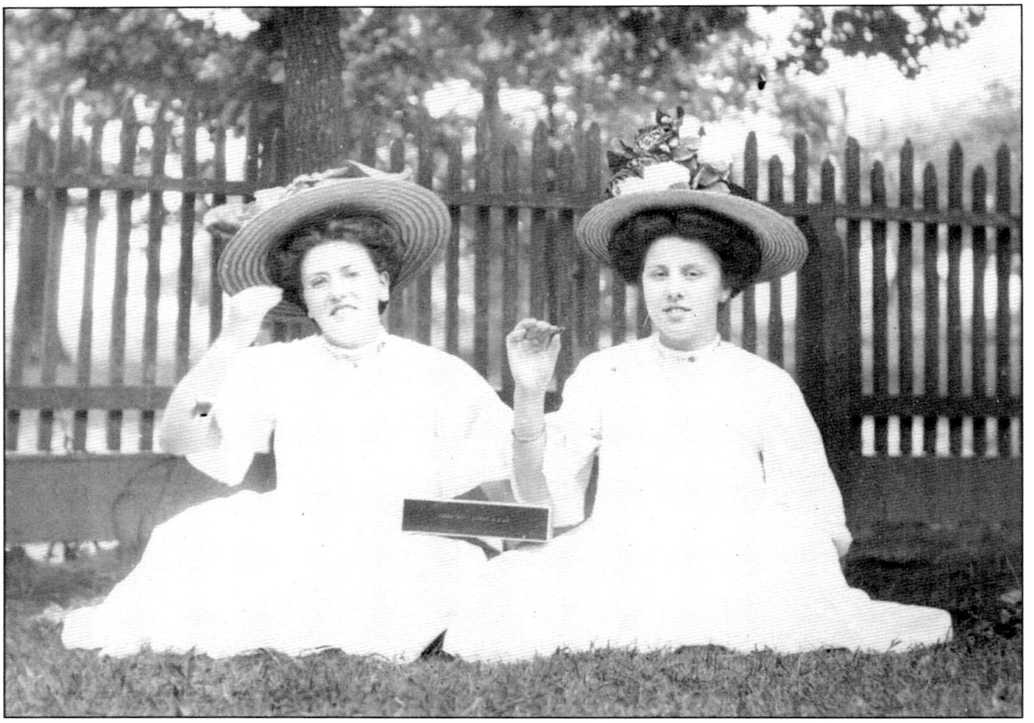

Sisters Ethel (left) and Blanche Spaugh are seated on the lawn of the Methodist parsonage. Their father, Lewis Spaugh, worked with the Spaugh family sawmill. (LHS.)

Dressed in fashionable clothing, Florence Holder (left) and Lillie Tuttle are standing at Shallowford Road in front of the Methodist parsonage. (LHS.)

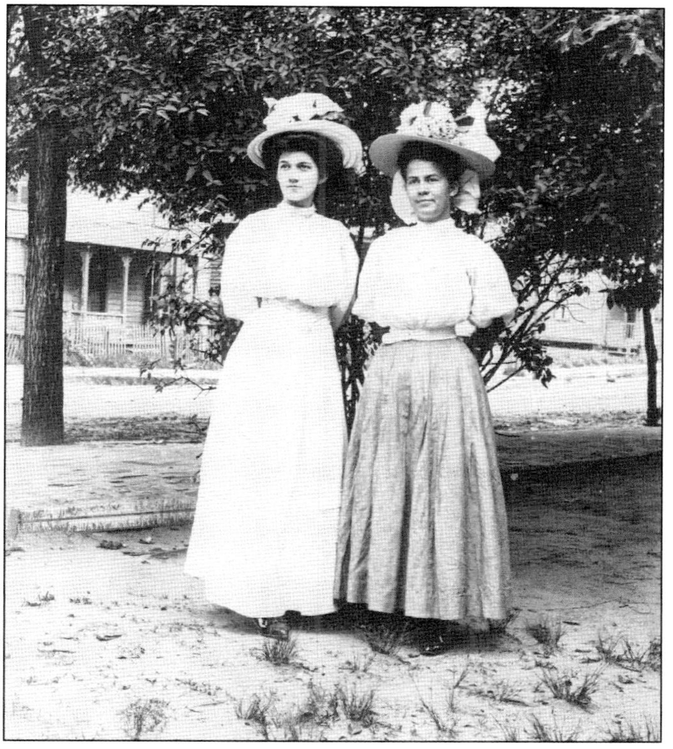

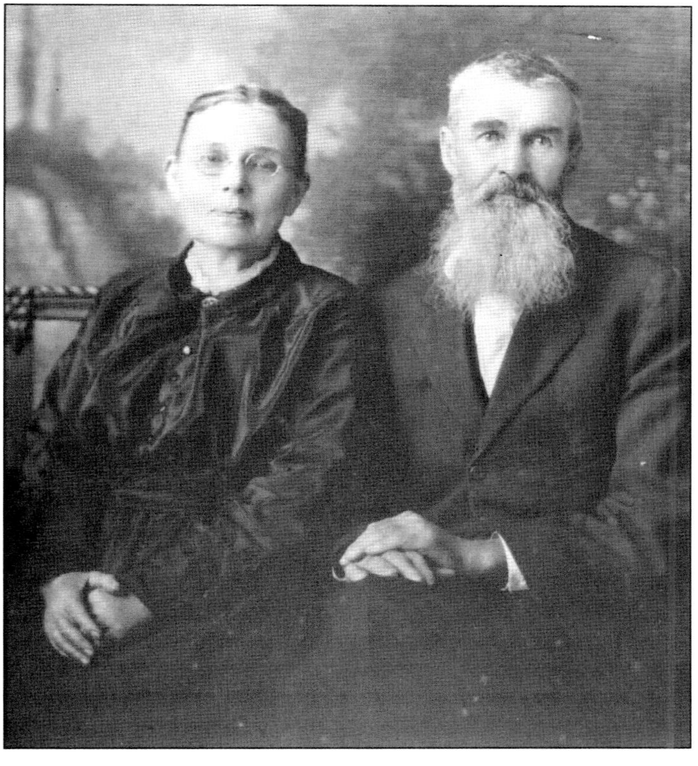

Abram Allen Styers and his wife, Millie Ann Crews Styers, resided in the western portion of the Lewisville community. Abram Styers operated the Styers Ferry on the Yadkin River, transporting people, horses, and wagons before bridges were built. Styers Ferry Road is named for this family and business. (LHS.)

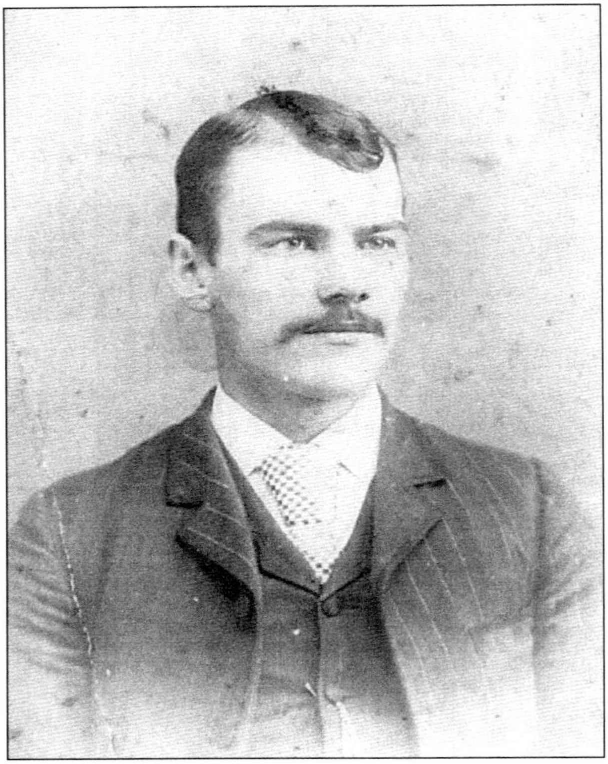

Thomas Albert "Ab" Craft lived in the heart of Lewisville with his wife, "Susie," and 12 children, where they were active members of the community. (RC.)

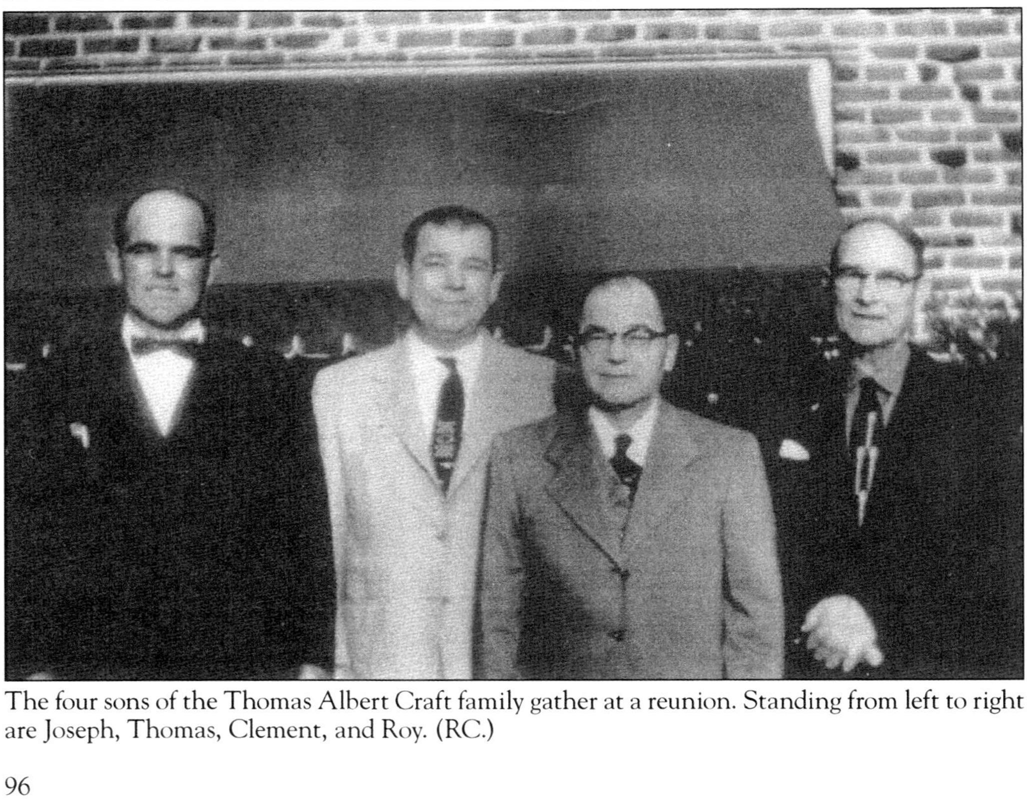

The four sons of the Thomas Albert Craft family gather at a reunion. Standing from left to right are Joseph, Thomas, Clement, and Roy. (RC.)

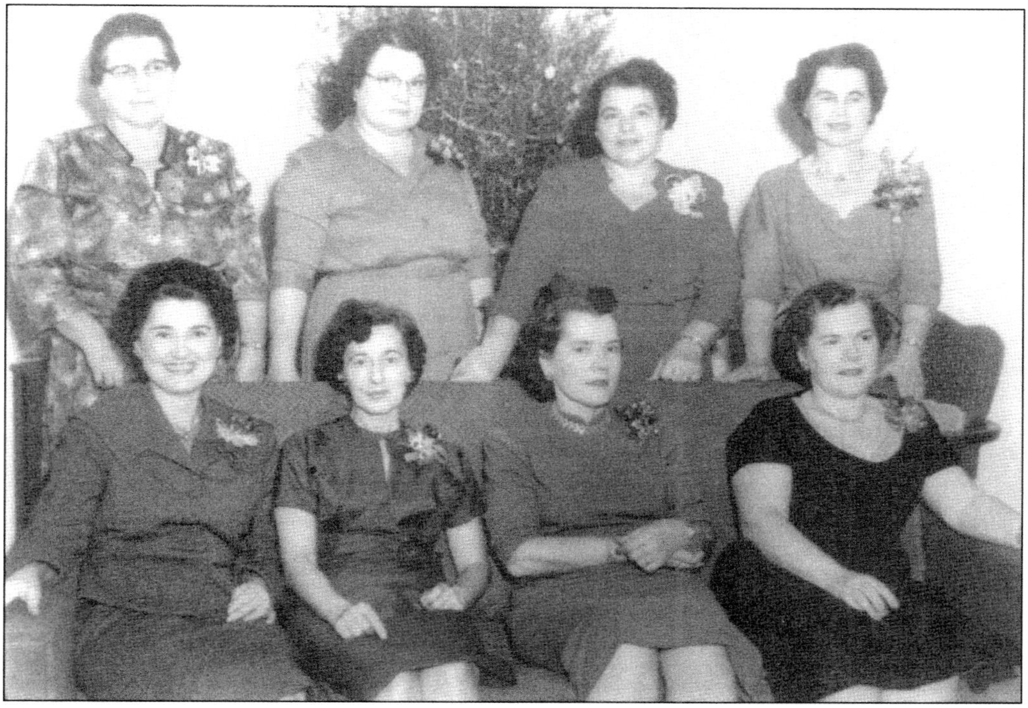

Eight daughters were born in the Thomas Albert Craft family. From left to right are (seated) Alberta, Blanche, and twins Lucille and Lucy; (standing) Millie, Edna, Elma, and Margaret. (RC.)

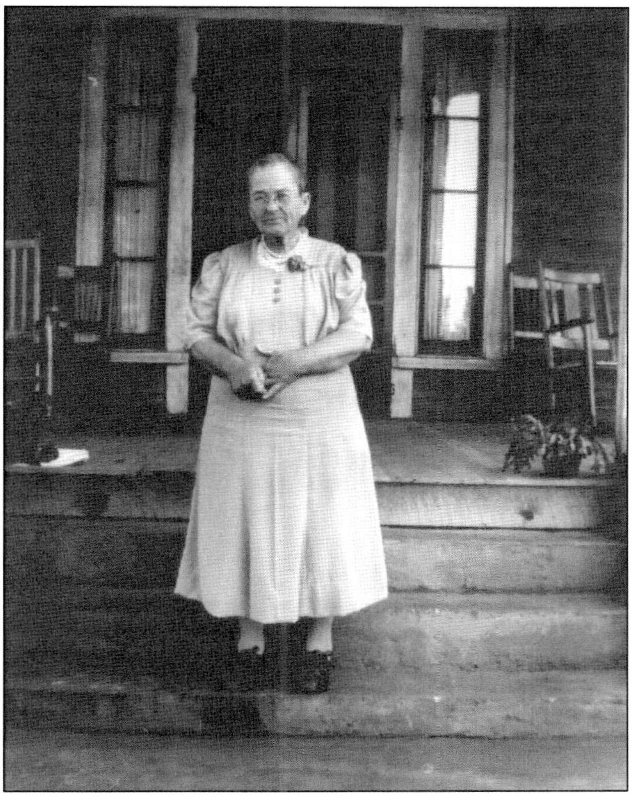

Eliza Sue "Susie" Styers Craft stands on the front steps of her home. She and her husband, Ab, raised 12 children. The Thomas Albert Craft house stood in the vicinity of the new town hall today on Shallowford Road near Lewisville School. (RC.)

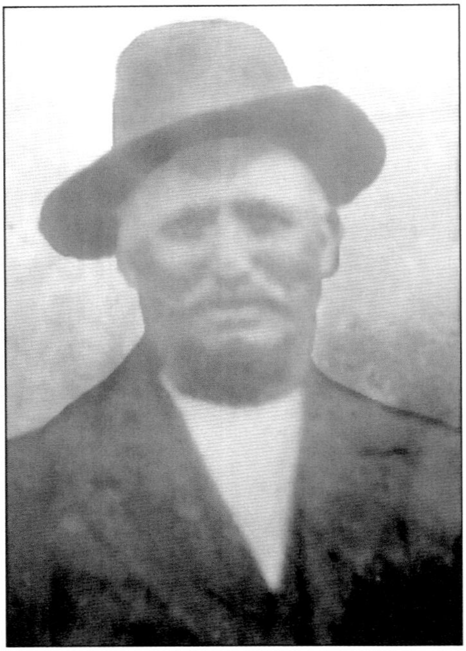

John Joe Jackson "Jack" Kiger and his family lived in the George Nissen House on Shallowford Road, and they later relocated to farm an extensive acreage of land on Williams Road near the Yadkin River. (FB.)

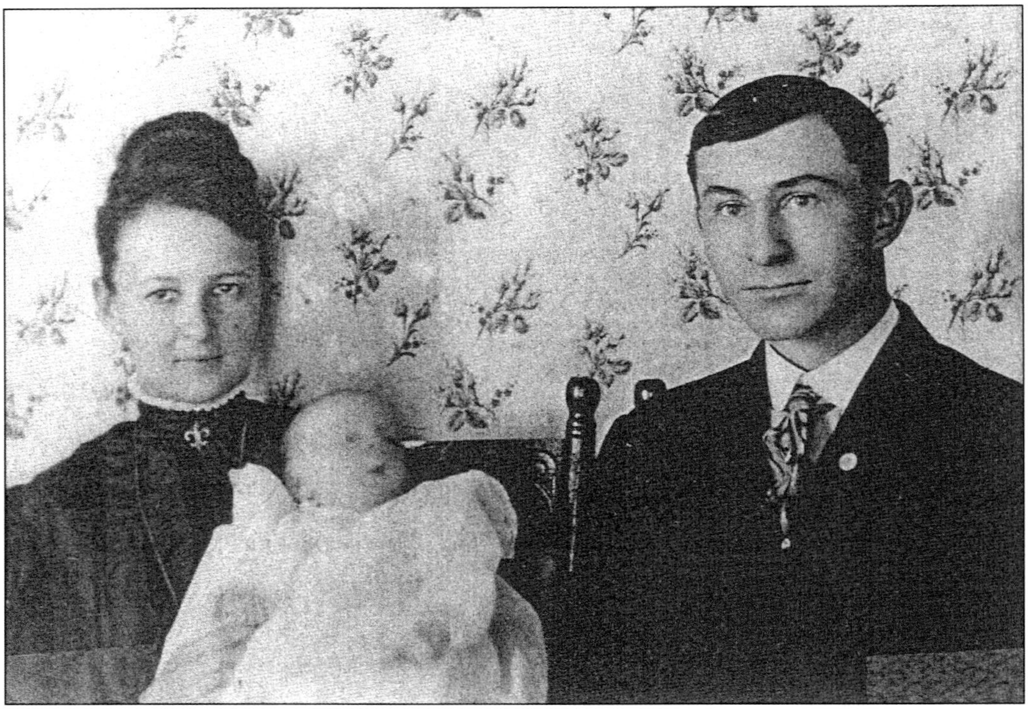

William Stedman Kiger, son of Jack Kiger, was a farmer and merchant living in Lewisville. His wife, Bertie Fulk Kiger, is holding their firstborn child, Ruby Mary Almira Kiger. As a young teen, Bertie was one of the girls in the community who learned social graces in the home of Betty Nissen Laugenour, The girls served tea and refreshments to Mrs. Laugenour's friends who visited her country home. (LCH.)

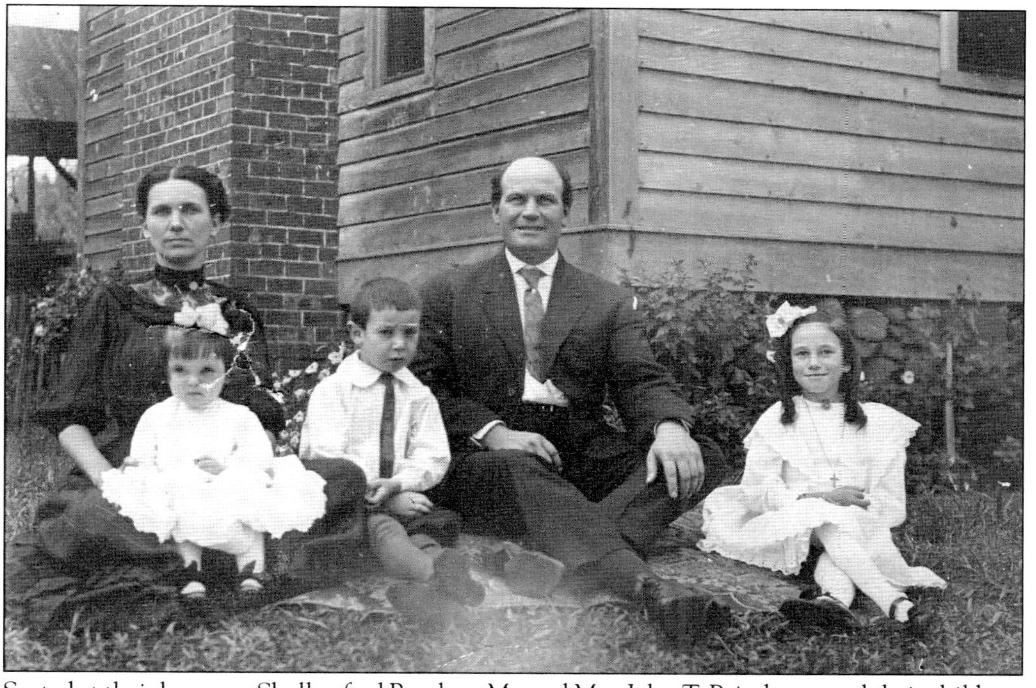

Seated at their home on Shallowford Road are Mr. and Mrs. John T. Poindexter and their children, from left to right, Gladys, Hubert, and Vivian. Mr. Poindexter operated a general store next to his home in Lewisville. The post office operated in his store from 1914 to 1919. (NGC.)

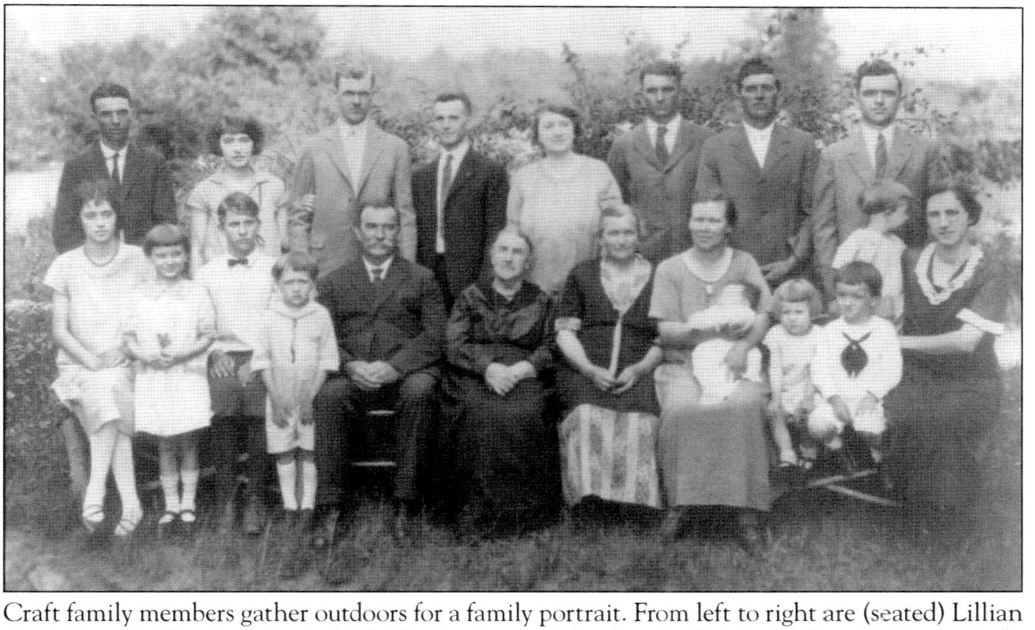

Craft family members gather outdoors for a family portrait. From left to right are (seated) Lillian Craft, Doris Miller, Paul Craft, I. J. Miller Jr., James Columbus Craft, Martha Jerusha Casey Craft, Lillie Doub Craft, Lina Johnson Craft, Louise Craft, Pauline Craft, J. H. Craft Jr., Clyde Craft, and Dora Mock Craft; (standing) Spencer Craft, Mattie Craft Lasley, Ray Lasley, I. J. Miller, Pearl Craft Miller, Winburn Craft, Arthur Craft, and James Henry Craft. (FPC, HL.)

Young girls model the latest fashions of 1929 at Will Jones home place. Posing are, from left to right, Vina Petree, Lucille Jones (Hill), Doll Jones (Jones), and Stella Jones (Reich). (MRB.)

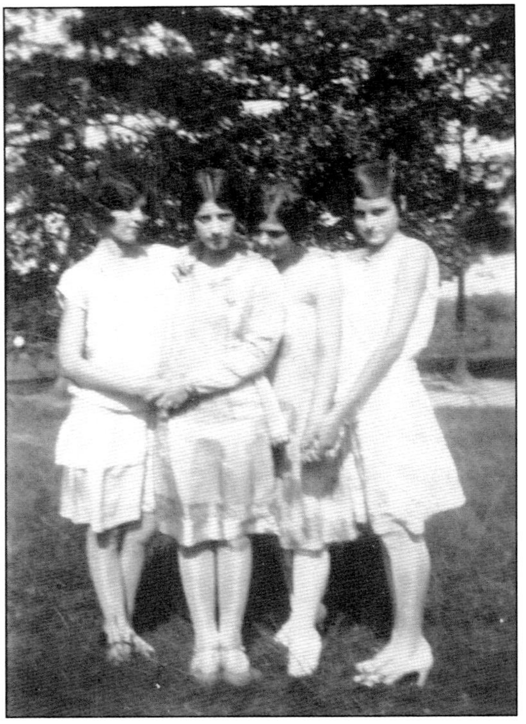

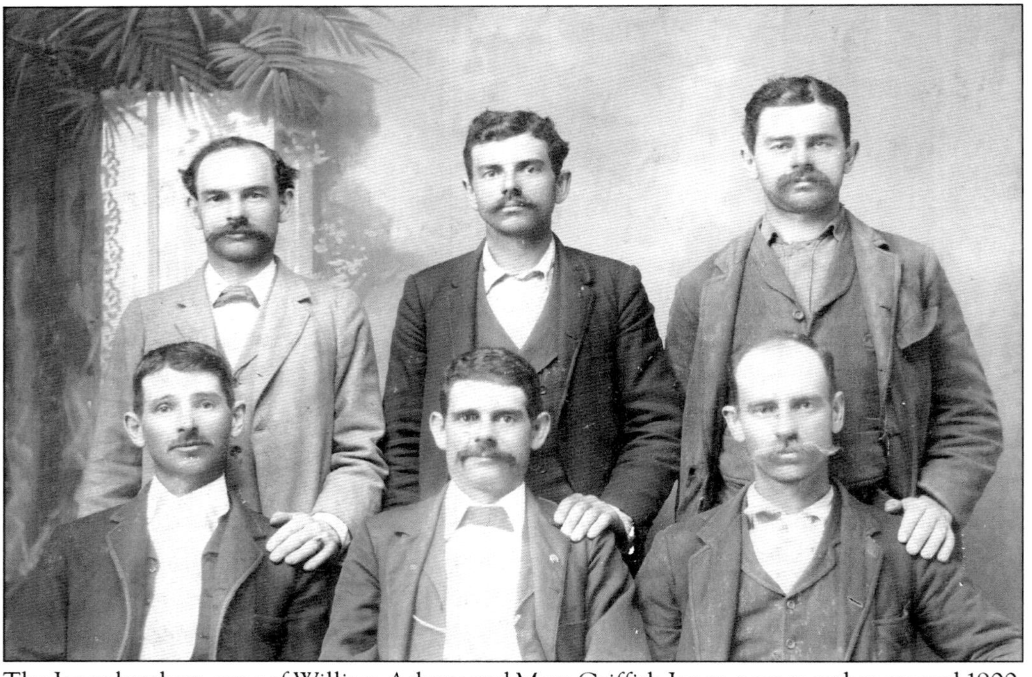

The Jones brothers, sons of William Asbury and Mary Griffith Jones, pose together around 1900. From left to right are (seated) Leon Reid, Enoch Wesley, and John Elery; (standing) Joel Alvis, Albert William, and Bertley Monroe Asbury. Their father served in the Confederate army and fought in the Battle of Second Manassas. (SJ.)

Ellery Holder and his wife, Cora, pose on the steps of their home, which was located on Lewisville-Clemmons Road at the site of the present-day fire department building. The Holders farmed surrounding acreage. Their sons, Matthew and Ervin, established the Lewisville Furniture Company in the 1930s, manufacturing kitchen and dinette furniture on family property located across from Jack Warren Park. (EH.)

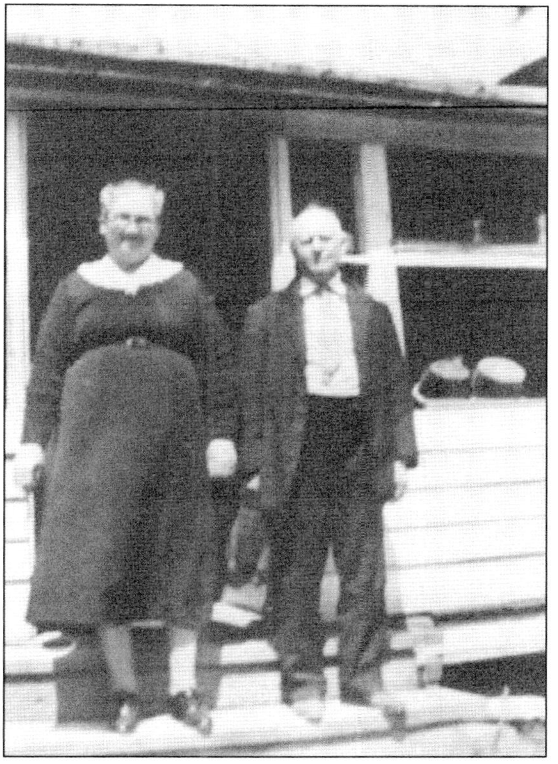

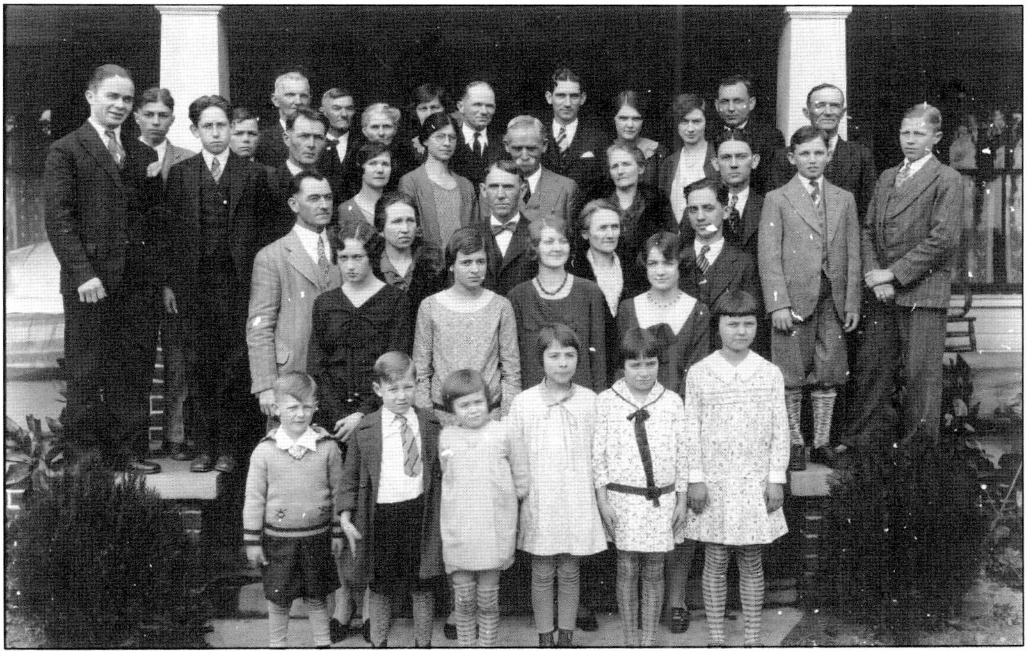

The Waggoner and Hauser families who resided in the Lewisville community gather for a family portrait. Some of their family farms were located on Hauser Road and the surrounding area. (NGC.)

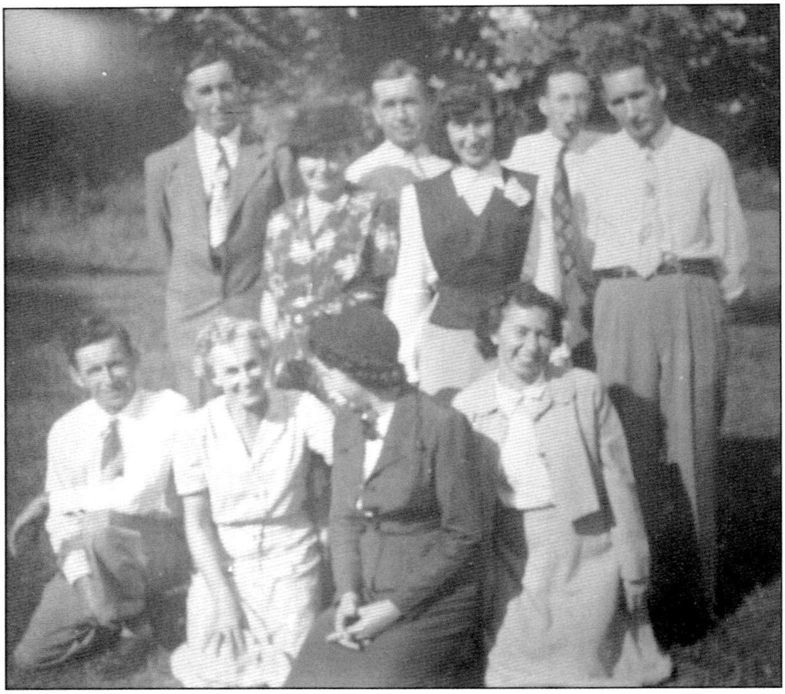

The Huffman brothers and sisters were active members of the community and here they gather for a portrait together. Posing from left to right are (kneeling) Joseph Huffman, Bertie Huffman Poindexter, Mary Sue Huffman Shields, Katherine Huffman Gough; (standing) Baxter Huffman, Rebecca Huffman Winfrey, Felix Huffman, Ruby Huffman Reich, William Huffman, and Robert Huffman. (LCH.)

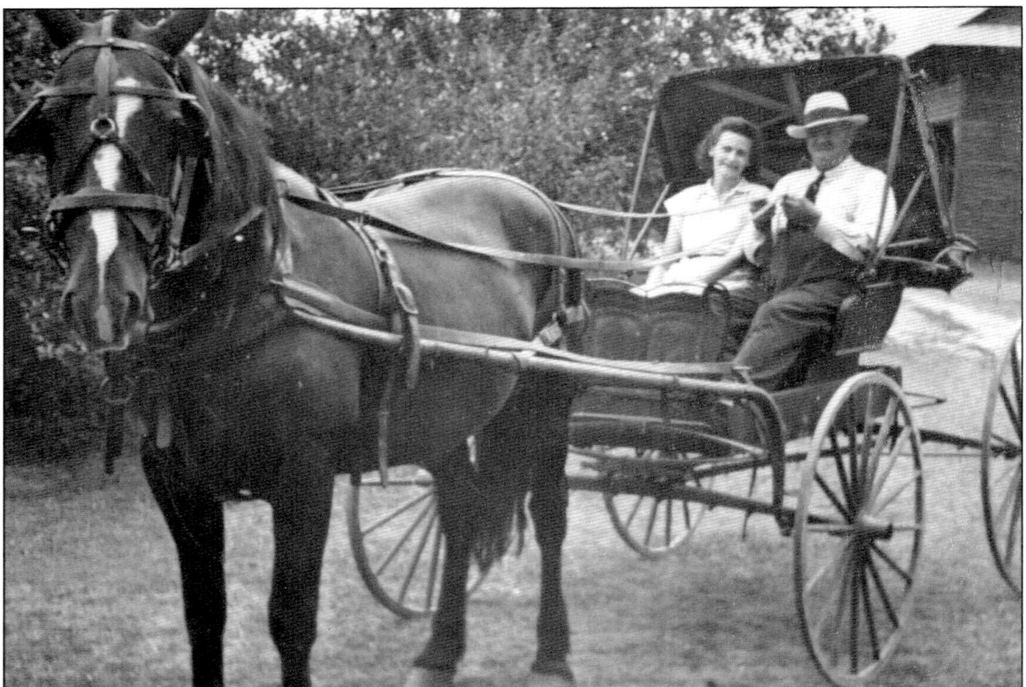

Joe Doub and daughter Mildred Doub take a ride in a horse and buggy. (FPC.)

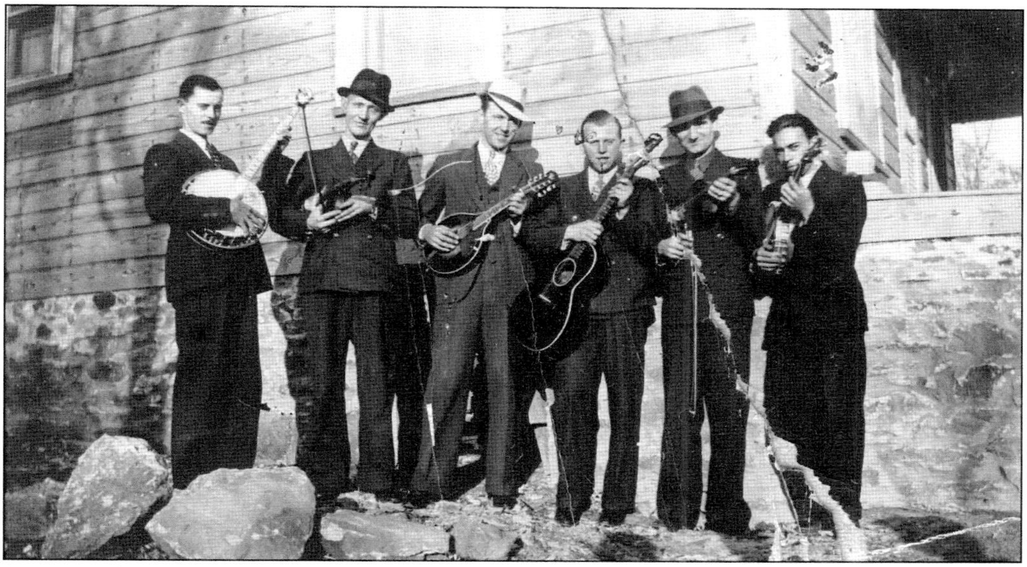

A group of men gets together to play a few tunes at the Dotson home place on Concord Church Road. Strumming and fiddling are, from left to right, ? Dotson, ? Adams, Spencer Reich, Jewel Reich, and two unidentified men. (MRB.)

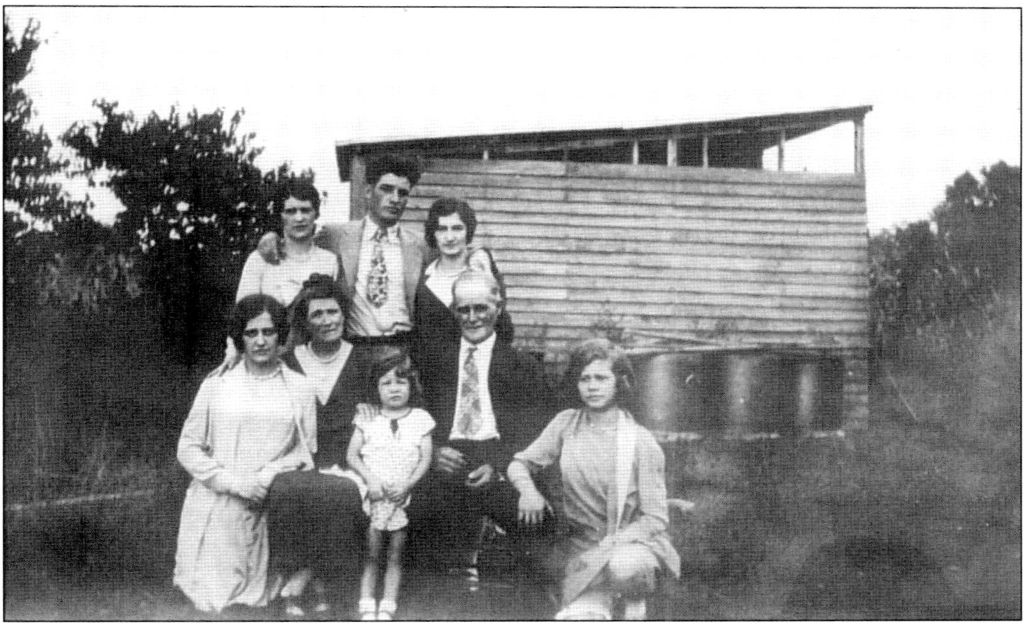

The Martin family lived in the house on Shallowford Road next to Jasper Howard "J. Howard" Moser's Store. Gathered in their yard beside the first Moser Store building are, left to right, (first row) Johnsie, Bertha Alice, Ruth Jean, Walter, and Sarah Alice; (standing) Elsie, Thomas Shermer, and Mary. (NGC.)

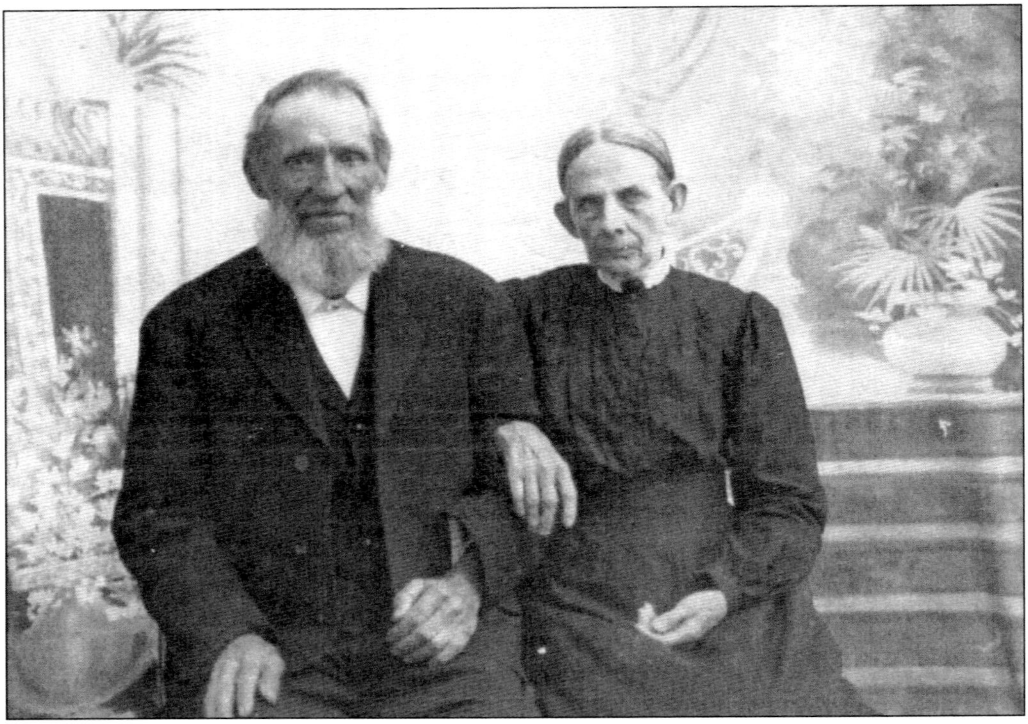

Albert W. Craft and his second wife, Jane Vest Craft, resided in Lewisville, where he served as a Methodist minister. He is the son of Vachel Craft and was a founding member of Lewisville United Methodist Church. (NGC, SJ.)

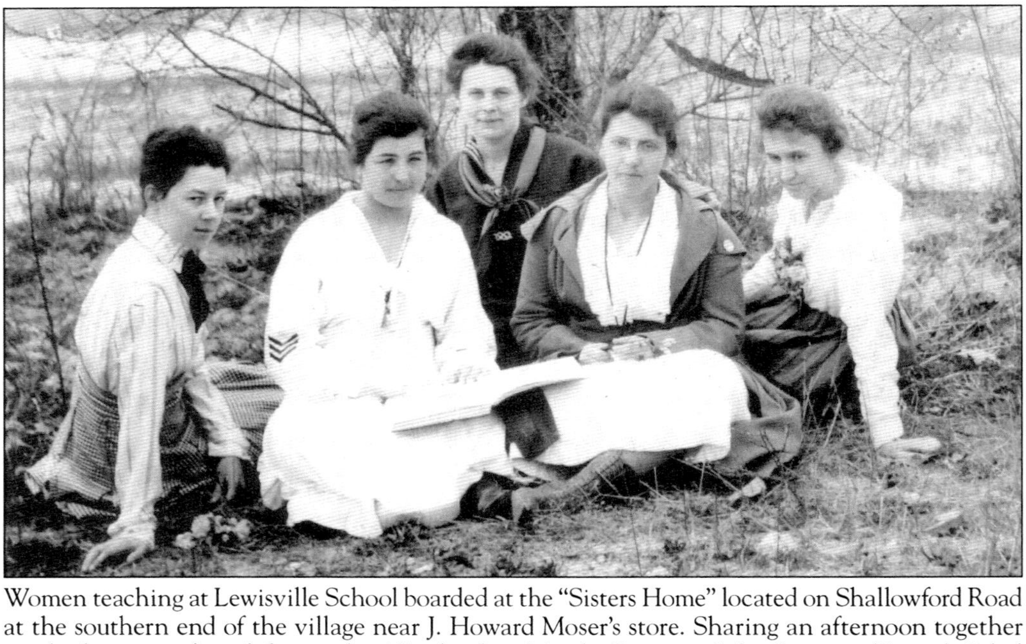

Women teaching at Lewisville School boarded at the "Sisters Home" located on Shallowford Road at the southern end of the village near J. Howard Moser's store. Sharing an afternoon together on the lawn are, from left to right, ? Beckerdite, Myrtle Caviness, Julia Stimson (Green), Ethel Spaugh (Mock), and Ethel Whitman (Doub). (NGC.)

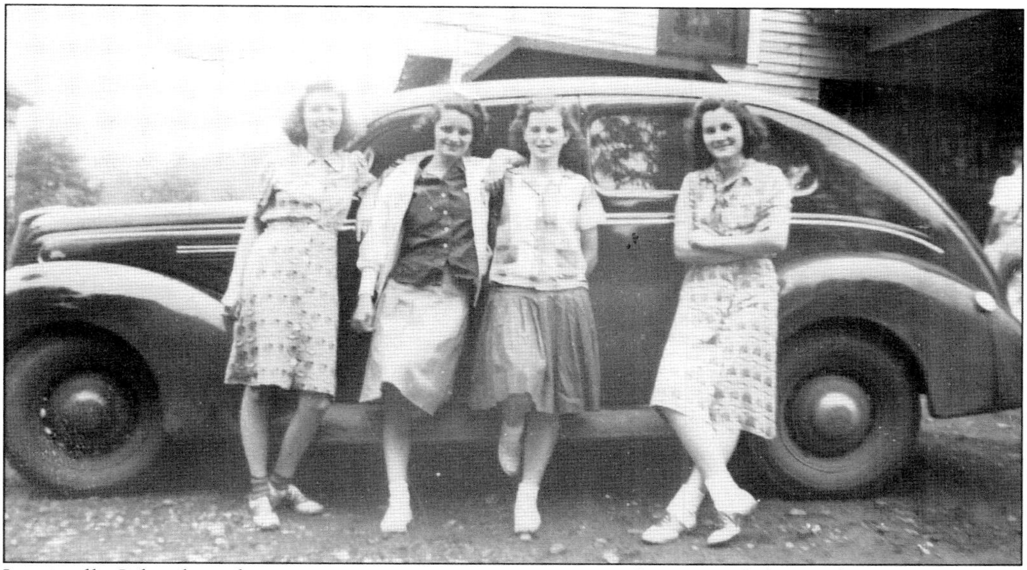

Lewisville School coeds pose next to a car on an outing together. From left to right are Mary Alice Fulk (Warren), Gay Smith, Jean Davis (Ray), and Katie Lee Mock (Graves). (MAFW.)

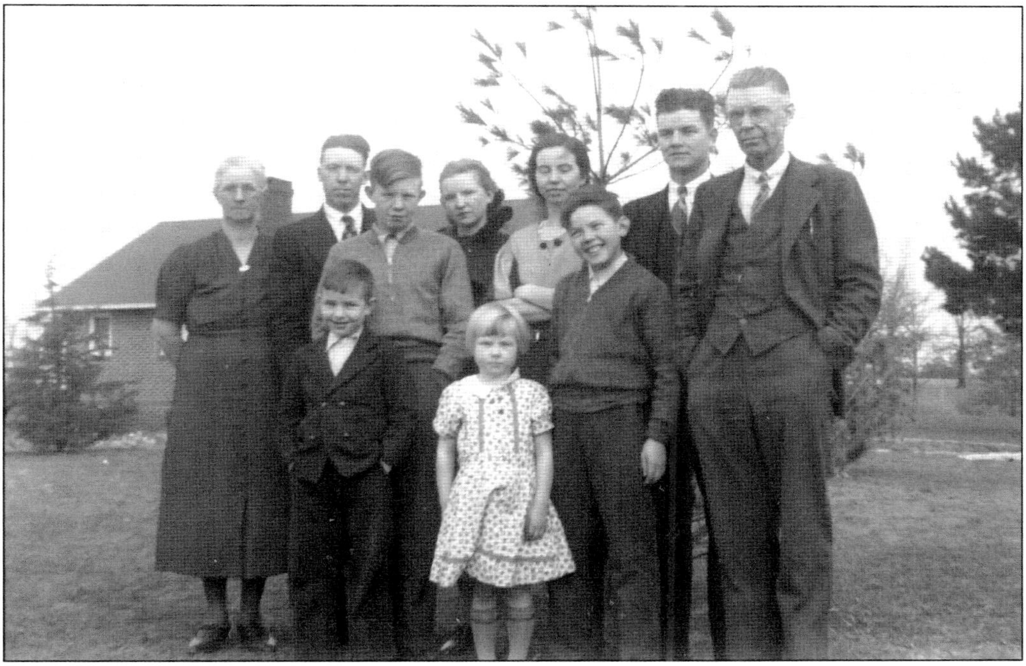

Fielden and Ollie Jennings moved to Lewisville in 1925 with their family to own and operate the Lewisville Roller Mills. Several generations of Jennings worked in the family business located on Shallowford Road. Gathered near their home are the youngest children standing (first row), from left to right, Roy, Grace and Hale; (second row) Mother Ollie and children Gwyn, Charlie, Elva, Ethel, Paul, and Father Fielden. (DP.)

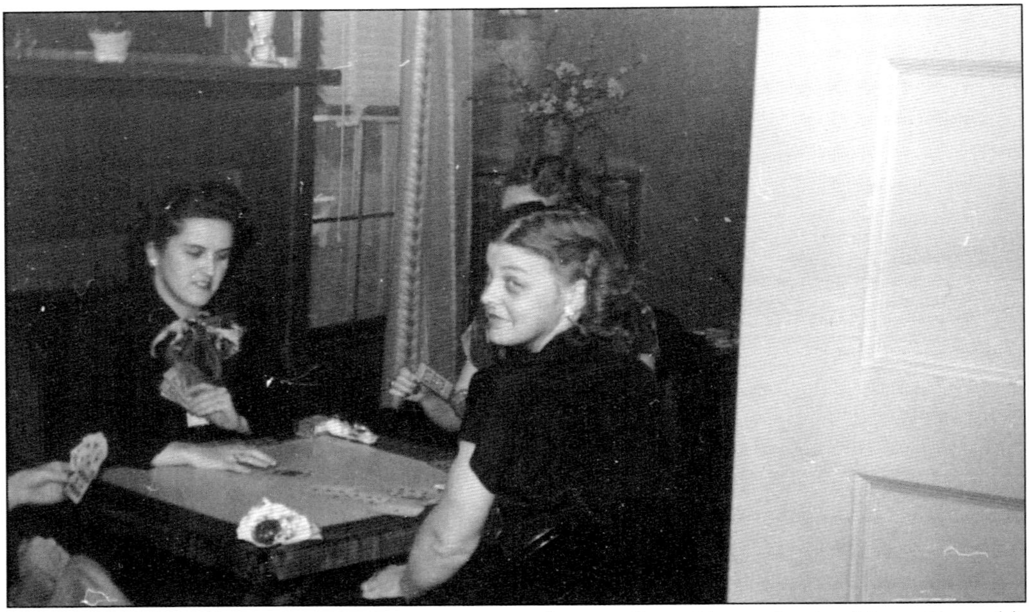

Bridge clubs have been a popular activity among Lewisville residents. Louise Moser Reynolds looking over her shoulder and Lillie Belle Kiger Mock enjoy a game of bridge with friends in a club member's home. (MAFW.)

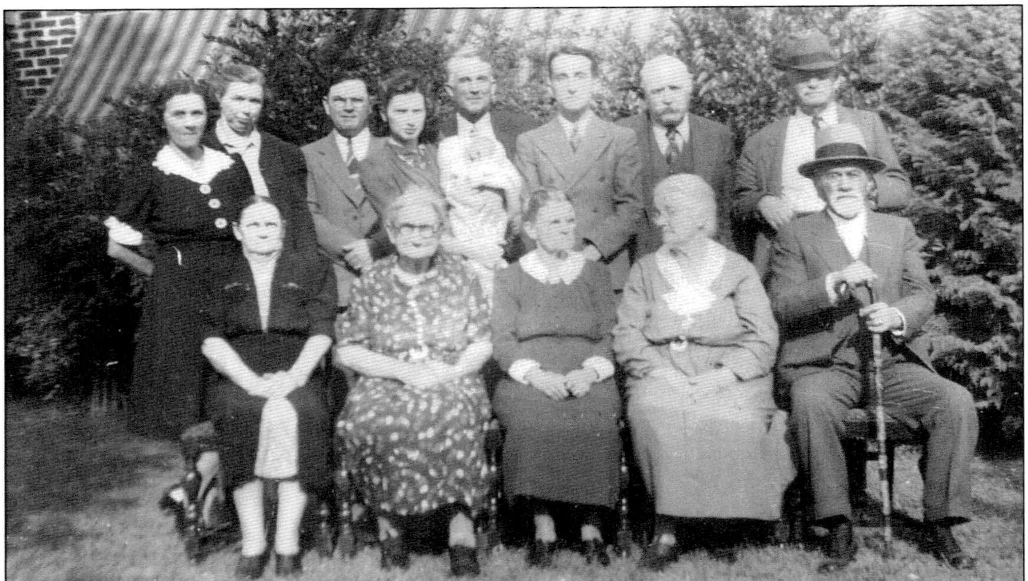

In 1941, baby Philip Allen Mock is held by his parents, Mary and Philip Mock, and surrounded with generations of grandparents and great-grandparents. From left to right are (first row) great-grandmothers Ellen Kearney Beroth, Cora Sprinkle Spease, Lucetta Crater Harper, Ellen Thomasson Mock, and great-grandfather Henry Harper; (second row) grandmothers Anna Harper Mock and Mary Spease Beroth, grandfathers Marvin Beroth, Jasper Mock, and great-grandfathers Walter Spease and Victor Beroth. The family gathered for this photograph at Marvin Beroth's home. (GCD, JL.)

For many years, Vern Conrad worked as the caretaker of Lewisville School's building and grounds. In 1953, the students dedicated their school annual, *La Ha Sa*, to him, in recognition of his many years of faithful service: "A busier man than he you'd find nowhere." (LHS.)

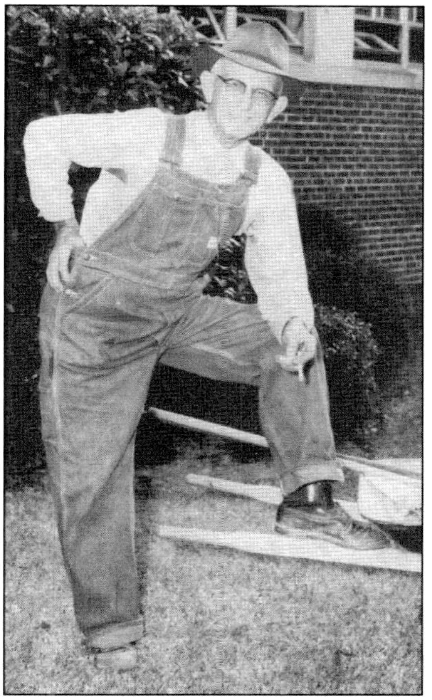

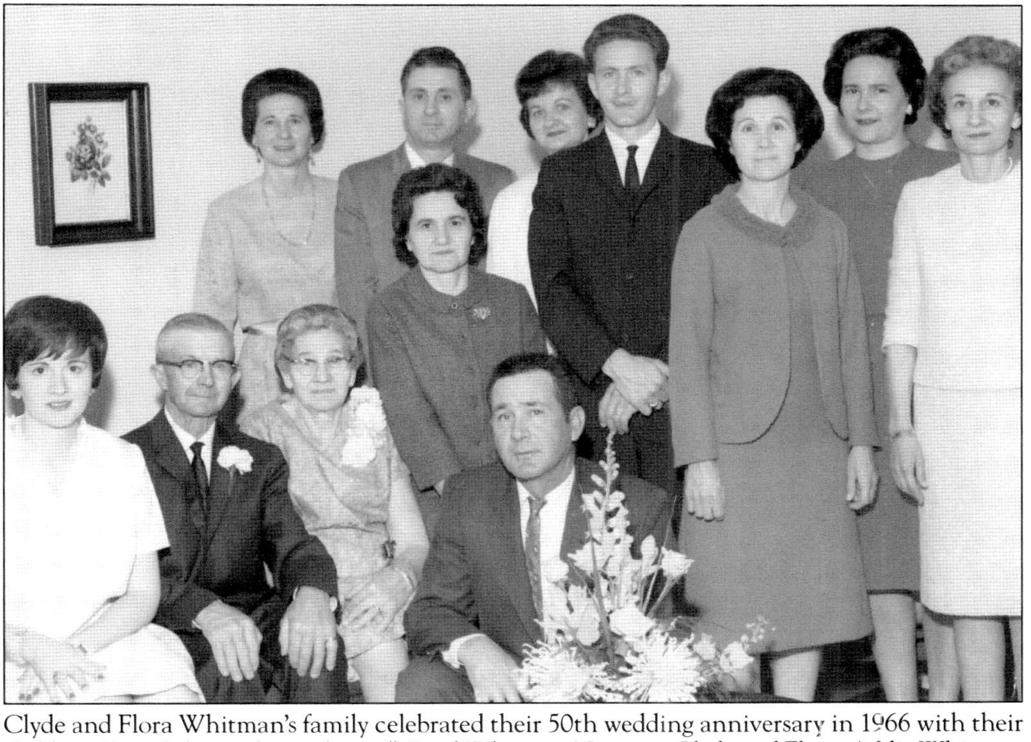

Clyde and Flora Whitman's family celebrated their 50th wedding anniversary in 1966 with their children. From left to right are (seated) Pearl Whitman Norman, Clyde and Flora, Addie Whitman Taylor, and William Whitman; (standing) Martha Whitman Trent, Roger Whitman, Frances Whitman Hauser, C. H. Whitman Jr., Della Whitman Trent, Louise Whitman Huffman, and Mary Whitman Livengood. (PWN.)

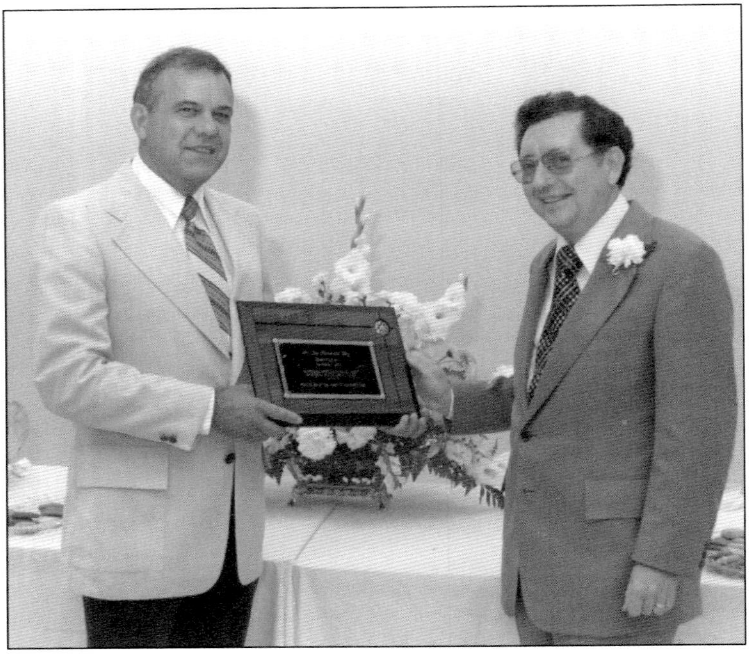

On October 1, 1978, Tom Voss honors Dr. James "Jim" H. Hampton for 25 years of service in Lewisville on "Dr. James H. Hampton Day." Dr. Hampton was a family-practice physician for 40 years in the community and beloved by all. He was honored as Citizen of the Year in 1969 by the Lewisville Civic Club and on March 29, 1994 at a second Dr. James H. Hampton Day on the occasion of his retirement. Dr. Hampton passed away in 2009. (MV.)

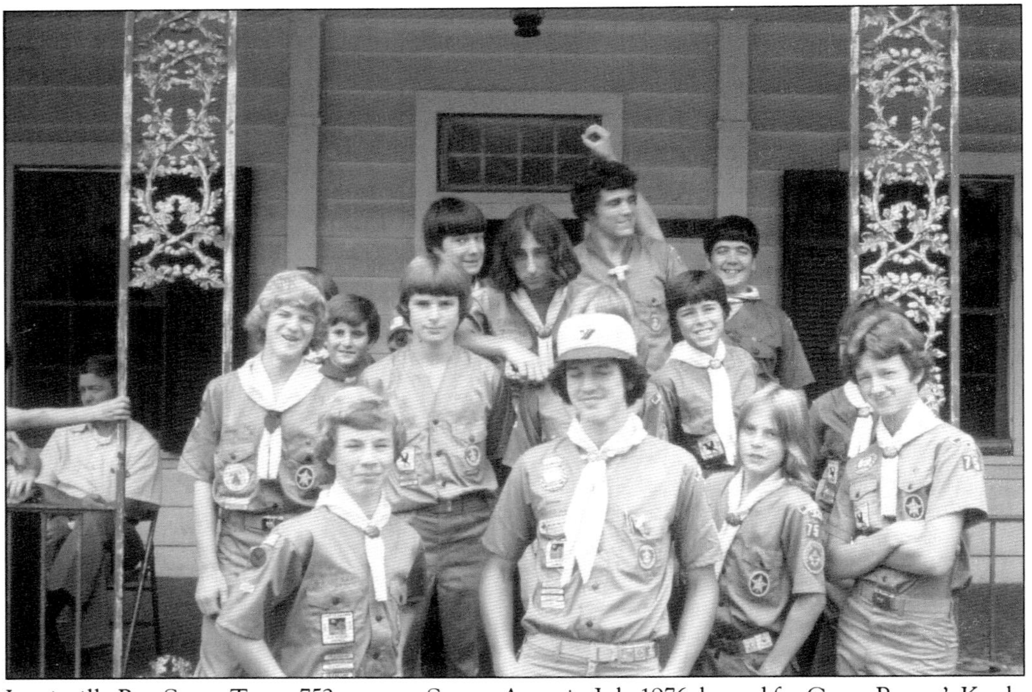

Lewisville Boy Scout Troop 752 poses at Sunny Acres in July 1976, bound for Camp Raven's Knob. Scouting began in 1937 in the Lewisville community, with interruption during World War II. The Lewisville Civic Club revived scouting after the war, sponsoring Troop 752. In 1987, Boy Scouts celebrated 50 years of scouting activities in the Lewisville community. (MIJ.)

Seven

COMMUNITY LIFE

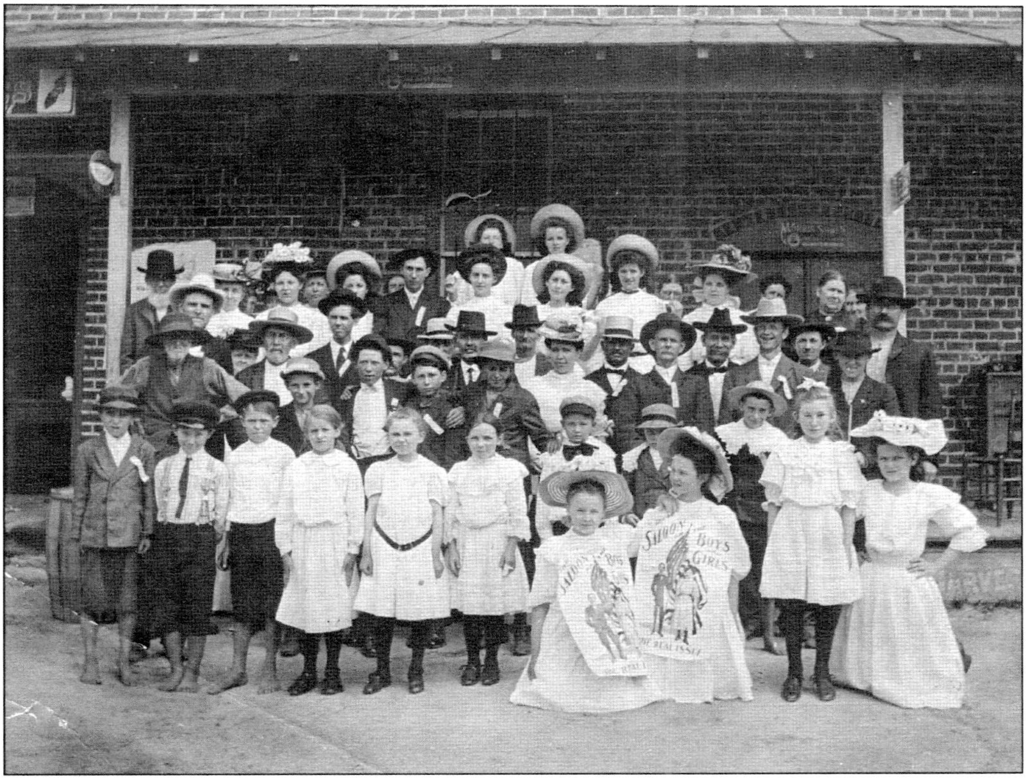

The Prohibition rally around 1908 at Eugene H. Wright's Store on Shallowford Road raised social consciousness among citizens of the day. Adults, teens, and children gathered together with signs proclaiming, "The Saloon or the Boys and Girls – The Real Issue." Wright's Store was a community gathering place and a center for the life of the people in the late 1800s and early 1900s. It was located across from the blacksmith's shop and near the tavern and campground, where weary travelers stopped on their way, after crossing the Shallow Ford. (LHS.)

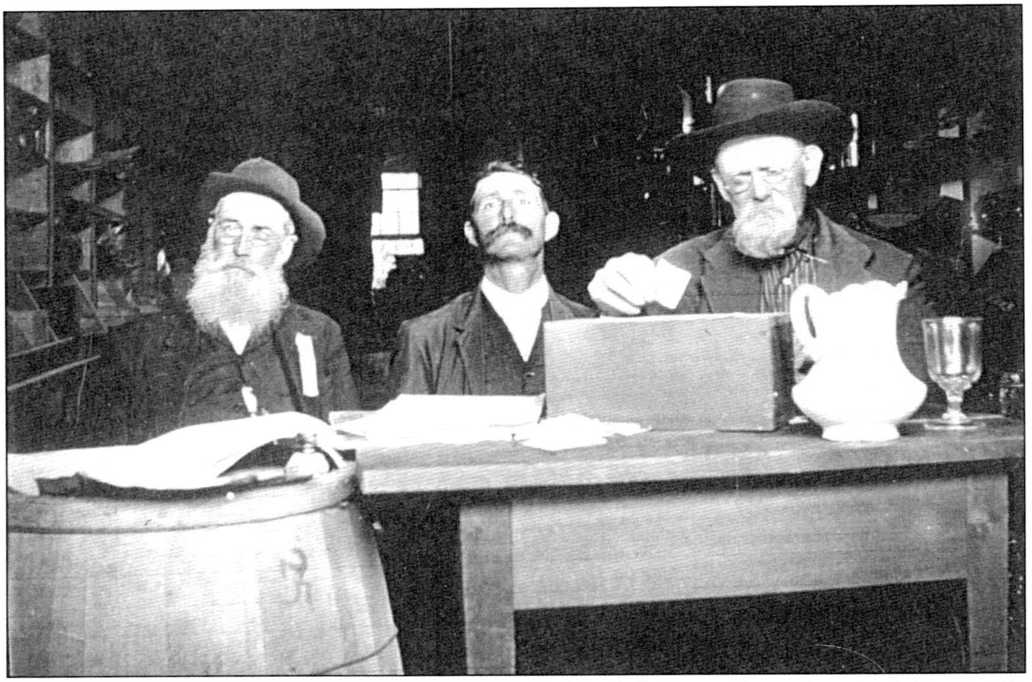

Elections brought many citizens out to vote at E. H. Wright's Store, the voting site in Lewisville for many years. Charlie Doub (center) joins fellow men in casting their votes. Women had not earned the right to vote at this time. (LHS.)

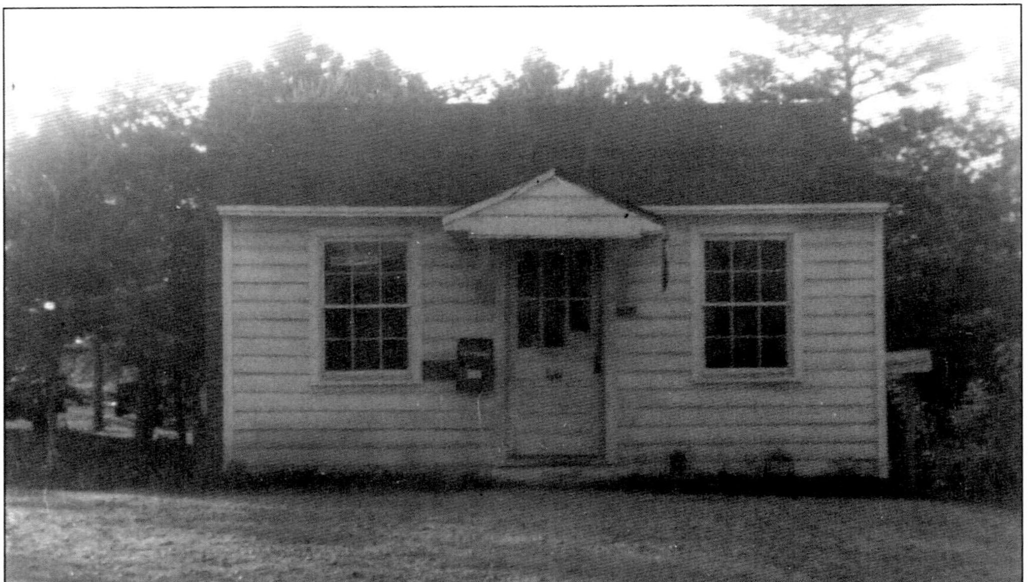

The first freestanding post office building on Shallowford Road was built by the Stimson family in 1942. Myrtle Stimson served as postmistress from 1942 to 1960. Prior to this building, the post office was housed in various stores, depending on the political party in federal office and the politics of the store owners who served as postmasters. (DS.)

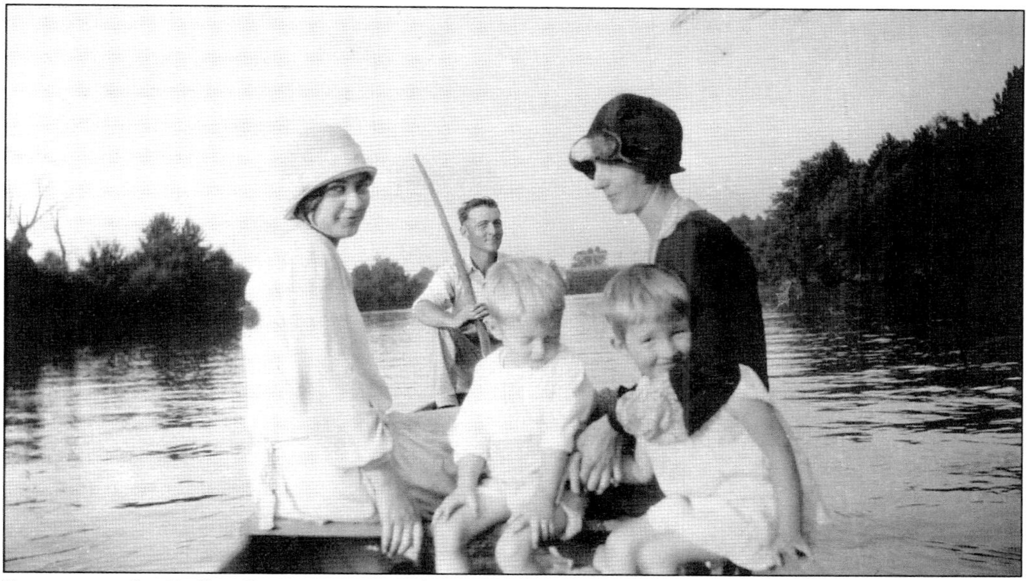

Boating on the Yadkin River was a popular outing for families and friends in the 1920s. The adults riding in the boat are, from left to right, Myrtle Waggoner, Balfour Mock, and Maude Cornelius Fulk. The children are Thomas Fulk (left) and Mary Alice Fulk (Warren). (MAFW.)

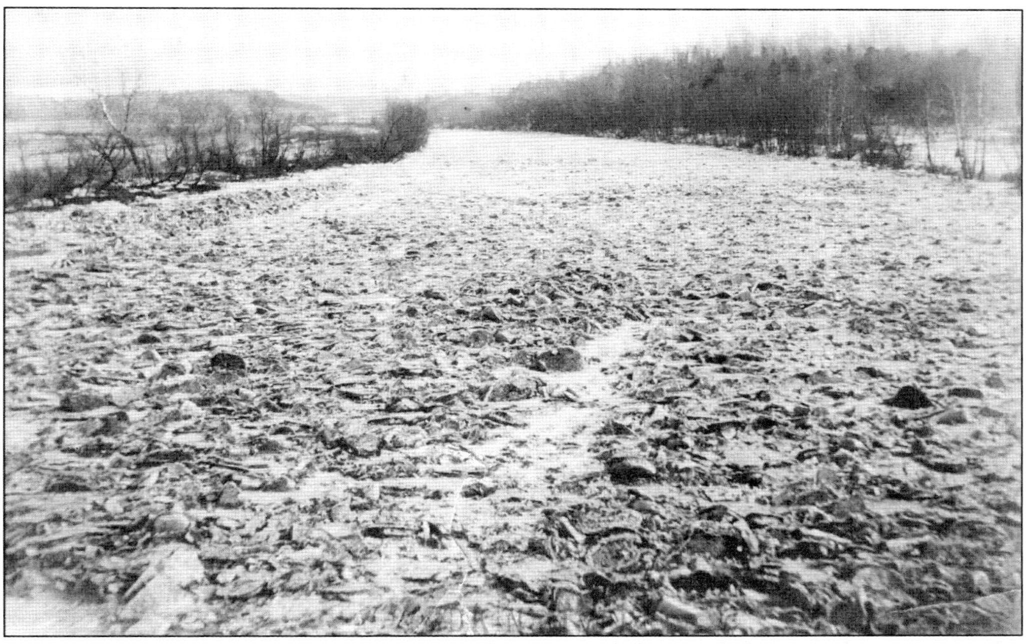

In January 1918, the Yadkin River was frozen, prohibiting fishing or boating on the river. (MAFW.)

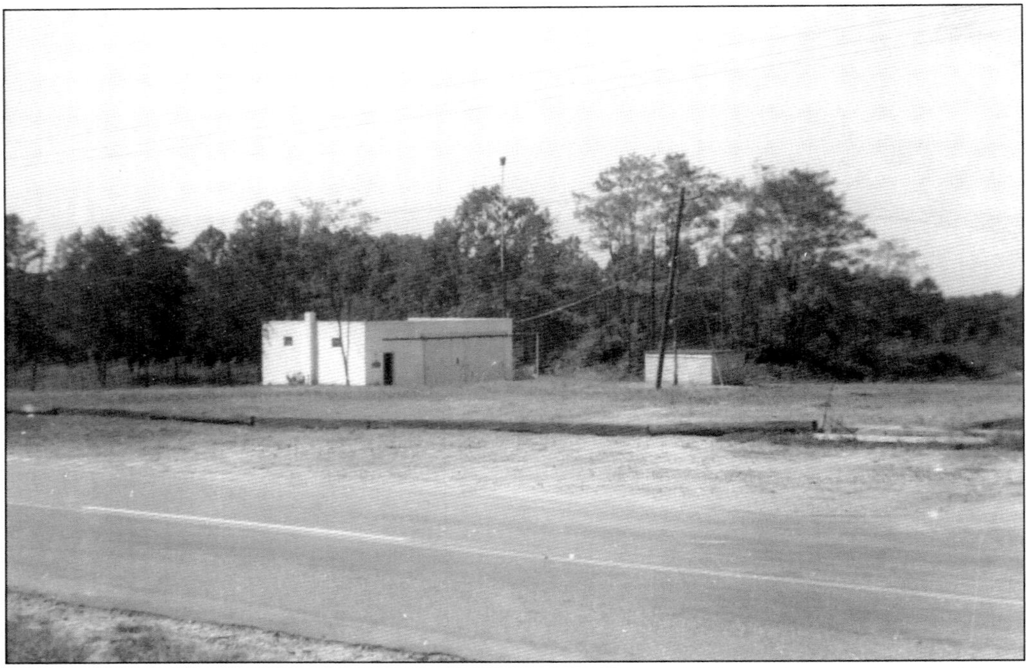

The first Lewisville Volunteer Fire Department station built in 1951 stood on Shallowford Road near the intersection of Lewisville-Vienna Road. The first fire chief was Glen Galloway "Buck" Reynolds. (LCC.)

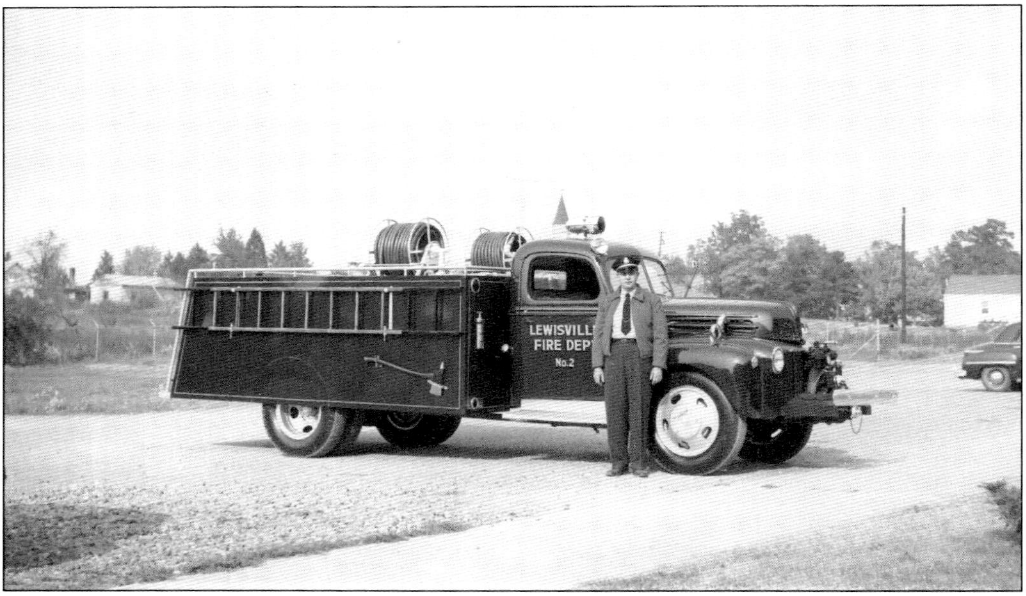

An early 1952 fire engine was built by volunteer firemen to service the Lewisville community. The Lewisville Volunteer Fire Department began on September 22, 1951, with a reconditioned army crash truck and 35 volunteers. The Lewisville Civic Club led the effort to establish the fire department by providing the organization with the original funds of $4,000. (LCC.)

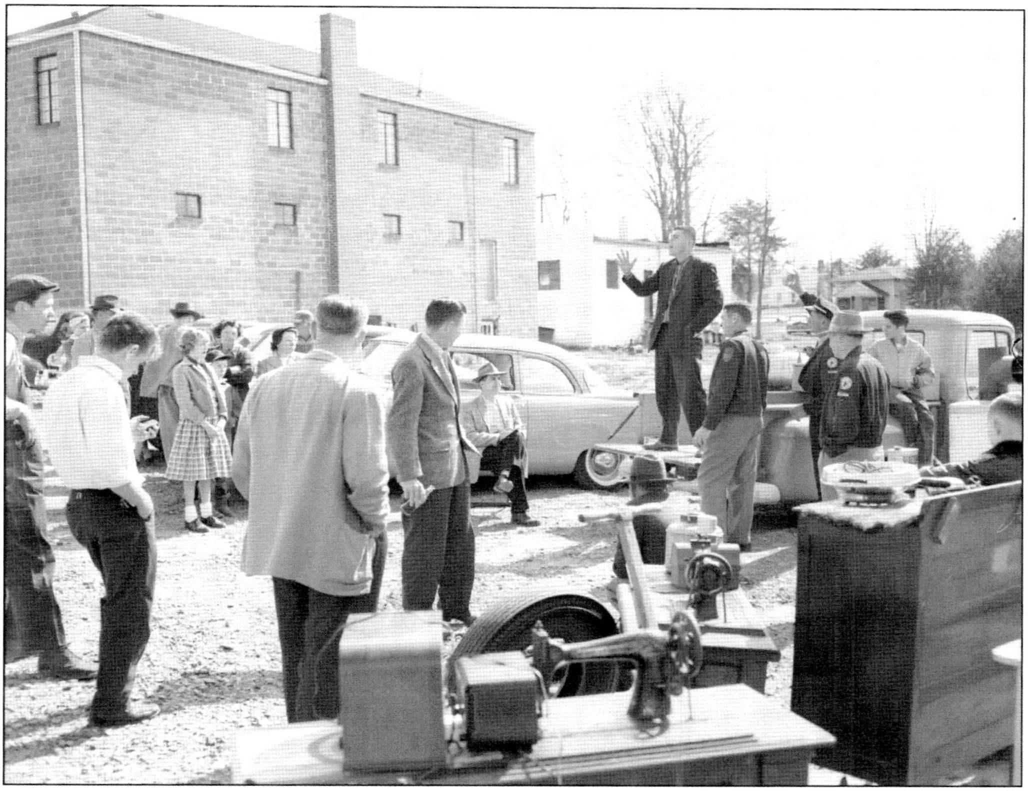

Auction sales were a popular means to raise funds for the volunteer fire department. Citizens donated items to sell, and all proceeds went to build and maintain the station and firefighting equipment. This sale was held between the fire station and the Masonic building on Shallowford Road. (MV.)

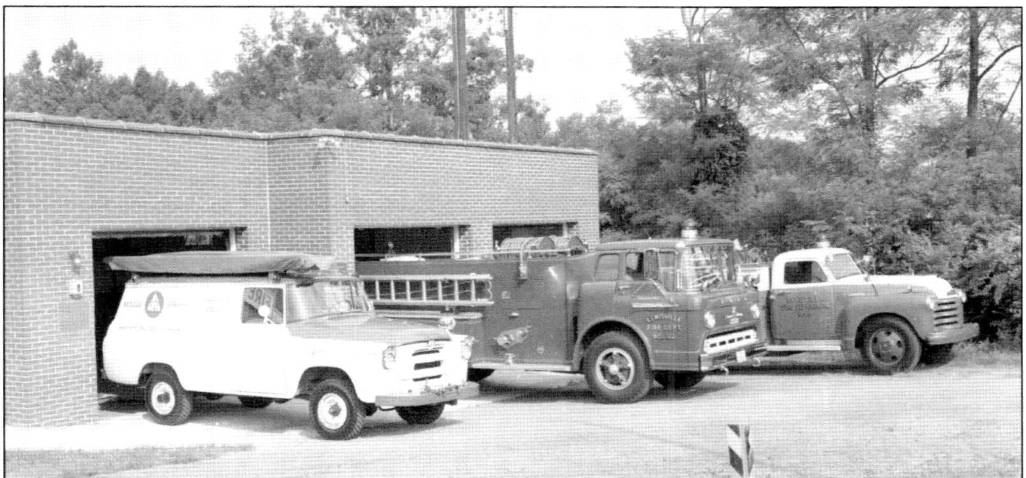

The second Lewisville Volunteer Fire Department station was built near the first structure. Three bays provided space for two fire trucks and one rescue squad vehicle to be housed under one roof. (MV.)

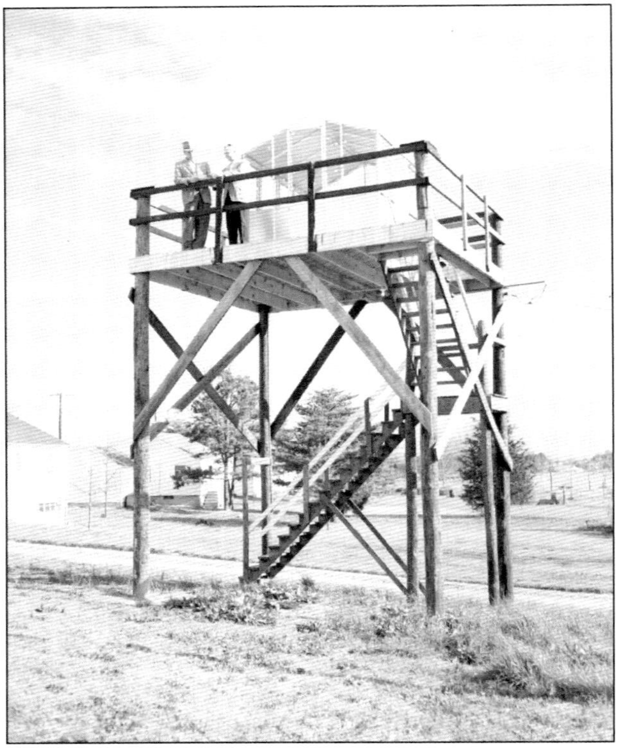

A ground observer post was activated on April 15, 1957, which stood near the fire station at the intersection of Lewisville-Vienna and Shallowford Roads. Built by the Lewisville Volunteer Fire Department under the supervision of the U.S. Air Force, this observer post was manned several hours a day by volunteers who recorded plane sightings, reporting certain ones to the filter center in Charlotte, North Carolina. During the cold war years of the 1950s, civil defense measures were stressed in all communities. (MV.)

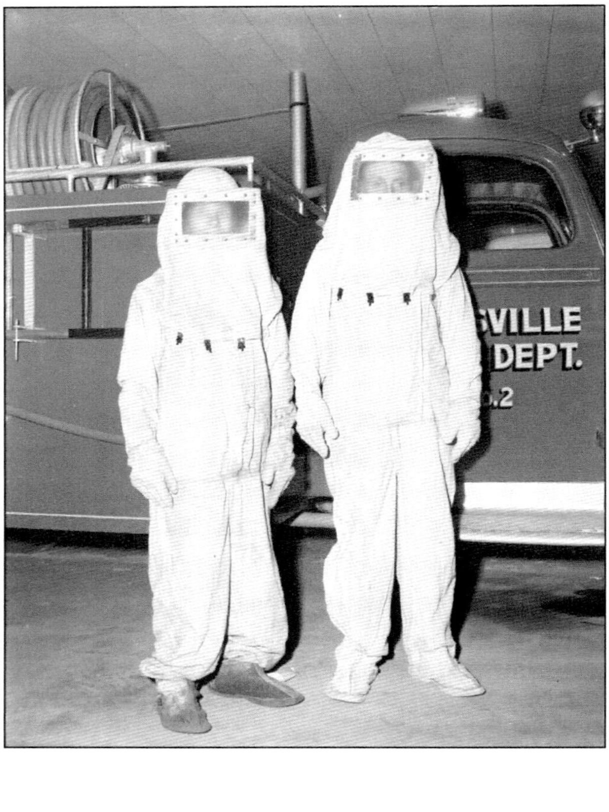

In February 1955, volunteer firemen Ralph Hicks (left) and Bynum Plunkett try on new asbestos suits, which allowed them to enter burning buildings more safely. (MV.)

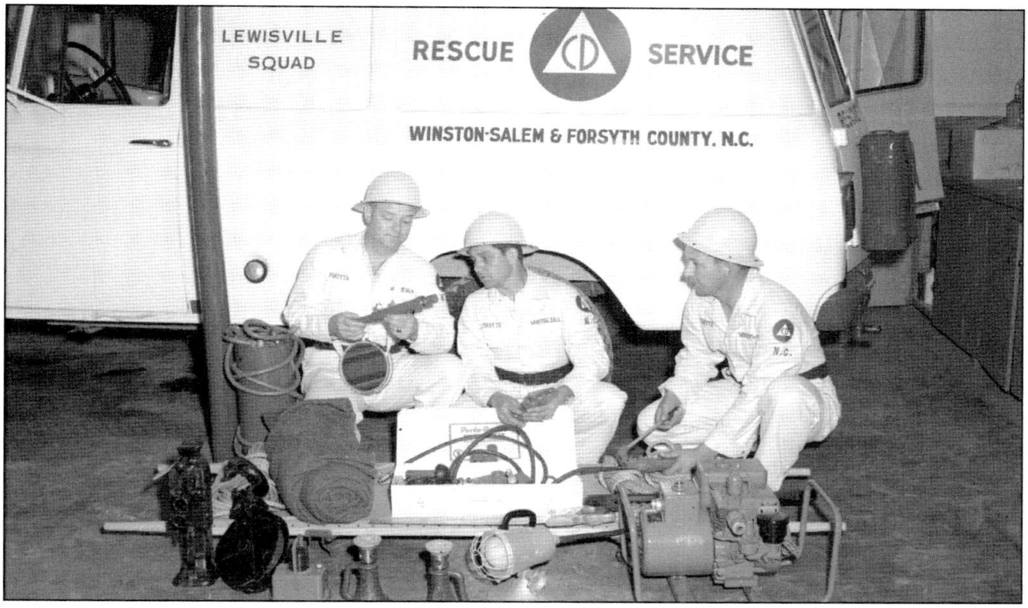

The Lewisville Rescue Squad was manned by volunteer citizens trained to assist in crisis situations, such as fires, automobile accidents, and stranded boaters and swimmers. The first rescue squad truck arrived at the Lewisville Volunteer Fire Department on March 25, 1959. Squad members are, from left to right, Paul Jennings, Robert Hicks, and Henry Farmer. (MV.)

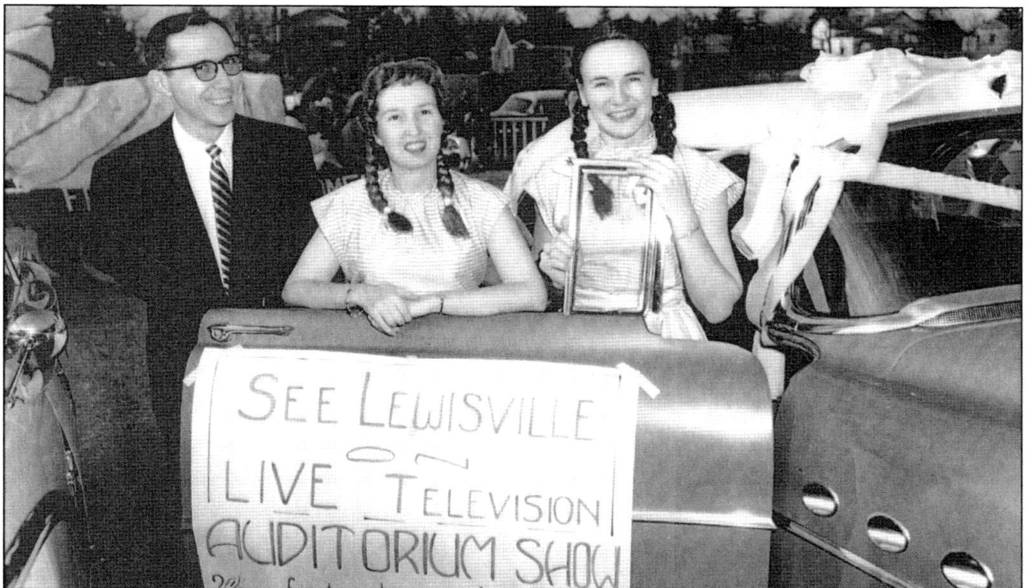

Fred Moser, Mary Alice Fulk (Warren), and Ruth Reynolds (Hartle) are among the citizens dressed to entertain and raise money for the volunteer fire department at the 8th-annual Fall Festival. Featuring a live television broadcast, the event took place at Lewisville School on December 3, 1955. The Fall Festival, which began in 1947, was cosponsored by the Lewisville School PTA and the Lewisville Volunteer Fire Department as a fund-raiser for both organizations by the 1950s. (LCC.)

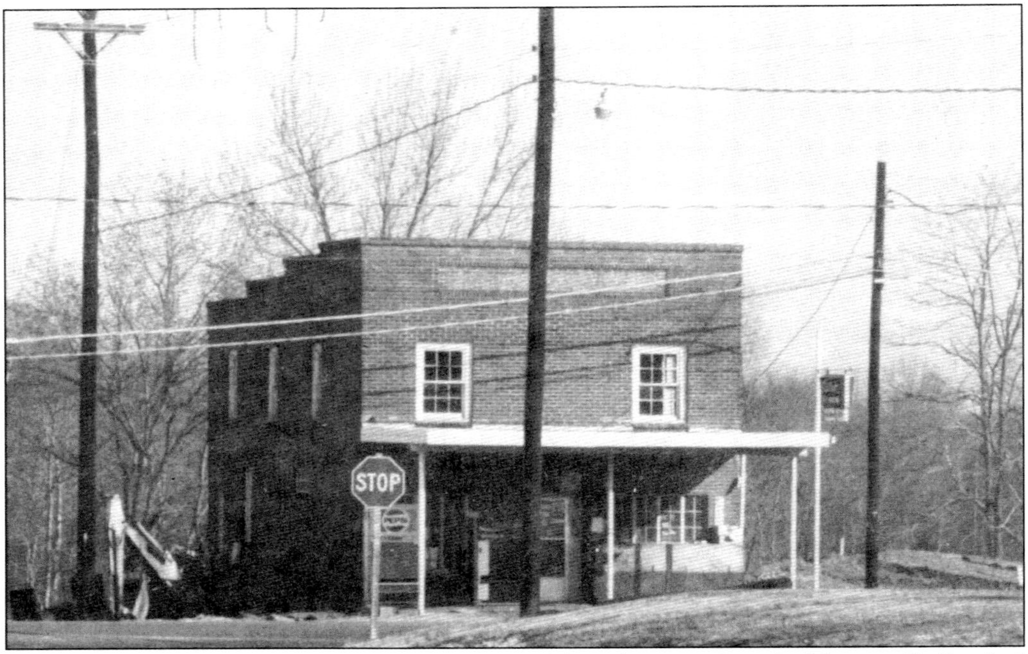

West Bend Masonic Lodge rented the second floor of the Whitman's Store building on Shallowford Road from 1931 until 1949 for their meetings. Prior to this time, they met from 1890 until 1931 in a two-story building in West Bend, which also housed the West Bend Academy for several years. (WBL.)

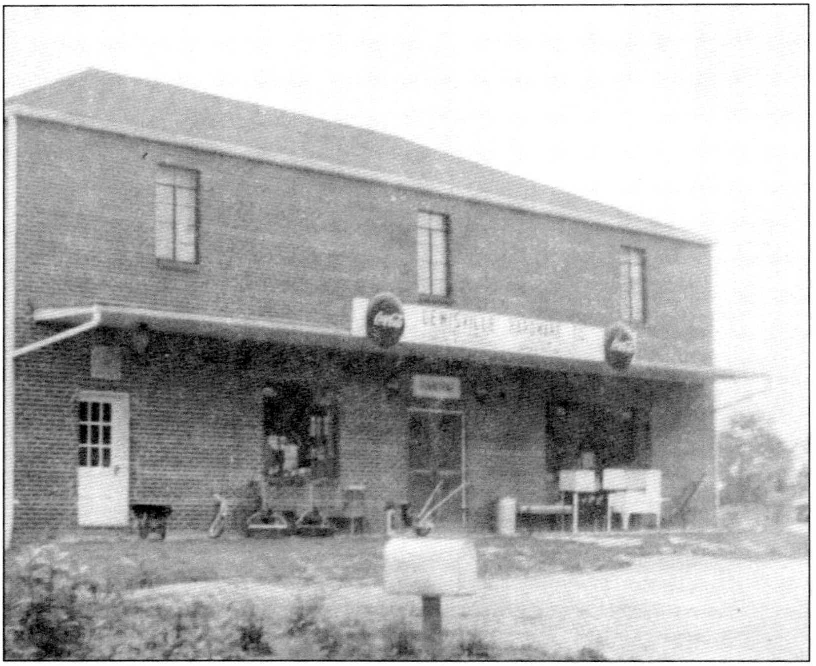

The first meeting in the new Masonic Lodge was held December 16, 1949. Members of the West Bend Lodge sacrificed and worked hard to raise $12,000 to pay for the new building, located on Shallowford Road. (WBL.)

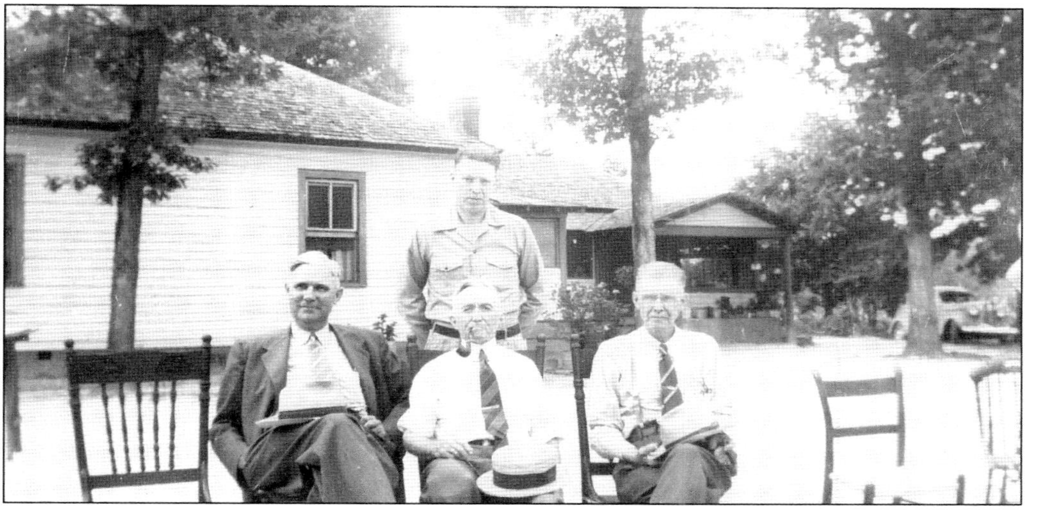

The Albert William Jones home was the meeting place for this West Bend Masonic Lodge gathering. Forsyth County sheriff Ernie Shore was the guest speaker. Seated from left to right are Ernie Shore, Smith Williams, and Fielden Jennings. Standing is Gwyn Jennings. Ernie Shore played professional baseball with teammate Babe Ruth on the Boston Red Sox and New York Yankees teams prior to his career as sheriff. (MAFW.)

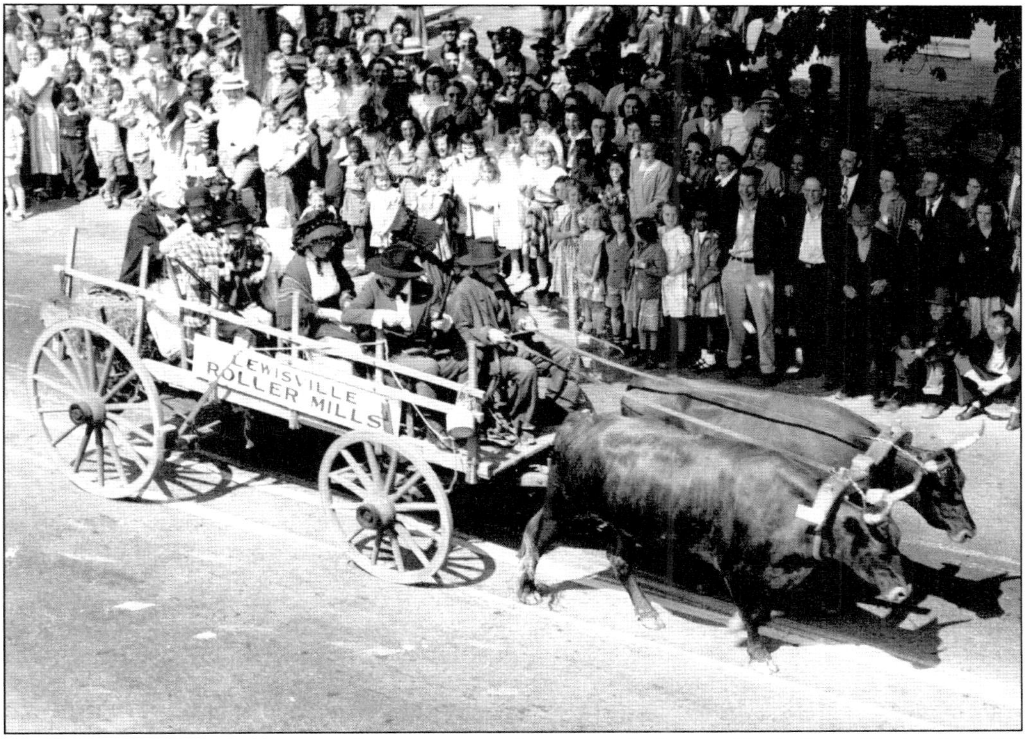

The Jennings family drove an ox-drawn wagon advertising the Lewisville Roller Mills in the 1949 Forsyth County Centennial Parade, held in downtown Winston-Salem. Thousands of citizens turned out for the parade celebrating Forsyth County's 100th anniversary (1849–1949). (RJ.)

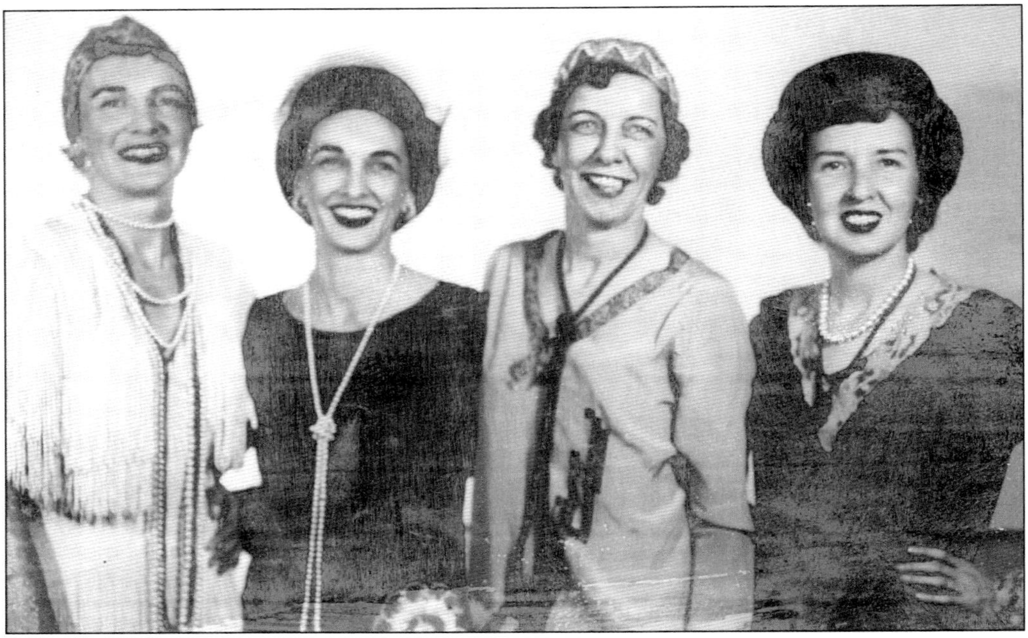

The Civic Club and residents of Lewisville held fund-raisers to collect money for community projects, such as supporting the volunteer fire department, building roads, and school expansions. A 1920s gala was held at the Lewisville School auditorium in the 1950s. From left to right are Ruth Reynolds (Hartle), Billie Conrad (Crawford), Doris Stimson (Hauser), and Mary Alice Fulk (Warren). (MAFW.)

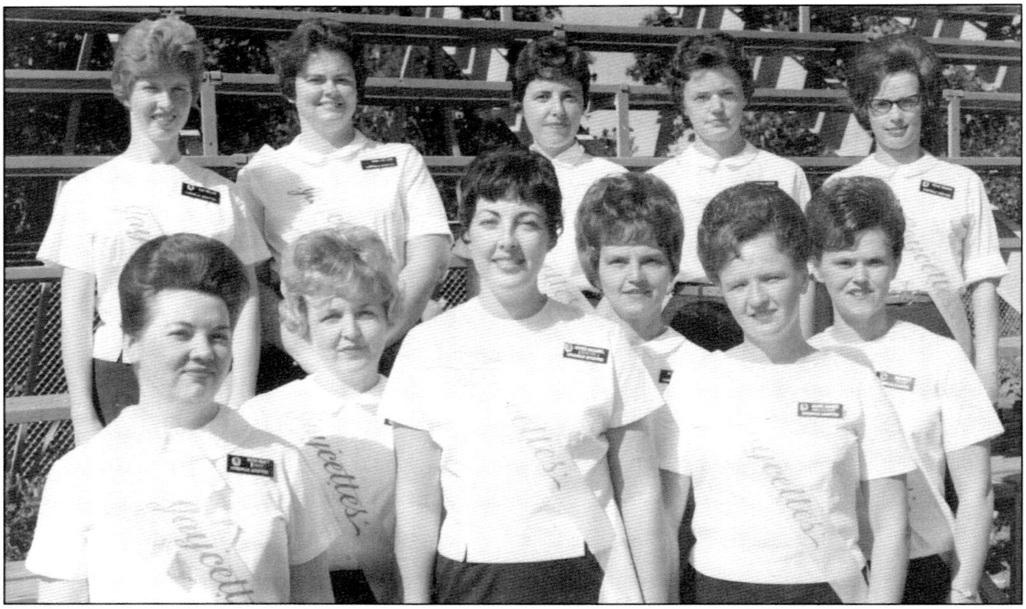

Lewisville Jaycettes organized in 1968–1969 with an active membership. Standing from left to right are (first row) Pres. Ruth Craft, Treasurer Ruth Tally, Sec. Astrid McDaniel, Dir. Betty Matthews, Vice President JoAnn Hauser, and Dir. Ann Craft; (second row) Kay Miller, Cora Lee Lane, Jean Pearce, Barbara Knouse, and Helen Pendergrass. (JRC.)

The Lewisville Horse Show was a popular event in the 1960s and 1970s, raising money to build a community center. The 10th annual show in 1975 was sponsored by the Lewisville Civic Club and the Lewisville Jaycees. (LCC.)

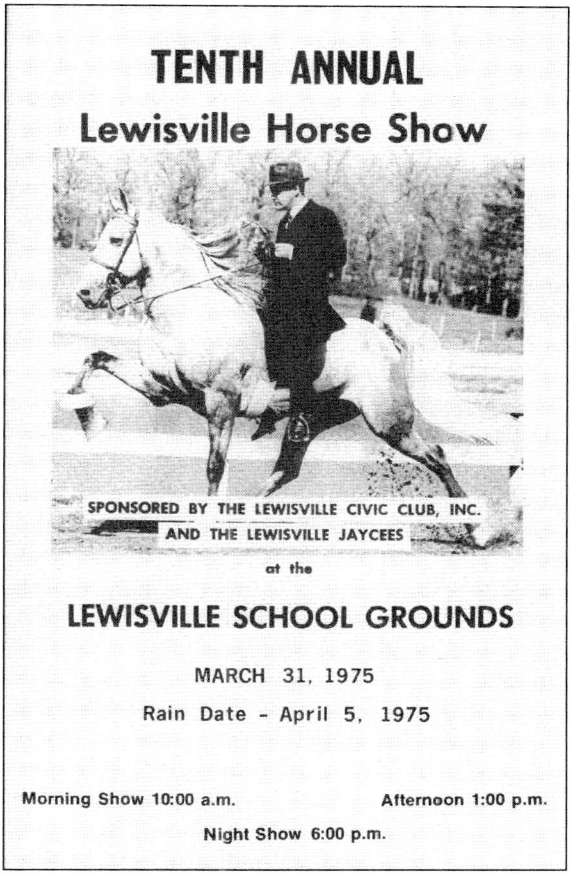

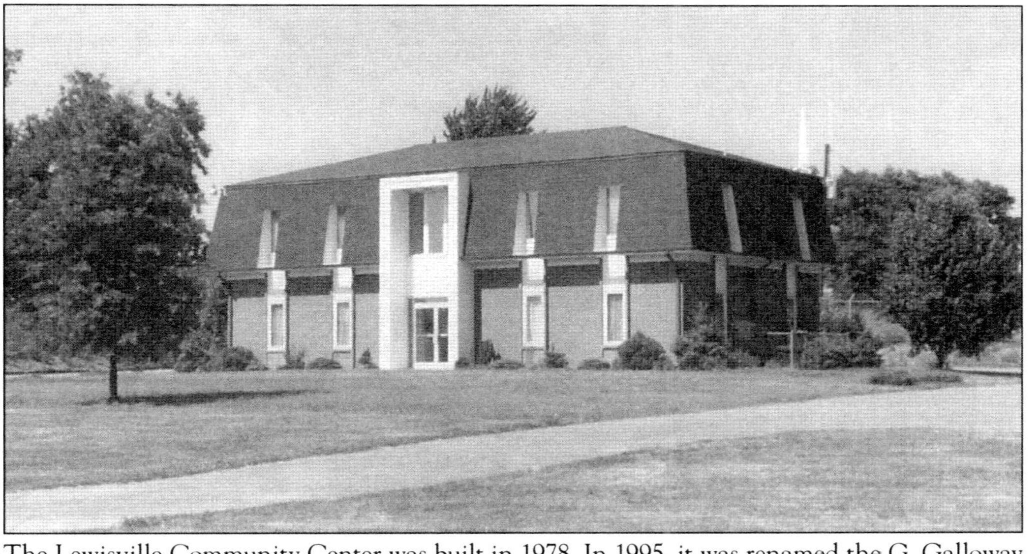

The Lewisville Community Center was built in 1978. In 1995, it was renamed the G. Galloway Reynolds Community Center honoring civic leader Glen Galloway Reynolds. Architect David Rierson drew the plans for the building at no cost to the Lewisville Civic Club. (LH.)

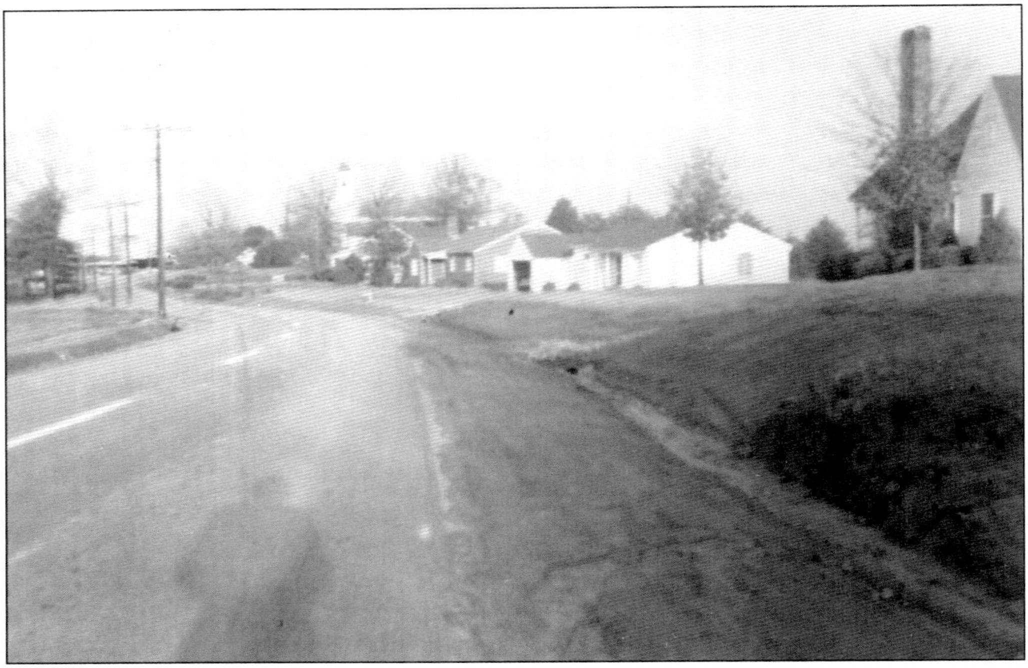

The Lewisville Civic Club raised funds to widen Shallowford Road in the 1950s, providing a pedestrian space for children walking to school and to other destinations in central Lewisville. (LCC.)

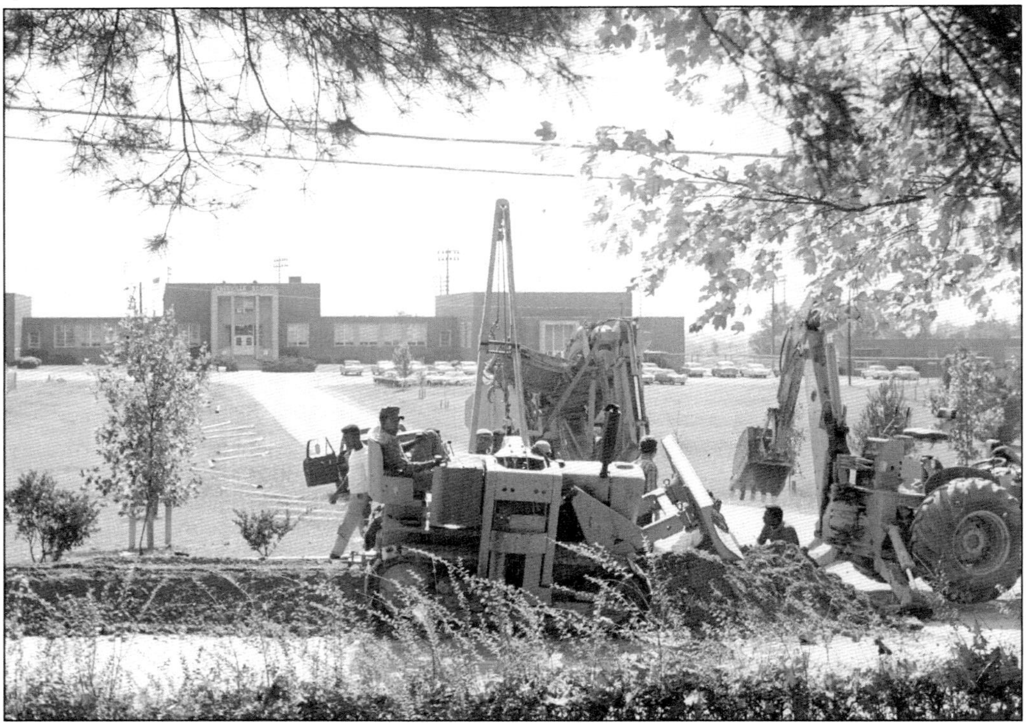

Workmen dig along Shallowford Road in front of Lewisville School, where Forsyth County installed a waterline in the Lewisville community. (LHS.)

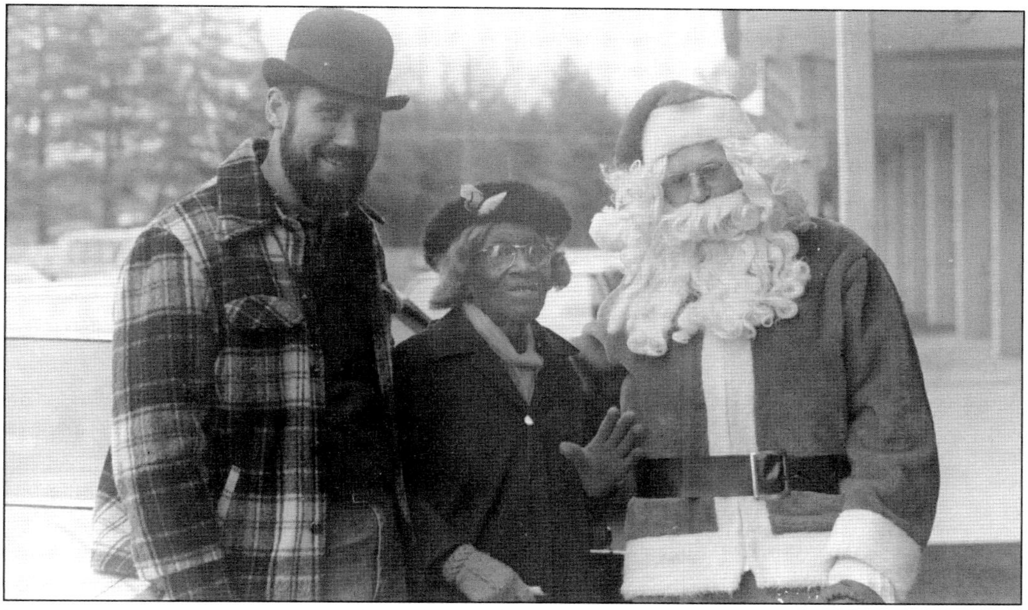

Betty Lyons was honored as grand marshal of the Lewisville Christmas parade. Honorary mayor John Craft (left) and Santa Claus (Jody Holder) join Betty in the annual town event. Betty lived to age 119, one of the town's longest-living citizens. (MV.)

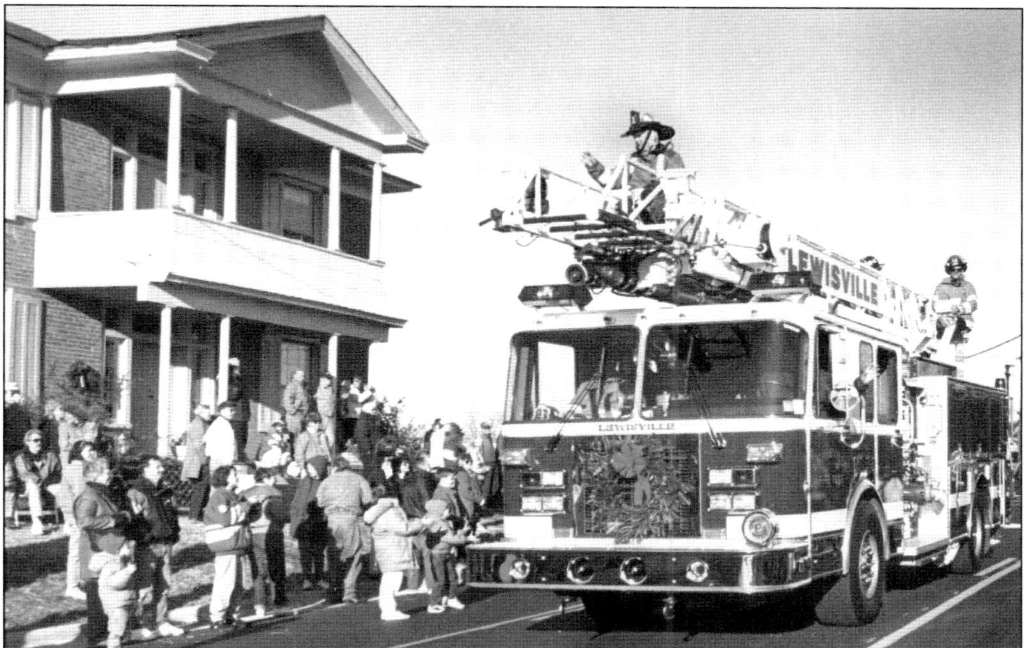

The annual Lewisville Christmas parade has drawn large crowds of people since 1981. John Craft and Margaret Pilcher organized the parade and coordinated it for many years. In the early 1990s, the Lewisville Civic Club took over the sponsorship. The Lewisville parade has become one of the best in the county. A Lewisville fire truck passes the Laugenour House, with firemen throwing candy to excited parade attendees in the 1980s. (MV.)

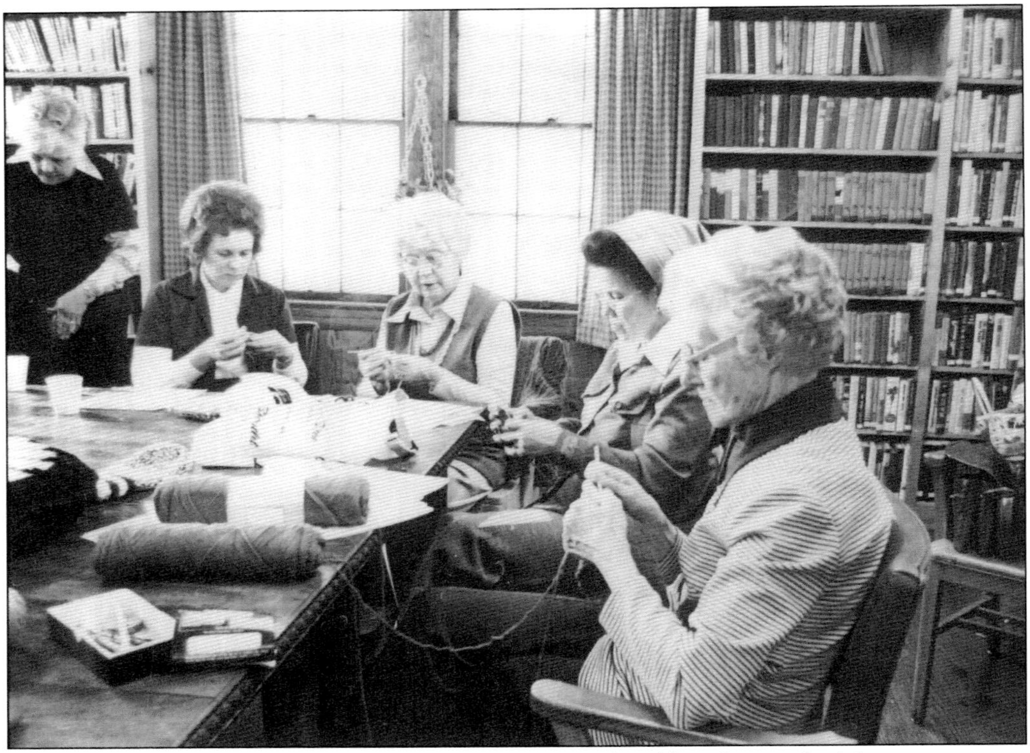

Sunny Acres was the first location of the Lewisville Branch Public Library, which began operation in December 1970. The library was located on the side porch of the expansive house, and it provided space for children's story times, art shows, and needlework classes, until the library moved to another location in 1977. Crochet classes in the 1970s were attended by, from left to right, Dorothy Moser Holder, Anne Boger, Margaret Barclay, Lillie Hicks, and Dela Gordon. (LHS.)

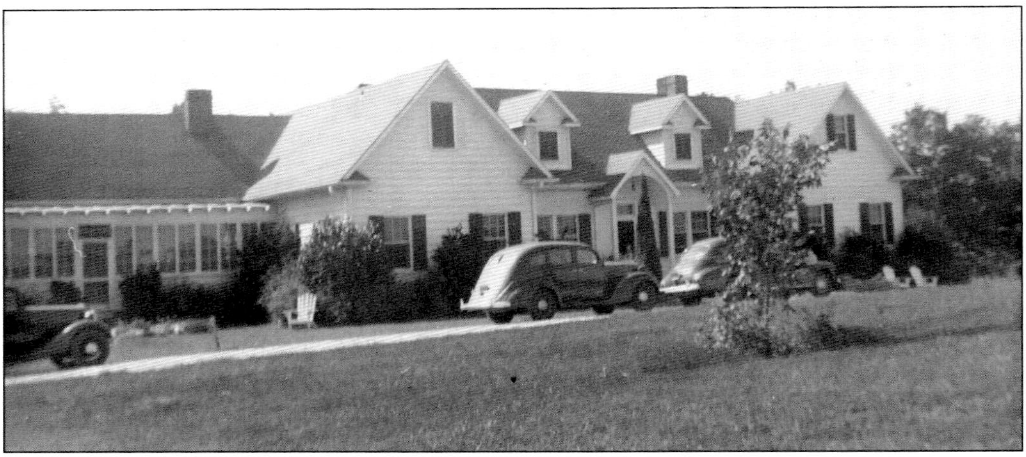

Sunny Acres initially served as a country retreat for underprivileged children when it opened in the 1930s. The spacious, picturesque home was located at the turn of Shallowford Road for many years. Built by Anna Ogburn, Sunny Acres also served as a Methodist retreat and eventually became a community and business center when Dr. James Hampton purchased the property in 1961. When it was torn down in the 1980s, a shopping center was built on the site. (LHS.)

Eight

Our Eyes Are on the Future

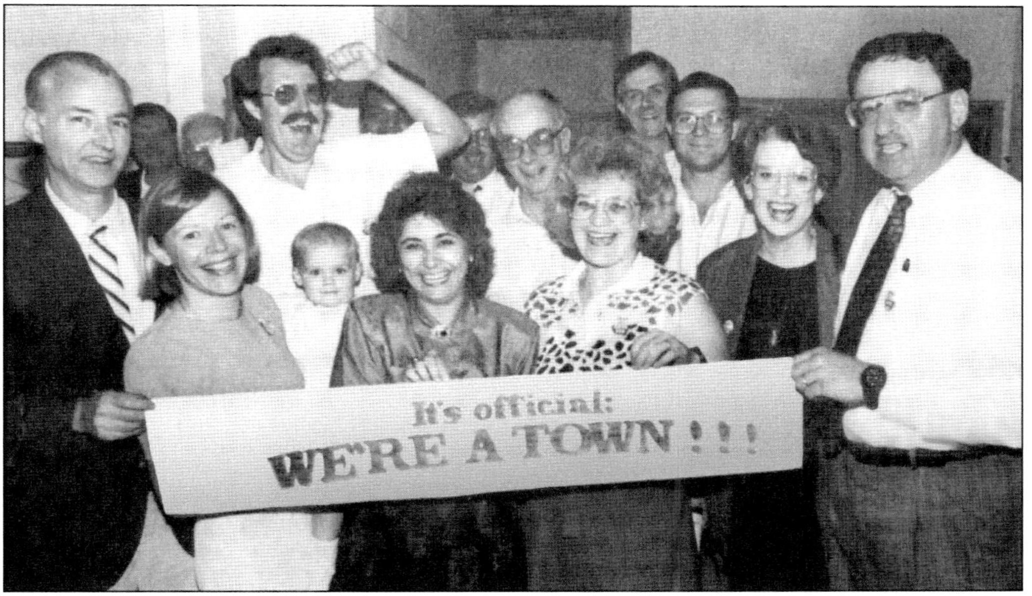

On the evening of August 13, 1991, Lewisville officially became a town, with a 3-1 vote in favor of incorporation. The interim council and incorporation steering committee celebrating together from left to right are (first row) Dan Jennings, Linda Rohr and daughter Anna Louise, Marcia Enns, Doran Tate, and Hank Chilton; (second row) Kyle Stimson, Frank Foster, and Anthony San Filippo; (third row) Ken Sadler, Steven Garland, and Gordon Bingham. (CM.)

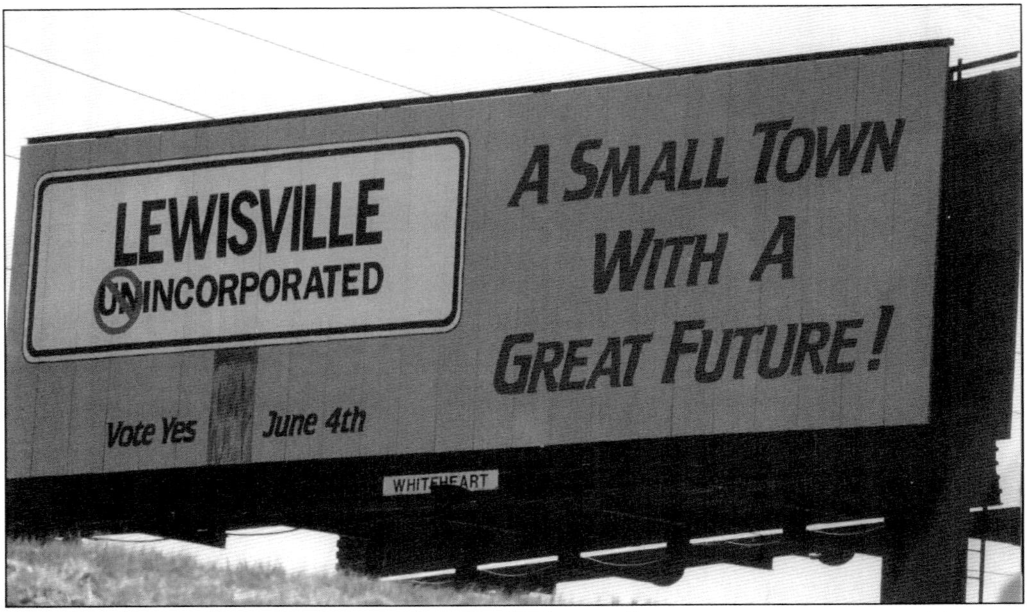

A billboard on Highway 421 passing through the Lewisville community encourages citizens to vote "yes" for incorporation on June 4, 1991. (LHS.)

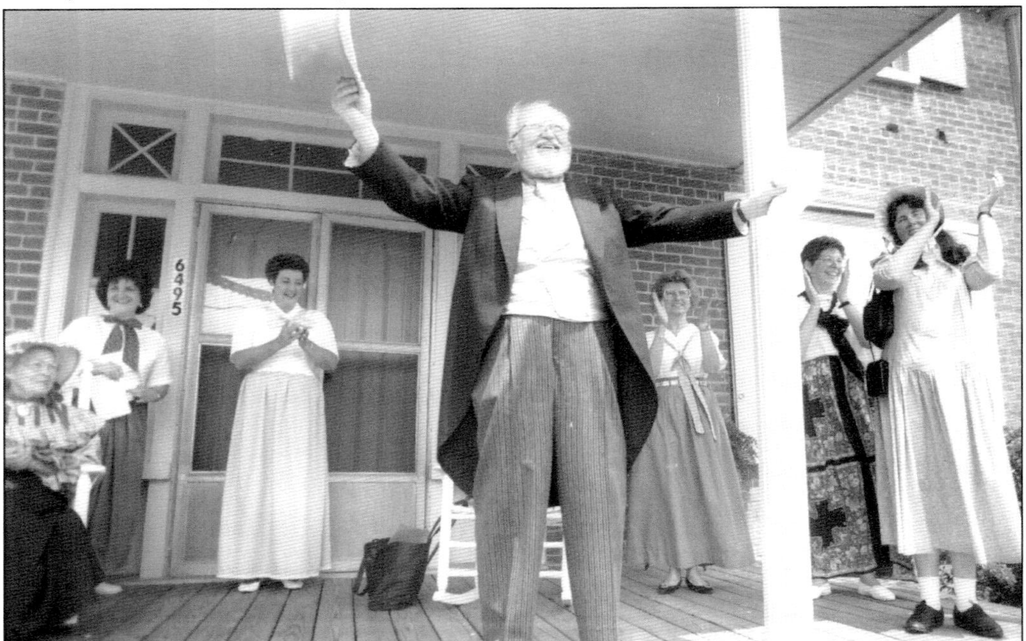

At the Lewisville Lawn Party held on May 16, 1992, Kent Mathewson portrays Lewis Laugenour welcoming citizens to Lewisville on the steps of the Laugenour House. Seated at left, Marianna Mathewson portrays Mary Elizabeth "Betty" Laugenour. Lewisville Historical Society members standing on the porch are, from left to right, Edie Turner, Astrid Saylor, Margaret Boggs, Mary Gaines, and Merrikay Brown. (LHS.)

The first elected officials of the Lewisville Town Council pose at the Lewisville Town Hall on Shallowford Road, from left to right, (first row) Mayor Hank Chilton, Ken Sadler; (second row) Lynn Thrower, Jane Welch, and Marcia Enns; (third row) David McKee and Dan Jennings. (LHS.)

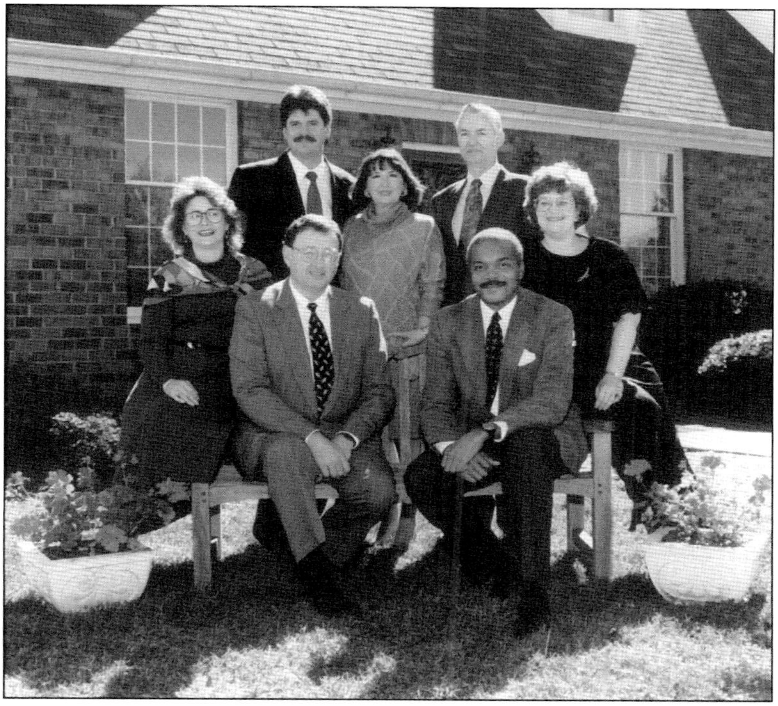

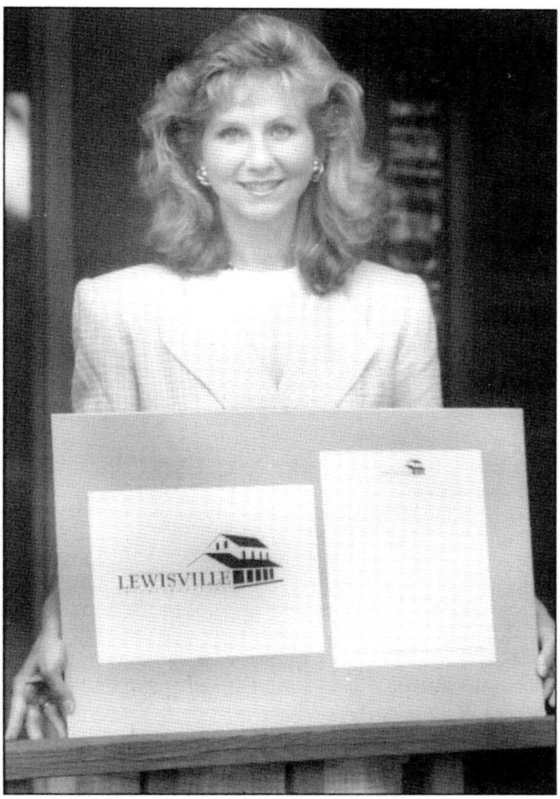

The town logo was designed by Tracy Daniel Heriot, who was a graphics design major from Appalachian State University. The logo, a stylized rendering of the Lewisville Roller Mills, represents the town's past and future. The Lewisville Beautification Committee, then headed by Doran Tate, held a contest for the logo, and Heriot's design was adopted in 1992. (LHS.)

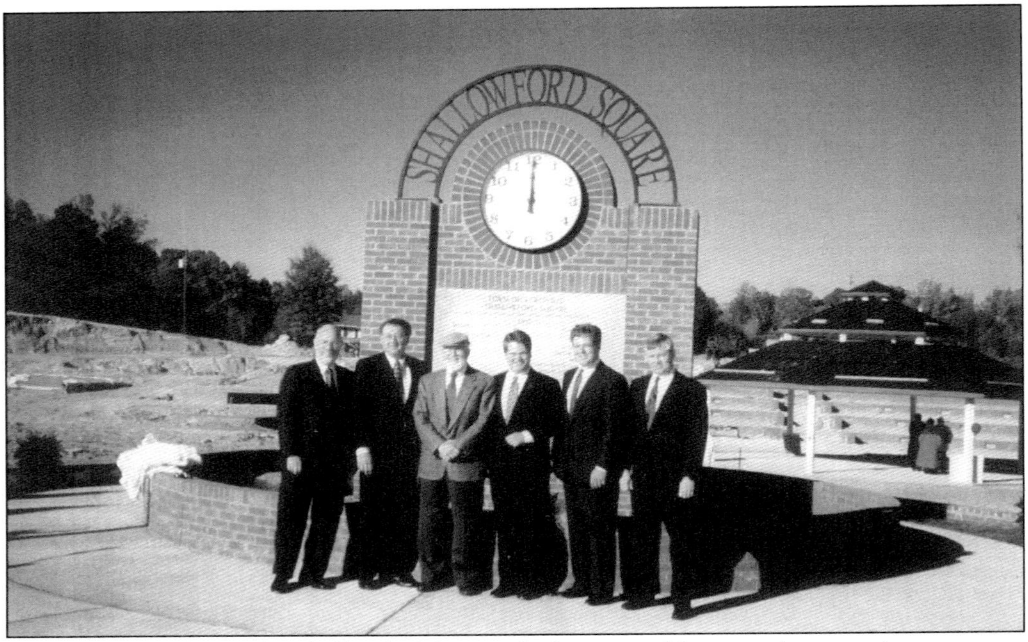

Civic leaders gather at the Shallowford Square clock, a new addition to the central town square in Lewisville. Standing from left to right are Bob Stebbins, Hank Chilton, Kent Mathewson, Dick Stahura, Lang Wilcox, and John Whitson. The Shallowford Square was completed in 1997 and is the hub of the town's activities. (LHS.)

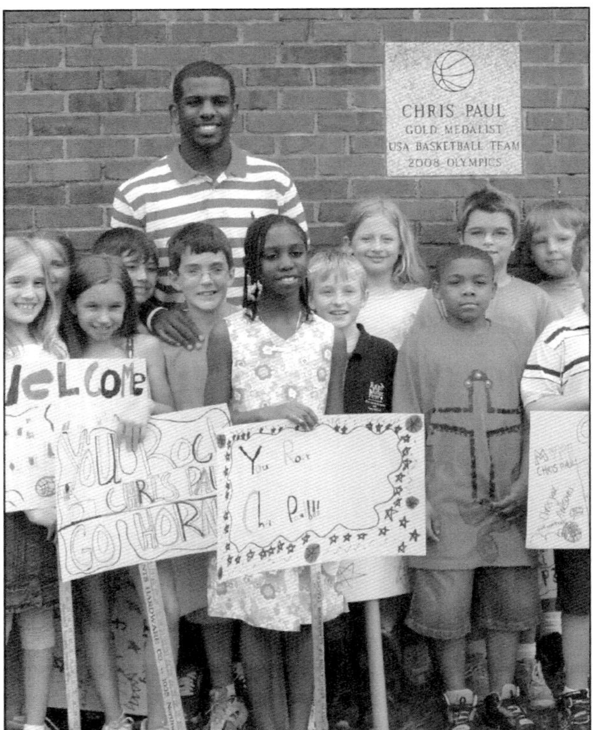

Chris Paul and students from Lewisville Elementary School celebrate the unveiling of a plaque in his honor at Shallowford Square in 2009. A native of Lewisville and. a graduate of West Forsyth High School, Chris was a star on the Wake Forest University basketball team, plays professionally for the New Orleans Hornets, and earned an Olympic Gold Medal on the USA Basketball Team in 2008. (LHL.)

Bibliography

Dalton, Mary Haynes. *West Bend (Little Yadkin Township), North Carolina: Historical Records and Memories*. Winston-Salem, NC: self-published, 2004.

Forsyth County Public Library. *The Changing Face of Forsyth County, North Carolina: A Guide to its Heritage and History*. Winston-Salem, NC: self-published, 2004.

Fries, Adelaide L., contributor and editor. *Forsyth: the History of a County on the March*. Chapel Hill, NC: University of North Carolina Press, 1976.

———, *Records of the Moravians in North Carolina*. Raleigh, NC: N.C. Department of Archives and History, 1968.

Lewisville Civic Club. The *Lewisville Citizen*. Lewisville, NC: Lewisville Civic Club, 1947–1961. Various issues.

Lewisville United Methodist Church. *Our Spiritual Heritage: A History of Lewisville United Methodist Church Lewisville, North Carolina 1878–1988*. Lewisville, NC. 1988.

Reynolds, Glen Galloway. *Shallow Ford Country*. Lewisville, NC: Ruth Reynolds Hartle and Louise Moser Reynolds, 1992, c. 1999.

Stimson, Richard Kyle. *The Great Philadelphia Wagon Road in Forsyth County, NC, 1750–1770: Historic Roads of Forsyth County*. Vol. I. Lewisville, NC: self-published, c. 1999.

Taylor, Gwynne Stephens. *From Frontier to Factory: An Architectural History of Forsyth County*. 2nd ed. Winston-Salem, NC: City-County Planning Board of Winston-Salem and Forsyth County, c. 1981, 1982.

Tursi, Frank V. *Winston-Salem: A History*. Winston-Salem, NC: John F. Blair, 1994.

West Bend Lodge No. 434. *West Bend Lodge No. 434 AF&AM, 100th Anniversary*. Lewisville, NC: self-published, 1990.

Williams, Lewis James III, et al. *Williams: 300 Years of Leadership in America: A History of the Descendants of John Williams of Llangolery, Wales*. Lewisville, NC: Panther Creek, 1997.

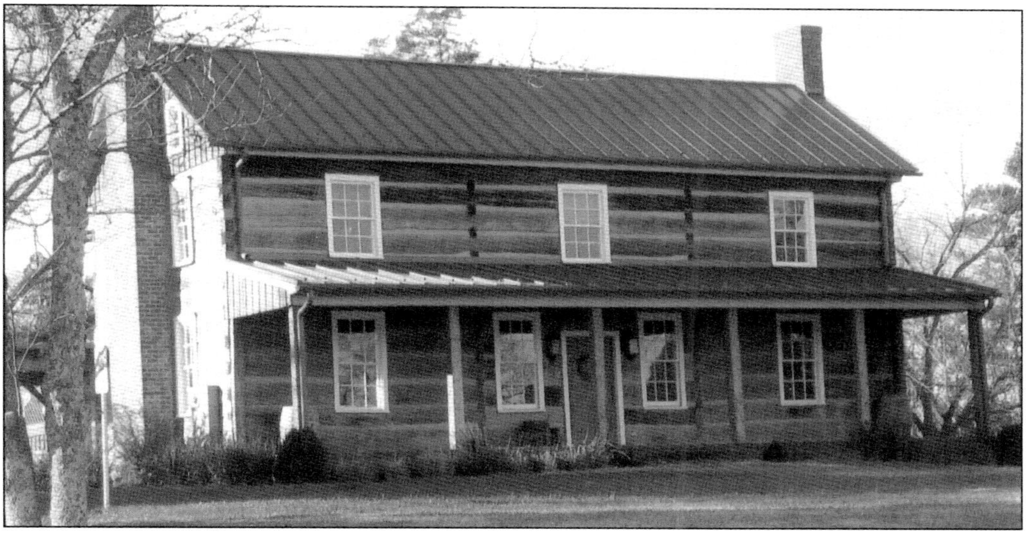

Established in 1972, Westbend Vineyards in Lewisville was the first winery operating in the Yadkin Valley of North Carolina. Today over 30 wineries operate in this emerging Yadkin Valley industry, which draws many tourists to the area. The Joel Benjamin Hauser Cabin was built around 1850 and today is restored for use on the Westbend Vineyard property for a variety of social events. (DMJ.)